Native American Aliens _____

Recent Titles in
Contributions in Legal Studies
Series Editor: Paul L. Murphy

The Origins of the American Business Corporation, 1784-1855: Broadening the Concept of Public Service during Industrialization
Ronald E. Seavoy

Prologue to Nuremberg: The Politics and Diplomacy of Punishing War Criminals of the First World War
James F. Willis

The Network of Control: State Supreme Courts and State Security Statutes, 1920-1970
Carol E. Jenson

Drugs and Information Control: The Role of Men and Manipulation in the Control of Drug Trafficking
Jerald W. Cloyd

State Supreme Courts: Policymakers in the Federal System
Mary Cornelia Porter and G. Alan Tarr, editors

The Future of Our Liberties: Perspectives on the Bill of Rights
Stephen C. Halpern, editor

Tightening the Reins of Justice in America: A Comparative Analysis of the Criminal Jury Trial in England and the United States
Michael H. Graham

The Development of Law on the Rocky Mountain Frontier: Civil Law and Society, 1850-1912
Gordon Morris Bakken

Clients and Lawyers: Securing the Rights of Disabled Persons
Susan M. Olson

The New High Priests: Lawyers in Post–Civil War America
Gerald W. Gawalt, editor

The Little Rock Crisis: A Constitutional Interpretation
Tony Freyer

Nuclear Weapons and Law
Arthur Selwyn Miller and Martin Feinrider, editors

Native American Aliens

Disloyalty and the Renunciation of Citizenship by Japanese Americans during World War II

DONALD E. COLLINS

CONTRIBUTIONS IN LEGAL STUDIES, NUMBER 32

Greenwood Press
WESTPORT, CONNECTICUT · LONDON, ENGLAND

Library of Congress Cataloging in Publication Data
Collins, Donald E.
   Native American aliens.

   (Contributions in legal studies, ISSN 0147-1074 ;
no. 32)
   Bibliography: p.
   Includes index.
   1. Japanese Americans—Legal status, laws, etc.
2. Japanese Americans—Civil rights.   3. Japanese
Americans—Evacuation and relocation, 1942-1945.
4. Citizenship—United States.   I. Title.   II. Series.
KF7224.5.C64   1985   940.53′15′03956   84-25239
ISBN 0-313-24711-0 (lib. bdg.)

Library of Congress Catalog Card Number: 84-25239
ISBN: 0-313-24711-0
ISSN: 0147-1074

First published in 1985

Greenwood Press
A division of Congressional Information Service, Inc.
88 Post Road West, Westport, Connecticut 06881

Printed in the United States of America

10 9 8 7 6 5 4 3 2 1

Dedicated to
Wayne M. Collins,
Horace Montgomery,
my wife Fay,
and children
Sean, Charles, and
Frances Fay Collins

Contents

Illustrations		*ix*
Preface		3
1 Introduction		5
2 Evacuation: From Freedom to Concentration Camps		12
3 The Registration Crisis: Segregating the ''Disloyal''		22
4 The Failure of Moderate Leadership in Tule Lake		35
5 Martial Law and the Rise of the Radical Underground		47
6 Prelude to Renunciation: The Growth of Terrorism and Fear		64
7 Renunciation of Citizenship		84
8 Reaction against Renunciation: The Retreat from ''Disloyalty''		105
9 The Renunciation Cases: The Restoration of Citizenship		123
Appendix One	The Case against the Renunciants	*145*
Appendix Two	The Case for the Renunciants	*155*
Appendix Three	The Renunciants Speak for Themselves	*169*
Notes		*175*
Bibliography		*199*
Index		*211*

Illustrations

Between pages 46 and 47

1. Pre-construction site of Tule Lake Relocation Center

2. A lone Nisei crosses a firebreak through mud in Tule Lake

3. Guard tower, wire-mesh "man-proof" fence, and gate guard

4. Radicals drill in honor of the departure of 171 pro-Japan leaders

5. Bugle corps of the *Hokoku Seinen-dan*

6. *"Banzai!"* salute to departing radical leaders

7. "Lay-down" strikers forcibly removed from Tule Lake

8. Renunciants sign repatriation papers under orders of the Department of Justice

9. Renunciants and their families are searched for contraband

10. Tule Lake residents depart voluntarily for Japan

Native
American
Aliens _____

Preface

During a brief three-month period in 1944–45, 5,589 persons, one in every fourteen American citizens of Japanese descent, gave up their citizenship in the land of their birth. Most lived in Tule Lake Segregation Center, one of ten concentration camps (euphemistically called relocation centers) created by the United States government to house its resident West Coast Japanese population at the beginning of World War II. Preceding this apparently disloyal act, the renunciants had suffered numerous hardships at the hands of their government. They had been subjected to loss of homes, jobs, pets, and everything that went with life in normal American communities. Along with their parents, they had been incarcerated in isolated camps, based on race alone (Caucasian German and Italian enemy aliens and their children were not imprisoned as a group). And finally, they had been transferred to a special segregation center, based on a poorly worded and planned questionnaire that tended to register frustration, confusion, and fear more than disloyalty. Because of this, plus other problems enumerated in this book, it is my contention that few of those who renounced their citizenship were truly disloyal to their country; rather, they were reacting to real and imagined events which were often beyond their control. This work examines the cultural, sociological, psychological, and historical factors that, in combination, resulted in mass renunciation of United States citizenship and concludes with the twenty-two-year legal fight for restoration of American nationality.

Perhaps the single most important individual in this volume is neither a renunciant nor a Japanese American. Without the full cooperation of San Francisco attorney Wayne M. Collins (no relation) with the author, this story could not have been written; and without his dedication to civil liberties and perseverance in the face of government and American Civil Liberties Union opposition, many renunciants might have never remained in their native country, nor regained their American citizenship.

Collins was a fiery, volatile lawyer, with a quick temper, who was proud of his ability to "out-curse anyone." These characteristics were combined with a staunch determination to defend civil liberties. He was a graduate of San Francisco Law School and a classmate of former California Governor Edmund G. Brown. Collins' involvement in the defense of Japanese American rights during and after World War II is impressive. He argued the case of Korematsu v. the U. S. before the Supreme Court and wrote amicus curiae briefs for Hirabayashi v. the U. S. and *Ex parte* Endo. He put up an energetic defense of Iva Toguri D'Aquino (Tokyo Rose); and although he lost the case, he was able to prevent later efforts to deport her to Japan. Collins never forgave the government for its wartime treatment of persons of Japanese descent. In 1972, he told the author, "I am the only person in the world who is still angry."

The author wishes to express special thanks to two historians, whose aid was invaluable in the writing and publication of this book. Professor Horace Montgomery of the University of Georgia provided guidance through all stages of writing. His advice that "the historian's job is to synthesize" contributed greatly toward preventing the volume from becoming burdensomely long. Professor Roger Daniels of the University of Cincinnati, one of the leading historians of the Japanese in the United States, is owed appreciation for his reading and criticism of the manuscript. It was through his encouragement that this work was finally published.

1

Introduction

Loyalty is especially important during time of war. It is necessary for a government to know whom it can trust in order to protect itself at home while its armies are fighting on the battlefields. But how can a government determine the loyalty of its citizens? This problem faced the United States in the early years of World War II, and in the attempt to find a solution the nation committed what has been termed its "worst wartime mistake." It committed this mistake by making race the sole basis for judging the loyalty of the Japanese American minority living on the West Coast. During the first year of the war, 112,000 persons of Japanese descent were incarcerated without the benefit of hearings or trials. It was widely assumed that this racial minority was the most dangerous element in our society. Widespread acceptance of this belief on the West Coast permitted the government to subject them throughout the war to a mass probing and surveillance process which was almost certainly without parallel in American history.[1] Nowhere in the nation did any single group encounter the sustained nativist assault that was directed against California's Japanese.[2] This unjust discrimination and imprisonment strained the loyalty of both the United States–born Japanese, known as Nisei, and their alien parents (Issei). While the vast majority acquiesced in these hardships, a sizable minority broke under the strain and renounced their American citizenship. Thus, an official federal policy of determination of loyalty by race drove many otherwise loyal citizens to an act which most were soon to regret.

In July, 1944, Congress passed an amendment to the Nationality Act of 1940 which made it possible for United States nationals to renounce their citizenship during wartime while still residing within the country. This legislation was the climax of three years of efforts by congressional leaders from the Pacific Coast to rid the nation of what they considered to be an undesirable race. While the act was a somewhat diminished version of what they actually desired, that is, to rid the United States of its entire Japanese population, it did succeed far beyond their expectations.[3] As a result of what amounted to a policy of persecution and imprisonment by their government, 5,589 Nisei gave up the land of their birth in a mass movement during the months of December, 1944 and early 1945. Thus, one out of every fourteen American citizens of Japanese descent renounced his citizenship and became in fact a "native American alien."

In order to understand this act of apparent disloyalty (i.e., renunciation of citizenship) by such a large number, it is necessary to begin with a brief geographical, historical, and sociological analysis of the Japanese community in the United States just prior to World War II. Although the mass renunciation of nationality came about because of events following America's entrance into the war, conditions in the community during the four decades preceding 1941, while not sufficient to cause renunciation, did contribute to the state of mind that made this action possible.

The problem of the Japanese American has historically been associated with the Pacific Coast. From the very beginning, Japanese immigrants had tended to settle in that region. According to the census of 1940, 89 percent of the nation's 126,947 Japanese were located in the three Pacific Coast states. The greatest concentration, however, was in California, which had three-fourths of the national total, with Los Angeles alone possessing 29 percent.

The failure of the Japanese to disperse among the native population of the West Coast resulted in ethnic communities which tended to retain the cultural characteristics of the Japan the immigrant Issei generation had known in its youth. Much of this heritage was passed on to their Nisei children who, although United States citizens by birth, and were becoming increasingly acculturated through attendance at American schools and other (generally minimal) contacts with the Caucasian population, spent much of their time in the unacculturated homes of their parents. Nisei sociologist Harry Kitano describes the Japanese American community as a "subculture" which followed, in varying degrees, the norms, values, and culture of early twentieth-century Japan.[4] This is significant in that when war, evacuation, internment, and renunciation of citizenship came, many, if not most, Japanese Americans tended to act in accordance with their cultural heritage.

Kitano's analysis reveals a community in which family, status, and hierarchy were relatively permanent and important. The father's position as head of the family was absolute and unquestioned. Respect for and obedience to authority extended to all levels of society so that acceptance of the dictates of family, community, groups, cliques, and government was expected without dispute. The Japanese was a "team player," which meant subordination of one's own needs and interests for the common good of the family or group was expected.[5]

The strength of the family is regularly cited in the literature as the factor chiefly responsible for maintaining ethnic Japanese solidarity and distinctiveness. The transmission of traditional ethnic-moral values was largely accomplished by means of *Shushin* instruction, a major child-rearing practice in Japan and among Japanese in this country, which stressed standards for proper behavior, respect for filial authority, and pride in the Japanese community.[6] Over two-thirds of the Nisei surveyed reported receiving *Shushin* instruction from their parents. In addition, Nisei were expected to attend Japanese language schools set up by their parents for instruction in the Japanese language and culture. Among the family and community values which the Issei attempted to pass on to the young were: conformism; regard for conventional behavior; obedience to rules and regulations; and yielding to others, even when unnecessarily provoked. Discipline was mandatory, and self-control, resignation, and gratitude were encouraged. There was also a heavy emphasis on "knowing one's place," so that age, sex (masculine superiority), class, family lineage, and other variables of social status were important.[7] Such cultural traits and parental pressures and influence played a part in the way in which Japanese Americans accepted or rejected various aspects of their evacuation and incarceration.

The family and community maintained the above system along with its norms and values through a highly effective system for social control which generally succeeded in preventing deviation by their members. Behavior was constantly rewarded, punished, reinforced, and reshaped by such techniques as emphasis on the dependence of the individual on his parents and community; fostering feelings of shame and guilt; appeals to obligation, duty, and responsibility; and the devastating use of gossip. The effects of these pressures were expressed by a Japanese American who wrote, "I felt [as if] my parents or others were looking over my shoulder at all times."[8] Many Nisei answering government forms, questionnaires, and interviewers were subjected to the same unseen, but nevertheless real, restrictions on freedom of action. Under such conditions it was the nonconformist who did not unquestioningly leave home and job to go obediently into concentration camps or who disobeyed parental desires or community pressures that he renounce his citizenship.

The events which finally drove the renunciants to give up the land of their birth were the unjust evacuation and incarceration imposed upon them during the years from 1942 through 1945. However, the process of making un-Americans out of the Japanese American minority actually began at the turn of the century when Japanese immigrants first began to arrive in this nation in large numbers. From that time through World War II, the West Coast was never without at least one powerful, zealous, and single-minded group devoted wholly to the purpose of preventing Japanese immigration and dispossessing as many as possible of the Japanese residents already established there. Groups of this type were especially numerous in the early 1920s and early 1930s.[9]

It was during the first quarter of the century that the anti-Orientalists had their greatest success in divorcing the Japanese residents from American life. The clearest early manifestation of the intense anti-Japanese feeling on the West Coast was a campaign of front-page headlines in the San Francisco *Chronicle*, begun in early 1905, which repeatedly informed Californians that the "Japanese invasion" was under way.[10] Within two decades, Japanese immigrants had lost practically every right that was normally held by resident non-Oriental alien groups. In 1908, pressure from the West Coast resulted in President Theodore Roosevelt's Gentlemen's Agreement with Japan to restrict the entry of Japanese laborers and farmers into this country. Except for the arrival of parents, wives, and children of immigrants already here, the Agreement for all practical purposes ended Japanese immigration to the United States. In 1913, the California legislature passed the first of the many alien land laws, soon to become common to the Pacific states, which was aimed directly at preventing immigration into the state and at driving out Orientals already there. By 1924, it was impossible for a Japanese alien to own land in most Western states. In 1922, a decision of the United States Supreme Court aided the racists by reaffirming that non-whites, except for Negroes, were ineligible for American citizenship, thus making for many firm loyalty to their adopted land difficult, if not impossible.[11] However, the greatest victory for the West Coast anti-Orientalists was their success in pushing through Congress the Immigration Act of 1924. This legislation forbade further immigration to the Japanese and had the effect of causing a continuous decline in the Issei population.[12] With the major goal of exclusion accomplished, anti-Japanese antagonism declined. It never fully disappeared, however, and was to reappear in full force after the outbreak of World War II.

The Japanese living on the West Coast in 1940 were composed of three quite diverse groups: the Issei parents, who had migrated from Japan and were still nationals of that country; their Nisei children, born in the United States and eligible for the citizenship of both nations; and the Kibei, a sub-group of the Nisei, who had received much of their education in Japan. The Issei made up only about 40,000 of the total 112,000 persons of Japanese descent on the Pacific Coast just prior to World War II. This number was steadily decreasing because immigration was prohibited after 1924. Denied a part in American life by legal and social discrimination, they lived apart from the native population and attempted to bring their children up in the culture of their native land.

The Nisei population totalled approximately 70,000 in 1940, of whom about 9,000 were Kibei who, although American citizens, were culturally closer to their Issei parents than to their United States–educated brothers and sisters. The practice of sending at least one child to Japan for training was common between 1920 and 1941 and was based on a preference for Japanese-style childrearing and education, a desire to maintain communication with the home country, and a pessimism about their future in the United States. The Kibei were sent to Japan at an early age and usually returned in their teens. They became exposed to the nationalism that permeated Japanese education at the time, and many of their ideas clashed with the more Americanized Nisei at home.[13] Because many developed "Japanesy" manners and spoke poor English, they were often objects of ridicule by the Nisei. In addition, their Japanese education earned them the distrust of Caucasian Americans and the suspicion of the United States government.[14] Some of the problems in the wartime relocation centers developed from these Kibei-Nisei quarrels.

Yet, the Kibei were not alone in feeling the frustrations of trying to make a life in the Caucasian culture of the United States. Actually, their Nisei brothers and sisters fared little better. United States citizens, and educated in American schools, they were idealistic and dreamed of success in their native country. They stressed education and had a higher educational level and lower crime rate than any other national or racial group in the United States. However, few were to see their goals attained before the end of World War II. The Caucasian community closed its doors to them. Those with college degrees often found that their professional talents were limited to their own people in the ghettoes of the West Coast; only menial jobs were available in the white community. Thus, to the Nisei, regardless of his qualifications, scientific laboratories and teaching were both closed; even civil service jobs offered slow advancement.[15]

Despite these hardships and the Nisei's efforts to win acceptance, their Oriental features proved a serious deterrent. Although Californians were willing to accept the children of Caucasian immigrants, they considered all persons of Japanese descent to be alien. As early as 1921, the Controller of the State of California predicted that once immigration was prohibited, the next objective of the anti-Orientalists would be to amend the United States Constitution to forbid citizenship to children of persons "ineligible to citizenship."[16]

The success of this objective depended on the ability of the anti-Oriental groups to discredit the citizenship of the Nisei. Various means were devised to arouse hostility. Typical was the "peaceful penetration" theory developed shortly after World War I. It was claimed that wives of Japanese immigrants were under orders from the Emperor of Japan to have a baby every year. Within half a century, these children, who were American citizens but loyal Japanese at heart, would outnumber the Caucasian residents and control California.[17] Further proof of their loyalty to Japan was their attendance at Japanese language schools and possession of dual citizenship. It was a widely accepted belief that of all immigrant children, only those of Japanese descent were incapable of loyalty to the United States.[18] This argument was repeated again and again both before and during World War II.

Aware that suspicion was directed against their Americanism, the Nisei made serious efforts to demonstrate their loyalty. Outside of the home they developed American dress and activities as thoroughly as any Caucasian. Their attendance at the language schools was done mainly at the insistence of their alien parents who were concerned that their children were unable to speak Japanese. As early as 1921, some Nisei successfully petitioned the Japanese government to remove its claims of citizenship on them. This was done solely to soothe American public opinion, as the Nisei themselves knew that it was impossible for Japan to enforce claims on residents of the United States. Nonetheless, such attempts to demonstrate their loyalty were unsuccessful until after the end of World War II.

Such political and social harassments made the Nisei constantly aware that citizenship for him was not equal to that of the Caucasian American. While such practices were in themselves not enough to turn the Nisei away from the United States, they nonetheless strained the ties that bound these young Japanese Americans to the land of their birth and helped to drive many of them to the breaking point. The process of making un-Americans out of almost six thousand otherwise loyal persons was well underway long before the December 7, 1941, attack on Pearl Harbor. The war that began on that day and the incarceration that followed were to complete the process.

2

Evacuation: From Freedom to Concentration Camps

The Japanese attack on American forces at Pearl Harbor, Hawaii, on December 7, 1941, had disastrous consequences for those persons of Japanese descent who lived on the West Coast of the United States. Four decades of anti-Japanese propaganda had made hostility to this racial minority a part of the mental climate of the region. Powerful and influential pressure groups, which included such organizations as the American Legion, the Native Sons of the Golden West, and the California Joint Immigration Committee, repeatedly passed resolutions calling for such anti-Japanese measures as denial of citizenship to persons of Japanese descent born in the United States, in clear violation of Fourteenth Amendment guarantees. The war and especially the sneak nature of the Japanese attack were a boon to persons who held these sentiments. It gave credence to the popular stereotype of the Japanese as sly, sinister individuals who were incapable of trust or loyalty. West Coast anti-Orientalists saw in the war an opportunity to rid that region, and perhaps the nation, of what to them was an unwanted and undesirable race.

Largely as a result of this intense regional animosity, the first year of the war saw some 112,000 persons of Japanese descent, including approximately 70,000 American citizens, forced into a change in their lives that may have been more rapid and more extreme than that suffered by any other group in American history. From a situation of relative comfort and security, they were plunged into one of uncertainty and anxiety. After many months, during which they were given conflicting instructions and orders by the United States government and

during which they had good reason to anticipate all manner of hardships and persecutions, they were ordered from their homes and confined in relocation centers, a euphemism for concentration camps. During
the process they became economically impoverished and lost most of
the status by which they could respect themselves. State, local, and
national authorities, as well as the press, radio, and general public of
the Pacific Coast, in effect, branded them as potential spies and sabo-
teurs. Although the United States was also at war with Germany and
Italy, aliens of these nations were treated with sympathy, and almost
no serious consideration was given to their removal. Only the Japanese
American was singled out for exclusion and detention.

There were few hints during the first month of the war to indicate
the coming wave of anti-Japanese hostility which was about to engulf
the helpless minority. While the racial issue was still important in California, it had subsided greatly since the anti-Oriental forces had succeeded in barring Japanese entry into the country through passage of
the Immigration Act of 1924.[1] Throughout December and early January, 1942, expressions of sympathy for the resident Japanese and confidence in their loyalty came from numerous sources. In Washington,
three members of the West Coast delegation read favorable statements
into the *Congressional Record*.[2] Letters-to-the-editor columns in the area
newspapers showed an effort on the part of the general public to avoid
the witch hunt that occurred during World War I against German aliens
in the United States. The press spoke out for an understanding of the
plight of the Japanese and praised them for their loyalty.[3] The hostile
voices of the many militantly anti-Japanese pressure groups of the region were not yet fully aware of the value of the war issue to their
objectives and remained conspicuously silent.[4] The month of December was a difficult one for the area's Japanese, despite the prevailing
favorable trend in public opinion. Immediately upon the declaration of
war, all citizens of enemy nations living in the United States acquired
the new status of enemy aliens and were subject to certain restrictions.
Funds were frozen, foreign language newspapers were closed, and travel
beyond a few miles was prohibited. Agents of the Federal Bureau of
Investigation (FBI) began a roundup of all enemy nationals it considered to be potentially dangerous to the security of the nation. The
Japanese community found itself bitterly divided and leaderless as
thousands were arrested, including its most respected leaders, whom
the Japanese American people believed were not threats to the national

security. Rumors were rampant as fear, confusion, and panic spread through the community. Stories of ill-treatment of those arrested by the FBI, which was equated with the dreaded "thought police" of Japan, spread. Many valuable and irreplaceable personal items were destroyed by persons who believed that those possessions would result in imprisonment. Late December brought fears of violence as a number of Japanese were attacked, with two killed. The number and frequency of attacks were greatly magnified by the anxious people.[5]

The Nisei accepted the fact that some restrictions would be placed on their alien parents by the government but believed that their own American citizenship would protect them from the same fate. The months of January and February brought disillusionment as they learned that many persons on the West Coast considered them to be even more dangerous than the aliens of all three enemy nations.[6] Although they had made serious efforts to prove their loyalty, they found that all was in vain. Offers to do civilian defense work were turned down, while most Nisei soldiers were either discharged or removed from coastal camps. Before long they were classified IV-C, unfit for military service because of ancestry.[7] Many were dismissed from city, county, and state jobs on the rationalization that it was impossible to determine the loyalty of a person of Japanese descent. Soon they began to hear demands for their removal to concentration camps, first from Congressman Leland Ford of California on January 21, then by a growing list of persons that included virtually every important politician, journalist, and anti-Orientalist on the Pacific Coast.[8]

Although there was little justification for the fears besetting the Japanese community in December, 1941, a hostile feeling that began to develop during that month grew in intensity during the first months of 1942. Events beyond their control were turning the tide against the Japanese Americans. With Japan winning the war in the Pacific, the public anticipated invasion by an enemy whose physical characteristics and nationality were identical to those of the resident Japanese. Actual attacks on coastal shipping and the shelling of the coast near Santa Barbara, California, were followed by numerous false or mistaken reports that local Japanese had signaled the enemy from shore.[9] On December 15, Secretary of the Navy Frank Knox gave apparent authenticity to reports of Japanese American aid to the enemy when, in the course of a press conference on the Pearl Harbor disaster, he used the term "fifth column," incorrectly implicating members of Hawaii's Japanese community in the attack.[10] Knox's accusation was given headline treatment on the frightened West Coast. Late in December, refugees returning from Hawaii told equally inaccurate stories of aid given to the attacking Japanese forces by local Japanese residents. By the end of January, most people who had previously expressed faith in the loyalty of the resident Japanese were clamoring for their evacuation and incarceration.[11]

February was the month of victory for pro-evacuation forces. The Army, represented by General John L. DeWitt, the West Coast anti-Japanese organizations, represented by the California Joint Immigration Committee, and the Pacific congressional delegation all presented almost identical recommendations for evacuation to President Franklin D. Roosevelt on February 13 and 14. Within a week, on February 19, the President responded to their petitions with Executive Order 9066, which authorized the Secretary of War, or any military commander designated by the Secretary, to establish "military areas" and exclude therefrom "any or all person."[12] On the following day, Secretary of War Henry L. Stimson empowered DeWitt, as Commanding Officer of the Western Defense Command, to carry out an evacuation within his command under terms of the executive order.[13] General DeWitt thus became the virtual military dictator of the Western United States, with power over the movement and freedom of its entire population.

The choice of DeWitt was unfortunate. His prejudice against the Japanese was known to the War Department and the Japanese community alike. His statement, "A Jap's a Jap," was widely quoted. And his letter of February 14, in which he recommended evacuation of the Japanese population, stands out for its lack of understanding of the Japanese problem:

In the war in which we are now engaged racial affinities are not severed by migration. The Japanese race is an enemy race and while many second and third generation Japanese born on United States soil, possessed of United States citizenship, have become "Americanized," the racial strains are undiluted. . . . It, therefore, follows that along the vital Pacific Coast over 112,000 potential enemies, of Japanese extraction, are at large today. There are indications that these are organized and ready for concerted action at a favorable opportunity. The very fact that no sabotage has taken place to date is a disturbing and confirming indication that such action will be taken.[14]

That DeWitt was selected by Secretary of War Stimson shows a complete disregard for the rights of the Japanese minority on the West Coast. From the moment of his appointment, evacuation became a certainty.

On March 2, 1942, General DeWitt issued Public Proclamation Number One, which defined the West Coast exclusion zone. He designated the Western halves of Oregon, Washington, and California as Military Area Number One and announced that all persons of Japanese ancestry would eventually be removed from that area "in the interest of military necessity." His use of the term "military necessity" left opponents of mass evacuation defenseless. It brooked no opposition from either public or civilian leaders, all of whom were forced to accept the judgment of the military.[15]

In issuing Public Proclamation Number One, General DeWitt ushered in a brief period of "voluntary" evacuation. He encouraged this by adding that those who moved into the interior immediately would probably not be disturbed again. Fortunately, only about nine thousand persons responded to his appeal to migrate eastward. These voluntary evacuees encountered a variety of troubles. Some were turned back by armed posses at the border of Nevada; others were put into jail and held overnight by panicky local peace officers; nearly all had difficulties buying gasoline; many were greeted by "No Japs Wanted" signs on the main streets of interior communities; and a few were threatened with possibilities of mob violence. Considered too dangerous to remain on the West Coast, these hapless evacuees were similarly regarded by people of the interior.[16]

Two organizations were established during March to aid in the movement of the evacuees to new locations. The Wartime Civilian Control Authority was a military organization created by DeWitt to control initial movement of the Japanese. A civilian agency, the War Relocation Authority (usually referred to as the WRA) was created by an executive order of the President on March 18, 1942, with a vague grant of authority to "provide for the relocation" of evacuees "in appropriate places" and to "provide for their needs and activities."[17] Milton S. Eisenhower, the WRA's director for the first three months, and his successor, Dillon S. Myer, both performed well in attempting a just solution to a difficult problem, which won them the lasting gratitude of the Japanese community. Despite the sincere efforts of these two men, the WRA committed grave errors, mostly through lack of experience and some mismanagement, which would eventually drive a significant number of Nisei to a renunciation of their United States citizenship.

As a result of the failure of voluntary evacuation, both the Western Defense Command and the WRA concluded that an exploratory meeting with officials of the Western states was needed immediately, both to eliminate some of the tremendous public confusion and to provide for future planning. Held in Salt Lake City on April 7, 1942, this meeting was an important turning point in the history of the WRA program. Representatives of every Western state except Colorado indicated a deep-seated distrust and dislike for the evacuees and an appallingly low concern for human rights or constitutional guarantees. The representatives refused to be a "dumping ground" for the displaced Japanese. As a result of this meeting, Director Eisenhower became convinced that moving the evacuees directly into private employment was unfeasible and that some form of detention on federally managed and Army-guarded projects was necessary. Therefore, the agency immediately stepped up its search for suitable relocation center sites and concentrated its attention on building an organization and preparing for reception of the evacuated people.[18]

In making its decision on the necessity of internment of the Japanese population, the WRA was faced with the serious constitutional question of whether it had the legal authority to detain American citizens without bringing charges against them. While the Fifth Amendment to the Constitution prohibits the federal government from depriving any person of life, liberty, or property without due process of law, the agency felt that the Constitution should not serve as a straitjacket in time of global war and that it should be interpreted in the light of existing circumstances. The WRA examined the majority decisions of the Supreme Court dealing with the scope of the war powers of the President and concluded that those powers were sufficiently broad to include detention of American citizens "to whatever extent it is reasonably necessary to the national safety in wartime." Thus, the WRA felt it had the authority to detain the Japanese if it could be shown necessary to protect national security.[19]

Once Director Eisenhower had decided on the necessity of detention, he immediately stepped up the search for suitable relocation center sites in which the evacuees might be housed until the problem of resettlement could be solved. Soon barrack cities began rising in ten locations between the Sierra Nevada Mountains of California and the lower Mississippi River. Since only two of these centers were ready for occupancy in the spring of 1942, when General DeWitt issued the first of his more than one hundred exclusion orders, temporary accommodations had to be provided by the Wartime Civilian Control Administration within the West Coast exclusion zone. Sixteen assembly centers were therefore quickly set up at race tracks, fair grounds, and athletic stadiums to receive the evacuees. Most evacuees spent from six weeks to six months here before moving to the more permanent relocation centers under the supervision of the WRA.[20]

Removal of the evacuees from their homes by the Army was swift and impressive. By late May, 1942, approximately sixty-eight days after the first exclusion order, all but a few thousand of the 112,000 Japanese American residents of the West Coast were confined in the assembly centers. Although great care was taken by the military to make the movement as comfortable as possible, the rapidity caused undue hardship. The WRA tried to make the evacuation as painless as possible by moving families and other basic units of the Japanese community intact. However, it could not hide the concentration camp atmosphere of the assembly centers, nor could it ease the minds of the evacuees. Fairly typical of the new camps was the one constructed at Santa Anita race track. Guarded by military police, it was surrounded by barbed wire and equipped with searchlights that played up and down its streets at night. Mail was censored, and no one was permitted to leave the grounds. Publications in the Japanese language were prohibited. Although barracks were constructed for the evacuees, adjacent horse stalls with their smell of manure were considered better shelters.[21] There was undeniably a serious morale problem as well as an undercurrent of resentment. People were discouraged, baffled, and cynical. No one knew what was in store. Rumors spread that they would all be bombed in retaliation for American losses in the Pacific or that those who protested about food or other conditions would be sent to hot and terrible places as punishment.[22]

In June, 1942, the next phase of the forced migration got under way as trains loaded with men, women, and children moved into the still-unfinished relocation centers under the supervision of the WRA. The break with the past was now complete. In the assembly centers they had known they were outcasts, but at least they were still near their own homes. Upon arrival in the distant camps, the new residents wrote back to friends telling stories of heat and dust, of fears about inadequate food and medical care, and of some hope of new freedom and possibilities for the future. Three of the relocation centers were filled by July. Manzanar Assembly Center in California was merely redesignated as a relocation center. In early May, Poston in Arizona received several thousand persons directly from their homes with no interval in assembly centers. Tule Lake in northern California and Gila in southern Arizona were opened in June and July. Minidoka in Idaho, Heart Mountain in Wyoming, and Granada in Colorado were opened in August. The last three, Topaz in central Utah and the two Arkansas centers, Jerome and Rohwer, were filled in September, October, and November.[23]

The relocation centers were built by Army engineers according to a plan designed for only a few years' use. They consisted of tar-paper-covered wooden barracks one hundred feet long grouped into blocks. Each block was composed of two rows of barracks between which were a messhall, a laundry room, a recreation hall, and latrine and lavatory buildings. Families were to sleep in the barracks; they were to eat, wash themselves and their clothes, go to the toilet, and play in the communal buildings in the center of the block. The evacuees found themselves in bare rooms about twenty feet square containing only army cots and blankets. Makeshift furniture had to be built out of scrap lumber. There was no running water. Cracks in the walls and floors offered little privacy or protection against the dust. Construction crews had cleared from the sites all trees, brush, and whatever greenery there had been. Earliest impressions of almost all who entered the centers were of the drabness and the isolation to which they were committed. Little wonder that staff and evacuees alike began their lives in these desolate places with a sense of despair.[24]

There were many young men for whom arrival in these unfinished relocation centers was the last straw. Their feeling of rejection by the United States, provoked by evacuation, was deepened by the remoteness of the centers and the abundant evidence of hasty and inadequate preparations. There was also the frustration of living under federal supervision. It was clear that food, shelter, and medical attention depended on a group of government employees who were to be found at the edge of the center in the administrative buildings. Waiting in line to perform almost every detail of daily living was to become a way of life. Discrimination in employment further increased the sense of frustration. Only the lowest supervisory jobs were entrusted to the evacuees, who could receive no more than twenty-one dollars per month while Caucasian employees received regular wages for the same work. At Manzanar, Poston, and Tule Lake, tensions mounted steadily during the summer and reached peaks in October and November, five or six months after their openings. The feeling of being imprisoned permeated the centers, and the young men came to speak of them as jails and prisons. Evacuees became deeply concerned about the crowded living conditions and problems related to food and health care. Most important in the development of rising tension in the centers was a deep distrust of the government and of the Caucasians who composed it.[25]

The first major protest against relocation center conditions came at the Colorado River project at Poston, Arizona. On November 18, 1942, two popular residents were arrested by the FBI following the beating of a member of the Nisei governing council. Belief that the men were innocent was widespread, and many feared they would not get fair treatment if they were sent to the hostile "outside" for trial. The community was convulsed as sentiment crystallized behind the arrested men. For the first time since evacuation, there was a sense of striking back at the oppressor. The Nisei council resigned after a petition for release of the men was denied. Evacuee leaders called for a general strike, while well-organized crowds kept night-long vigils at the jail.

Imprisonment of the suspects was merely the catalyst, however, for community sentiments which arose out of deeper issues. The real objectives of the evacuee leaders were law and order, smoothness in center operation, and genuine community organization. As this was precisely what the administration also desired, negotiations were held in which the two sides came to an agreement on the major issues. The crowds which surrounded the jail returned to their homes satisfied. In the meantime, one suspect had been released for lack of evidence, and the other was released for trial within the center.[26]

Within two weeks after the incident at Poston, a far more serious outburst occurred at the Manzanar Relocation Center following the arrest of three of the camp's more popular residents, who were accused of beating a member of the then unpopular Japanese American Citizens League (JACL). When one of the suspects was transferred to a jail in a nearby town, a mass meeting of several thousand residents was held. The Project Director appeared and agreed to return him for trial in the center. However, a dissident Nisei announced in Japanese that a significant victory had been won over the administration and called for another mass meeting later in the day.

The administration was surprised by this second gathering and called in the military police who were unable to disperse the crowd. The evacuees and soldiers lined up facing each other in an atmosphere of high tension. A rock-throwing melee followed, and tear gas was used. A young evacuee drove a car toward an Army machine gun and then jumped out. In the following confusion, shots were fired which killed two Nisei and wounded nine others. A general strike followed, while the camp remained under control of the military police. After a week, the Army was removed and a group of evacuees met with the Project Director. Within five days, an agreement was reached and the center returned to "normal." [27]

These two crises had vividly similar effects. They helped purge the communities of some of their early tensions and resentments and thereby improved stability. They also brought the administrators more closely in touch with the evacuees' view of life in the centers and revealed to them the crosscurrents that existed among the Japanese. Avenues for sound working relations between Issei and Nisei were now opened. The other eight centers benefitted by the experiences as responsible evacuee leaders worked with their camp staffs to avoid similar incidents.

In the eyes of the West Coast public, however, the Japanese American population appeared to be more disloyal than ever. Ignored were the facts that the evacuees had been imprisoned for the unexplained reason of "military necessity" or for their own "protective custody" and that they had not been charged with a crime nor given a hearing. It was not considered important that the rumors of aid to the enemy at Pearl Harbor had been proven false or that no Japanese American was found guilty of a single act of sabotage or espionage. The West Coast public accepted the fact of incarceration as sufficient proof of disloyalty.[28] Such misinterpretation added to the deteriorating public attitude. Under such conditions, even protests for fair treatment were misrepresented as disloyalty. Thus, one year after the entry of the United States into World War II, the process of making un-Americans out of many of the Japanese American minority was well under way.

3

The Registration Crisis: Segregating the "Disloyal" [1]

While conditions of life within the relocation centers were creating discontent among the evacuees, efforts by the WRA to find an acceptable alternative to concentration camp existence for the West Coast's Japanese population were being made increasingly difficult by a hostile mood outside the camps. The public, particularly on the West Coast, largely maintained an attitude of distrust, suspicion, and hostility. An opinion poll, taken in December, 1942, showed that only 29 percent of the Pacific area population were in favor of allowing the evacuees to return to their homes after the war, while 55 percent would permit either none or only those possessing American citizenship to return. [2]

Political and military leaders, including Governor Earl Warren of California and General DeWitt, spoke out sharply against the evacuees, as did many of the Western and Southern congressional delegations. The American Legion, influential newspapers in the West, and state legislators took up the cry to keep all persons of Japanese descent locked up. [3] Simultaneously, however, many of those who had been thrown in close contact with the evacuated people came to hold a different view. The War Department, which had remained suspicious of the Japanese population throughout 1942, came to realize that there were indeed evacuees who desired an opportunity to prove their loyalty. [4]

The Department's primary concern, however, was with restoration of eligibility in the Selective Service Program. Should this objective prove successful, other civil and constitutional rights would be returned. Such possibilities were also seen by the Japanese American

Citizens League, the Nisei organization which had from the beginning
urged cooperation with the government as the best policy for persons
of Japanese descent to follow.[5] Accordingly, in November, 1942, the
JACL petitioned President Roosevelt for a reinstatement of the draft
for citizens of Japanese descent.[6] These and other considerations convinced the War Department that the Nisei should be given an opportunity to demonstrate their loyalty through military service. Consequently, on January 28, 1943, Secretary of War Stimson announced
the formation of a special all-Nisei combat unit of five thousand members.[7] Army teams were scheduled to visit the ten centers beginning
on February 6, 1943, to register all male Nisei of draft age. A special
questionnaire, designed to test their loyalty and willingness to serve in
the armed forces, was to be completed by each.

The WRA, on the other hand, had a more humanitarian interest in
the evacuees. National Director Myer became convinced that life in
the centers was bad and that all loyal evacuees should have complete
freedom restored. He saw as the solution a segregation program which
would separate the evacuees by loyalty, with those acknowledged as
loyal to the United States being allowed to leave the centers for resettlement in areas to the east of the Pacific Coast.[8] Those designated as
"disloyal" would remain safely confined in a camp set aside for this
purpose.

Myer was quick to realize the benefit of mass registration of the type
proposed by the War Department as an aid to his relocation policy.[9]
Up to this time the greatest obstacle to such a program of relocation
was the slowness of leave clearance on an individual basis. It was clear
that a cooperative undertaking by the WRA and the War Department
was the solution needed to the tedious process of resettlement. The
former's suggestion for a joint operation was readily agreed to by the
latter.[10] Unfortunately, the registration program was poorly planned and
executed. As a result, a program that was humanitarian and laudable
in its objectives had the detrimental effect of moving thousands of otherwise loyal Americans down the road to rejection of the United States
and loss of citizenship.

It was generally believed among those government personnel involved that registration would prove an important step in removing much
of the discrimination against the Nisei. By accepting the call for service in the proposed all-Nisei combat unit they would demonstrate to
the country at large their essential loyalty. Besides actual military ser-

vice, the registration program would offer another way of demonstrating loyalty. Every male citizen of military service age was to fill out a questionnaire which, in addition to calling for basic personal information, would contain two loyalty questions. Numbered twenty-seven and twenty-eight on the questionnaire, they were conceived by the War Department as a way of testing Nisei loyalty. Number Twenty-Seven asked:

Are you willing to serve in the armed forces of the United States on combat duty, wherever ordered?

and Number Twenty-Eight asked:

Will you swear unqualified allegiance to the United States of America and faithfully defend the United States from any and all attack by foreign or domestic forces, and foreswear any form of allegiance or obedience to the Japanese Emperor, or any other foreign government, power, or organization?[11]

The War Department erred in the wording of Question Twenty-Eight. Many Nisei found it offensive. The reference to "allegiance . . . to the Japanese Emperor" was an indication of the emphasis which the government placed on the possession of dual nationality by many Nisei. However, to Nisei who had always thought of themselves as loyal American citizens, or who feared that a "Yes" answer might indicate a former allegiance to Japan, the question was abhorrent.[12]

The War Department realized the registration program would cause resentment in the camps and made serious efforts to prepare for it. Army teams were told they would be asking men to volunteer for an army that had only recently rejected them on suspicions of disloyalty. The first step in meeting evacuee hostility was a statement which was to be read by the captain of the Army team soon after arrival in each of the centers. The assembled Nisei were to be told that:

The fundamental purpose (of registration) is to put your situation on a plane which is consistent with the dignity of American citizenship. You may object that . . . your life here is not freedom. . . . Many millions of Americans agree with your point of view [or] we would not be here. . . . The [registration] is . . . an acknowledgment that the best solution has not been found for you . . . in your relation to the United States. . . . Your government would not take these steps unless it intended to go further in restoring you to a normal place in the life of the country, with the privileges and obligations of other American citizens.[13]

Preparations of the WRA for the registration program were less thorough than those made by the War Department. The WRA saw the program as a means of both reducing restrictions on Japanese Americans and providing information for an accelerated relocation program. Thus, registration was to be extended to all adults in the ten centers. Questionnaires similar to those prepared by the War Department for draft-age male Nisei were formulated for all Issei and female Nisei. The loyalty questions, Numbers Twenty-Seven and Twenty-Eight, were altered to read, respectively:

If the opportunity presents itself and you are found qualified, would you be willing to volunteer for the Army Nurse Corps or the WAAC (Women's Army Auxiliary Corp)?

Will you swear unqualified allegiance to the United States of America and forswear any form of allegiance or obedience to the Japanese Emperor, or any other foreign government, power or organization?

Although the two agencies' forms were basically the same, they differed in titles. The War Department form for male Nisei bore the Selective Service System seal and was entitled "Statement of United States Citizens of Japanese Ancestry," DDS Form 304-A. The WRA form was entitled "Application for Leave Clearance," Form WRA–126. Male Nisei were required to answer an abbreviated version of the WRA questionnaire at the same time they filled out the one for the Army. The fact that the Army questionnaire was voluntary while the WRA form was made compulsory for all evacuees led to serious difficulties later in the program.[14]

WRA officials did not follow the War Department's lead in attempting to allay fears and suspicions with a propagandistic approach to registration. They evidently assumed that registration would be taken as a matter of course by the evacuees and that affirmative answers to the loyalty questions would likewise be given. This assumption was apparently so strong that they did not even attempt to adapt the wording of the Army questionnaire for male Nisei to the far different outlook and problems of the alien Issei. Thus, no explanation was given for the obvious absurdity of asking alien males whether they would be willing to enlist in the Army Nurse Corps or the WAAC. The inference of forced resettlement into what the evacuees felt were hostile communities that might be drawn from the heading "Application for Leave Clearance" was also overlooked. The fact that asking aliens ineligible for American citizenship to forswear allegiance to the only country in which they possessed citizenship, and which would make them stateless and liable to punishment in Japan, was also not recognized until it had thrown many Issei into a state of confusion. Belatedly, Question Twenty-Eight was changed to read: "Will you swear to abide by the laws of the United States and to take no action which would in any way interfere with the war effort of the United States?" [15]

Unfortunately, the plans and preparation of the War Department and the WRA failed to consider fully the deep emotional effects of evacuation and incarceration in the relocation centers. These experiences had profoundly affected the attitudes of almost every adult evacuee toward these two agencies. Any new program could be viewed only in relation to what had already taken place. Confidence in the government's newly professed intentions could not be developed in a few days of discussion and explanation.

The mood of the centers when the program began was that of a people who felt they had already been well tested. They had been filling out forms and giving their life histories to various officials for many months. The Army, the Department of Justice, the Wartime Civil Control Administration, and the WRA were only the most important of the agencies questioning them. The tests had been intricate and abundant. Now came another. Most of the evacuees had been "almost questionnaired to death." [16] They had peacefully bowed to evacuation; they had refused repatriation applications which had been initiated by General DeWitt in his attempt to urge the evacuees to leave the United States; and male Nisei had previously registered their willingness to serve in the military through their local draft boards. To an overwhelming majority of the evacuees, particularly among the Nisei, it now seemed that it was the government's turn to prove good intentions. [17]

It quickly became apparent that the majority of Nisei were not ready to accept the program as a proper test to be complied with uncritically. They felt that the government should not only reopen Selective Service but also restore other lost freedoms to both Issei and Nisei. The issue as most Nisei saw it sharpened into the question: "Shall we go ahead and register under protest or shall we register only on condition that our full rights as citizens are restored?'' Very few were willing to register without at least a strong measure of protest.[18]

Life in the Japanese community had traditionally centered around the family, and family relationships were therefore strong. Because of the influence of the alien Issei parents over their citizen Nisei children, it is important to realize that the registration program seriously disturbed the Issei population also. Since American laws had denied them the right to apply for United States citizenship, the original Question Number Twenty-Eight obviously detrimentally affected them. A ''Yes'' would make them stateless while a ''No'' could conceivably lead to deportation. Another point of concern was the title of the Issei questionnaire, ''Application for Leave Clearance.'' Few Issei wanted to leave the centers while the war was still on. The idea of relocation centers as safe havens from the hostility of Caucasian Americans had crystallized by this time. Yet, since the registration was compulsory, they felt they were being compelled to leave the centers. They reasoned that if this were not the case, why should they be forced to apply for leave clearance. The government appeared to be moving in a direction which was contrary to their interests.[19] Issei were also opposed to the draft because it would divide the family.

The consequences of Issei opposition to registration were serious. Some Nisei bowed to parental will and freely gave negative responses to the loyalty questions. Others stubbornly resisted, subjecting families to intense conflict. Young men and women even came to avoid their parents, itself a humiliating experience, to escape the mortification of facing their embittered elders. Little wonder that under such circumstances hundreds of teen-agers should give in and answer the loyalty questions in the negative.[20]

Parental pressure was not the only force driving Nisei toward what would lead to a ''disloyal'' classification by the government. While a majority of them were willing to settle with a protest against registration and then answer the loyalty questions affirmatively, a large minority in most centers chose forceful ''Nos'' to the loyalty questions as their means of protest. The word ''No'' on the questionnaire was for them a symbol of protest against evacuation and all that had happened since then.[21]

The reaction against registration reached its greatest intensity at the Tule Lake center. An analysis of the registration there is instructive,

illustrating an extreme example of staff-evacuee breakdown in relations; the results of failure by the government to take advantage of the
influential evacuee community councils; and the reaction of evacuees
to registration. Such an analysis is also important since a large per-
centage of the evacuees segregated because of the WRA's program were
a direct result of the failure of registration in Tule Lake.[22]

News of the proposed registration reached Tule Lake residents through
the War Department release to the press on January 29, 1943. However, it was not until February 4 that the camp newspaper, the *Tulean
Dispatch*, made known the fact that registration for recruitment purposes would be correlated with a general registration for leave clearance. At the same time, it was stated that registration would not be
necessary in any of the centers for persons who had applied for repatriation. Despite efforts by the evacuee Community Council and Planning Board to obtain further information, the Tule Lake administration
put off all questions with the statement that further clarification would
be given by the Army team upon its arrival on February 6. Unfortunately, the Army team failed to arrive until February 9, and registration was scheduled to begin the following morning. This left insufficient time for an adequate explanation of the program.

Left in a state of uncertainty from January 29 to February 9 about
what they were to register for, why they had to register, and how registration was to proceed, the evacuees made their own definitions of
issues and procedures. The Army team and WRA officials finally met
with various evacuee groups during the day and evening of February
9. Questions were seldom accepted in these meetings unless they were
on a list of forty-two questions and answers prepared earlier by the
War Department. Furthermore, no time was allowed for discussion despite the anxiety of the evacuees to learn more about the program.[23]

As a result of this lack of information, the evacuees approached the
day of registration in an uneasy frame of mind and with profound doubts
concerning the meaning of the entire program. Little wonder many were
unwilling to fill out the questionnaires.[24] Reports began to circulate that
many Nisei and Kibei were tearing up their birth certificates upon
learning they were being asked to serve in the Army after having been
subjected to the indignity of evacuation, confinement behind barbed
wire, and the insults of the press.[25]

Conditions continued to worsen. In some blocks, agreements not to
register were being made. By the week's end, only a few had regis-

tered. Some who had registered were now asking to have their papers withdrawn. On February 14, the first of several petitions against compliance with the registration program was circulated. A stalemate had been reached.

On the evening of February 10, meetings were held in every block in the center, during which approximately 150 questions were collected. Three days later, these were submitted to the Project Director by the Community Council. On February 15, the Project Director and the captain of the Army team met with the Community Council, the Planning Board, and the block managers, offering answers to only fifty-eight of the 150 questions presented two days earlier. The Project Director contributed to the anxiety at this meeting by placing full responsibility for securing compliance with the registration program solely upon the Community Council and by threatening those evacuees who might interfere with registration with penalties of up to $10,000 and/or twenty years imprisonment under the Espionage Act.[26]

With the publication of this threat in the *Tulean Dispatch*, the situation in Tule Lake declined drastically. On February 17, the center administration publicly listed those blocks in which compulsory registration would be made. Tension quickly mounted, and in Block Forty-Two, one of those specified for compulsory registration, male Nisei overwhelmingly voted not to register. They sent representatives to other block meetings, urging adoption of opposition plans.[27] Meanwhile, many evacuees were beginning to see the possibility of avoiding compliance by invoking the administration's proviso that registration was compulsory "except for those who had requested repatriation." As a result, such large numbers began applying for repatriation or expatriation that an Army representative publicly announced that it was "a mistaken idea" to suppose "that if male citizens obtain repatriation blanks, they do not have to register." Angered by this contradiction in policy, fifty Nisei pushed into the administration building demanding application blanks but were refused.[28]

On February 18, the Tule Lake administration, feeling that opposition was led by pro-Japanese agitators, embarked on a policy of identifying, arresting, and removing the purportedly disruptive elements. The following day, a delegation of thirty-four Nisei youths, accompanied by a large crowd, demanded the right of expatriation in lieu of registration. Instead of complying, the Project Director demanded they register and, upon refusal, ordered their arrest. Two days later, a caravan of cars bearing administration officials, followed by jeeps and trucks carrying military police armed with machine guns and bayonets, moved into Block Forty-Two, picked up the Nisei youths, who were waiting with packed suitcases, and took them to the county jail. As they departed, an angry crowd shouted threats at the soldiers.[29]

Repercussions were immediate. Signs of panic among some evacuees appeared, with many deciding to register; others refused until those arrested were released. The Planning Board and Community Council met in emergency session and appointed a delegation to ask the administration for immediate release of the youths and to propose a new plan for registration. The delegation requested that no further arrests be made and proposed that registration questionnaires be submitted by mail or suspended until tension diminished. All requests and proposals were turned down. Faced with the unwillingness of the administration to make any concessions whatsoever, Planning Board and Community Council members resigned en masse.[30] The evacuee Community Council was never reestablished at Tule Lake.

Meanwhile the authorities found themselves seriously deceiving evacuees in regard to the arrested Nisei and the stated penalties for non-registration. Tule Lake officials had assumed that the failure of Nisei to register was a violation of the Selective Service Act. On February 26, however, it was discovered that the Army questionnaire was not compulsory, and the threats of fine and twenty years imprisonment were invalid. Nevertheless, no announcement of this fact was made to the evacuees, who continued to believe that they were violating the Espionage Act and the Selective Service Act by failing to register. Instead of informing evacuees of the error, the WRA continued its policy of arrests and sought refuge in the legalism that because non-registrants were violating administrative instructions they were liable to ninety days confinement in jail.[31]

The registration of citizens was originally scheduled to end on March 2, 1943. However, since only a third of the male and half of the female Nisei had registered by that date, it was extended until March 10. To the Nisei, in general, the Project Director issued a bulletin stating that those who did not meet the March 10 deadline would "be considered as having violated the orders of the War Department and the WRA and subject to such penalties as may be imposed." This threat was made despite the Project Director's knowledge that the War Department would impose no penalties and the WRA's power to punish was limited.[32] That the registration program at Tule Lake proved a failure could not have been surprising. Of a total of 10,843 Issei and Nisei eligible to register, approximately one-third, or 3,218, refused to do so. Another 1,238 gave "No-No" answers to the two loyalty questions, while thirty-five ignored them. Only thirty-nine Nisei from Tule Lake volunteered for military service.[33] In the other nine centers, only thirty-six persons failed to register.

Of 77,842 eligible registrants in all ten relocation centers, 74,588 eventually registered. Approximately 6,700 of them answered "No" to Number Twenty-Eight, the thoughtless loyalty question that asked American citizens to forswear loyalty to the Japanese Emperor and to swear allegiance to the United States; 2,083 qualified their replies in one way or another; 426 failed to answer this particular question; and the overwhelming majority, 65,312, answered in the affirmative.[34] Although the mass registration has been described by the WRA as "one of the most turbulent periods" in its history, the agency nevertheless accomplished the objectives it sought.[35] The backlog of application forms acquired through the program enabled the agency to speed up the relocation process. Whereas only 866 persons had been relocated during 1942, the number rose to 17,844 by the end of 1943.[36] Army recruitment was also a moderate success, over 1,200 Nisei volunteering for service from the ten centers. Of these, over eight hundred were chosen to form the original United States mainland nucleus of the 442nd Regimental Combat Team, which eventually won the respect of the nation and helped overcome the ingrained prejudice against Japanese Americans that had long existed on the West Coast.[37] It is important to note that many of those who were rejected for military service were excluded for such physical reasons as height and poor eyesight, and not for reasons of disloyalty.

One of the most unfortunate results of registration was its use by the government as a basis for judging the loyalty of the evacuees. While some may have given negative responses out of sentiment for Japan, the great majority did so for reasons which were totally unrelated to national loyalty. For a substantial number, it was a protest against the wartime treatment accorded them. Conditions in the relocation centers prior to registration also helped in determining responses. At Manzanar, for example, where 52 percent of the adult male citizens failed to give affirmative answers, the center had suffered from substandard physical accommodations, unfriendly relations with the staff and nearby towns, and frequent changes in project directors. In contrast, at Minidoka, where negative responses were few, conditions were comparatively good. Considering such factors as the foregoing, and others as well, negative responses to the loyalty questionnaires could more properly be attributed to discontent, fear, confusion, frustration, and disillusionment than to disloyalty to the United States.

Increasing pressures were being brought on the WRA to segregate those who had refused to answer the questionnaire or who had answered the loyalty questions in the negative. Chief among those exerting pressures for such a policy were the Army, the JACL, and overly anxious project directors who tended to magnify the disrupting influence of the "disloyals" among the evacuees. Also, on July 6, 1943, the Senate passed a resolution which requested the WRA to segregate "persons of Japanese ancestry in relocation centers whose loyalty to the United States is questionable or who are known to be disloyal."[38]

Less than two weeks later, on July 15, 1943, the WRA announced adoption of a policy of segregation which actually proved to be broader in scope than most of its proponents had advocated. Five classes of evacuees were listed for removal to a separate "segregation center": (1) aliens who applied for repatriation to Japan and had not withdrawn their requests by July 1, 1943; (2) citizens who had applied for expatriation to Japan; (3) those who had answered the loyalty question in the negative or had failed or refused to answer it; (4) persons who had been denied leave clearance for any reason; and (5) paroled aliens from Department of Justice internment camps who were recommended by that agency for detention.[39] The first two classes totalled 7,222 and constituted the largest number of segregants, while the registration program accounted for the second largest, with 4,785. In order to avoid family separation, family members were to be permitted to accompany the segregants to the new center. These "voluntary segregants" were the only persons in the "disloyal" camp who remained eligible for relocation, although resettlement was made difficult by the fact that the office for this purpose was closed for most of the life of the new segregation center.[40]

Tule Lake Relocation Center in northern California was chosen for transformation into the segregation center because of its large size and the fact that it contained more of the "disloyal" than any other evacuee camp. Although segregation was to have little effect on the nine "loyal" projects, there was nevertheless a substantial minority in those camps for whom the transfer meant reliving the nightmare of the original evacuation program. For the so-called "disloyal" evacuees, the new plan meant breaking up the household and going to still another strange place. Several thousand evacuees scattered throughout all ten centers were not ready to accept the move without active protest. In Tule Lake, the crisis reached major proportions. Unlike the other nine centers, here the "loyal" evacuees were expected to move. Four thousand refused; they remained with two thousand Tuleans, segregants as defined by WRA regulations. The larger groups did not act out of loyalty to Japan but for a combination of reasons including their disgust with the government's arbitrary behavior, their wish to remain in California, and their objection to another move.[41] Despite their acknowledged loyalty, these four thousand internees at Tule Lake were not made eligible for resettlement outside the centers and were as truly prisoners as any of the segregant classes.

As the date for transfer neared, the number of segregants grew. For various reasons many evacuees wished to join the "disloyals" in Tule Lake. For hundreds of "loyals" in each center, Tule Lake increasingly came to be looked upon as a place of security for the duration of the war, where they would be free from the draft, relocation, and the hostility of the Caucasian community. Some chose segregation merely because it was the only way they could return to California. People decided to ask for repatriation or expatriation because that was a means to Tule Lake. "Loyals" about to join "disloyals" talked friends into going; families compromised and went; the number of segregants steadily increased. Tule Lake became a temporary escape from what WRA policy-makers conceived as freedom through the resettlement program.[42]

During September and October, 1943, approximately 8,500 "loyals" and "disloyals" were transferred to Tule Lake to join the 6,000 old Tuleans who had remained in the center. Except for another 3,500, most of whom had to await the construction of barracks, the movement was complete by early November. Those who came to the segregation center hoped to find a haven from further uprooting and to settle down to a peaceful existence for the duration of the war. However, this was not to be the case. As they arrived at their new home, it was obvious that they were regarded as dangerous enemies. Leave clearance was denied, and no community government was to be permitted.[43]

Thus, within a year after their second evacuation since forcible removal from their homes, the ''disloyal'' evacuees had undergone still a third move, one that was to be a last straw in their relations with the United States. The public on the ''outside'' saw the sorting of the Japanese American population in terms of loyalty and disloyalty. Without doubt, only a small minority were enthusiastic supporters of Japan; most of them were at Tule Lake for far different reasons. Some were there looking for security, while others persisted in their protests over past treatment, even though they disliked the idea of being placed side by side with the Japanese patriots in Tule Lake. For these ''No'' answerers, segregation was further evidence of their persecution by the government, and they greeted it with defiance and cynicism.[44] ''Citizenship'' was a word with increasingly little meaning, and they were well on their way to using it as their last significant protest.

4

The Failure of Moderate
Leadership in Tule Lake

The residents of the new Tule Lake Segregation Center arrived in hopes of finding a haven from the fears, worries, and frustrations which they had experienced in the relocation centers. What they found was disappointing. There were many factors which worked against the fulfillment of their hopes. The camp was depressing. High winds constantly swept over the area, and in summer dust-laden air made breathing difficult, driving inhabitants indoors. In winter, the camp was covered with snow, and the shacks and barracks were cold. The flooring of the evacuees' residences contained numerous crevices through which summer dust and winter cold penetrated. Coal was scarce and rationed. Food was insufficient in quantity and unappetizing in quality. A newly erected heavy wire-mesh "man-proof" fence held them inside while elevated block houses and watch towers with armed sentries prevented escape. Outside the fence, a battalion of military police with armored cars and tanks stood in full view of the residents.[1] The WRA insisted that segregation was not punitive, but to many the facts seemed otherwise.

Another factor working against peace and harmony in the center was the nature of the population. The segregation program had made Tule Lake the most heterogeneous of all centers. Persons from throughout the Western states and Hawaii were brought in and scattered through every block in the camp. Moreover, as one staff member phrased it, a great many "people with problems" came to Tule Lake. There were greater numbers of poorer, rural people, unmarried farm laborers, and farm families who had not been doing well in the United States and desired to return to Japan to live out their last years.[2] While such persons truly desired to return to Japan, they equally wished to avoid the disruptive, radical, pro-Japanese movement and events that would soon begin to dominate life in Tule Lake.

Prospects for normal life in Tule Lake were lessened further by the fact that a great many of the less desirable elements from all of the centers were now gathered in one place. This was a natural result of the WRA's policy of isolating disruptive elements in one center so that loyal evacuees in the other centers would have a better chance for resettlement in "normal" communities away from the Pacific Coast states. Because of this, Tule Lake contained "virtually all the trouble-makers, the malcontents, the factious, the rebellious and frustrated, the draft-dodgers, the fanatics, the social misfits, the professional 'organizers', the petty 'politicians' and 'political' leaders, and their gangs of 'goons' and 'strong-arm' boys.''[3] Added to these were all of the anti-administration leaders and their followers who were now gathered together in Tule Lake.

The problem that was to have the most serious repercussions in Tule Lake was that of divided national loyalties. According to the WRA's *Administrative Manual*, the segregation center was for those persons "who by their acts have indicated that their loyalties lie with Japan, . . . or that their loyalties do not lie with the United States.''[4] Unfortunately, the segregation program failed to adhere to this statement and, accordingly, broke down on this point. Instead of creating a center solely for misfits and pro-Japanese individuals who were unacceptable in the other centers, the Tule Lake population included all shades of loyalty and disloyalty to the United States. Children who held status as loyal citizens were allowed to accompany segregant parents to the center, and Issei loyal to the United States likewise accompanied segregant children. Of the 18,422 persons segregated in Tule Lake, more than one-fourth, including 4,517 citizens, were classed as loyal to the United States.[5] The remaining three-fourths included a large number who were classified as disloyal but were in reality in Tule Lake for reasons totally unrelated to national allegiance.[6] As a result, at one extreme were individuals who were decidedly pro-Japanese, while at the other were a significant number who had no intention of going to Japan and felt no loyalty to Japan whatsoever. Between these two groups was the bulk of the population—the fence-sitters. Such persons did not look upon segregation as a final step committing them to inevitable expatriation or repatriation. Instead, many in this group felt that their decision to assume a disloyal status was retractable and that a choice could be made at a later time regarding life in the United States or Japan.[7] The gathering together in one camp of such diverse and antagonistic groups invited trouble.[8]

One of the first reactions of the transferred segregants to the segregation center was antagonism to the more than six thousand Old Tuleans (the name given to residents of the center before segregation who chose to remain rather than move to one of the relocation centers). Not only was a larger proportion of the older residents loyal to the United States, but they held on to the best jobs and best apartments, while the newcomers were widely scattered throughout the project, separated from friends, crowded into inferior residences, and left with the worst employment.

The transferees quickly assumed leadership in the "pursuit of the Japanese way of life," which had been promised by the WRA. Buddhist religious ceremonies flourished, and Christian activities were relegated to a minor place. A group of older Issei organized a Japanese Language School Board and made plans for the establishment of Japanese language schools. This was a popular program since a large number of Nisei had merely a smattering of Japanese or an imperfect knowledge picked up in the preevacuation language schools. Some felt strongly that learning Japanese was an important preparation for life in Japan.[9] These schools later became important agencies for indoctrinating youth with pro-Japanese propaganda.

A minority of the transferees immediately set out to demonstrate forcefully that Tule Lake was created for Japanese, not Americans. Although most of the leaders in the pro-Japan group were alien Issei, many of their followers were youthful Kibei. The latter were looked down upon by the majority of the Nisei in the relocation centers because of their imperfect English and lack of familiarity with American ways and etiquette. Many of the Kibei took as license the designation of the center as a place where people could live like Japanese. Their harsh treatment of Nisei girls, their objection to American dancing, and their support of Japanese language schools were all expressions of their newly found status, and they were busy trying to pull into line the "loyal" evacuees who had accompanied the "disloyal" segregants to Tule Lake.

The WRA agreed with the view that Tule Lake was to be regarded as a place for evacuees who wanted to pursue a Japanese way of life. In most respects, the segregation center was to be run much as were the other centers, with the exception of evacuee government and education. Self-government, as established at other centers, was not allowed, although a democratically elected Representative Committee could be organized in order to act as an advisory council to the administration and as a liaison between the residents and the project director. The evacuees were also permitted to establish Japanese language schools (at their own expense) and to carry on various Japanese ceremonies and cultural activities, since these were in keeping with a preparation for life in Japan. Freedom of religion was granted, with the exception of "State Shinto, which is nationalistic rather than religious in character."[10]

The WRA's regulations for Tule Lake were not all of a benevolent nature, however. This was particularly true in the administration of justice. The project administration was given sweeping powers to act as law-maker, prosecutor, and judge. It could decide what acts were offenses and what court—federal, state, or segregation center—would try the case.[11] The camp administration was also permitted to "restrict the movement and activities of persons whose *influence* [italics by the author] or actions may be disruptive of the operations of the Center" and to transfer such persons "either to a separate area within the Center [i.e., a prison within a prison] . . . or to an isolation center outside the project." Since this was considered "purely an administrative arrangement to secure the peaceful and orderly administration of the Center," an individual could be arrested and held without charges upon merely "an administrative determination of the Project Director."[12] Under this regulation, over three hundred evacuees were later arrested and held for periods up to eleven months without charges or hearings of any kind. Such regulations led sociologist Rosalie Hankey Wax to describe the Tule Lake administration as "a benevolent 'democratic' dictatorship."[13]

The earliest leaders to arise were reasonable and moderate men, despite the fact that they had been among the anti-administration leaders in their former relocation centers. Their rise to control in Tule Lake came about as a result of a series of evacuee protests to the project administration concerning working and living conditions. On October 7, 1943, the administration abruptly terminated the employment of forty-three members of the evacuee coal crew who had vigorously protested the discharge of three co-workers for alleged insubordination. Consequently, the workers approached several transferee leaders who had been known in their former centers for aggressive anti-administration attitudes, including Taro Watanabe (pseudonym), an Issei, and H. Doi (pseudonym), from Heart Mountain.[14] They took the matter to the administration, which not only rehired the men but was forced to make certain concessions. This affair strengthened the position of these leaders with the population and demonstrated the ability of the evacuees to force the administration to back down.[15]

Shortly after this dispute, a serious accident occurred which precipitated a deepening split between residents and administration and the formation of an unauthorized evacuee government. On October 15, a farm truck overturned and five men were gravely hurt, including one who died soon afterward. In protest, hundreds of angry farm workers left the fields and returned to the center. They refused to work at the farm unless safeguards against further accidents were set up and adequate compensation for the injured persons was provided. At the same time, the farmers realized that the work stoppage, with the consequent loss of thousands of dollars worth of crops, offered an unparalleled opportunity to alleviate other grievances and to improve living conditions.[16]

The morning after the accident, representatives of the farm workers met with the evacuee leaders who had assisted the coal crew in its successful dispute with the administration. During the afternoon of that same day, the block managers met, agreed to support the farm workers, and then began the process of forming an organization to represent the entire camp. That evening sixty-four representatives were chosen in block by block elections. The body thus formed was called the *Daihyo Sha Kai* (Representative Body). George Kuratomi of the Jerome Relocation Center and H. Doi of Heart Mountain were elected chairman and vice-chairman, respectively. On October 17, the day after the election, the farm group formally placed all of its proposed negotiations with the administration in the hands of the *Daihyo Sha Kai*.[17]

Aside from the fact that the entire evacuee community planned and organized this popular representative body in only one day, the most striking aspect of the new organization was its democratic character. Persons who had been segregated purportedly for having renounced democracy were now behaving like genuine democrats. At the first meeting of the *Daihyo Sha Kai*, chairman Kuratomi calmed the more vociferous delegates and opposed a number of drastic actions which might have alienated the administration. After agreeing upon a program for negotiating the farm situation with the administration and agreeing to continue the work stoppage, the *Daihyo Sha Kai* focused its attention on settling some of the basic grievances of the residents regarding center living conditions.[18] The newly formed evacuee government assigned each problem to a particular committee, which in turn conducted investigations and met with residents to discuss the problem and to consider solutions. The central, and most important, subcommittee was the Negotiating Committee, made up of seven members, one from each ward in the camp, plus the chairman and vice-chairman of the *Daihyo Sha Kai*.[19] The purpose of the Negotiating Committee was to negotiate the problems of the residents with the administration.[20]

The Tule Lake administration, meanwhile, was totally unaware of the plans and activities of the residents in establishing the *Daihyo Sha Kai* and of that organization's preparations for negotiating a solution to the farm situation and the improvement of living conditions.[21] As a result, the administration, concerned with the possible loss of the valuable farm crop, issued an ultimatum to the farm workers to send an official spokesman to discuss the problem by 8:30 A.M., October 21, or the Army would be requested to harvest it, with its consequent loss to the evacuees.[22] In response, the farm foremen informed the administration, on October 20, that they had delegated responsibility for contact with the government officials to the Negotiating Committee and that the farm laborers could not return to work until the planned negotiations had been completed.[23] On the following day, Ray Best, the project director, invited "any representative committee to discuss any problem" with him. The *Daihyo Sha Kai*, however, was less interested in a rapid settlement than in marshalling the people's grievances in an orderly and impressive form so that genuine concessions could be obtained.[24]

Before Best's offer could be acted upon, however, tension and anti-administration feeling reached a new height as a result of preparations for the funeral of Kashima, the farm worker killed in the accident. His death had moved the people deeply. According to one Nisei, "they felt that the people who got hurt represented the whole center. They wanted to give Kashima an honorable funeral because he represented

all of us."[25] The desire for an honorable funeral resulted in a proposal
to have a public ceremony. Consequently, Best was approached separately by representatives of the *Daihyo Sha Kai* and the farm workers
for permission to hold a public funeral to honor the dead worker. Best
curtly refused the evacuee proposals, which he took as demands that
challenged the power of the WRA.[26] The *Daihyo Sha Kai* was angered
by Best's refusal and decided that the funeral would be held, with or
without authorization, on the project's outdoor stage on October 23.

The open defiance of the residents in holding the funeral was countered the following day with an act designed to render the evacuees
powerless. Best telegraphed the project directors of the Topaz and Poston
centers, requesting that evacuees from these projects be recruited to
harvest the crop at Tule Lake. This move was carefully kept secret
from the residents of Tule Lake, and even the project directors to whom
the request was made were misinformed about the situation.[27] This plan
would take from the residents their only important bargaining point in
their quest for better camp conditions—the fact that a valuable crop
would be lost unless they, themselves, agreed to harvest it.

On October 26, 1943, three days after the funeral, the *Daihyo Sha
Kai* finally completed its investigations of camp conditions and was
ready to accept Best's invitation to discuss project problems. The meeting
was dominated by the administration's trump card—the fact that Best,
unknown to the center's residents, had called for evacuees from other
centers to harvest the crop. The Project Director received the members
of the Negotiating Committee courteously and listened to their requests. He gave the Committee no encouragement on the farm incident
or on the food situation, but he was extremely affable and agreeable
on other matters. He was particularly reassuring on the matter of community government. As a result of this friendly meeting, the Negotiating Committee was optimistic. Best had treated the Committee as if
it were already a fully constituted advisory board.

The good will was shattered two days later, on October 28, however, when the administration bluntly announced that the entire eight-
hundred-man farm crew had been fired. The next day, the residents
learned through the newspaper that "loyal harvesters" would soon arrive. As a result, even the most timid and conservative persons were
outraged and joined the hotheads in denouncing the "double-crossing"
WRA and the "double-crossing loyal Japanese" strikebreakers.[28] The

administration had united the entire camp by its actions. The hostility between the Old Tuleans and transferees was submerged in common hostility to the administration.

The *Daihyo Sha Kai* made plans to strike back through a proposed meeting with WRA National Director Myer, who was scheduled to arrive in Tule Lake on November 1, 1943. When the project administration refused to arrange a meeting between Myer and the Negotiating Committee, camp leaders decided to force a meeting. In order to demonstrate that they had the support of the whole camp, *Daihyo Sha Kai* representatives appeared at all of the messhalls at noon and announced that Myer would meet with the Negotiating Committee that afternoon and would speak to the people. All were exhorted to attend.[29]

The demonstration was made entirely without warning to the administration. After lunch, a veritable multitude, estimated at between five thousand and ten thousand persons, streamed toward the administration area. Upon seeing this, Myer and Best were alarmed. However, when the two men saw that the crowd included both old and young, mothers with babies, and children of all ages, they became convinced that no violence was intended. Most of the crowd came as a gesture of support for the Negotiating Committee, since resentment against the administration was intense. *Daihyo Sha Kai* leaders were unwilling to risk a slackening of interest during the meeting, however, and groups of young men were assigned to block any efforts of the crowd to return to their barracks.[30]

After Myer found himself virtually imprisoned in the administration building by thousands of evacuees, he agreed to see the Negotiating Committee. Some evacuees, without instructions to do so, guarded the doors to see that no Caucasians left. During the two-and-a-half-hour conference, Best and Myer made no concessions on important points but were agreeable and cooperative on minor issues. Myer repeatedly stated that he would accept no demands but would consider requests or suggestions. He also refused to recognize members of the Negotiating Committee as representatives of the people, saying "You folks are serving in a temporary capacity until a truly representative committee has been chosen," and "I don't know how many people you represent."[31]

The *Daihyo Sha Kai* had planned the demonstration as a peaceful show of force in hopes of enhancing its negotiating power with the administration. However, an unrelated act of violence that occurred just as the meeting was about to begin had serious repercussions in the segregation center. While the crowd was gathering around the administration building, some young men entered the hospital, sought out the very unpopular chief medical officer, Dr. R. Pedicord, and gave him a severe beating. Although the administration recognized that the attack was an isolated incident, this and the fact that evacuee guards had prevented staff members from leaving the surrounded administration building struck fear into many of the project's Caucasian personnel. False rumors spread that there had been knives and other weapons among the demonstrators and that there had been attempts to set the buildings on fire. Some staff members became so hysterical with fear that they would not sleep in the project, going instead to nearby towns for safety.

On November 2, 1943, the Caucasian employees of Tule Lake held a series of meetings. The results were that some staff members resigned, while others demanded that a fence be erected between the administration building and the evacuee areas. Military protection was also demanded, including machine guns and tanks. Such staff fears were quickly reacted to: the military stood in readiness to occupy the center upon the summons of any Caucasian Internal Security Officer; a high barbed wire fence was erected separating the evacuee section from the Caucasian section; and sentries were placed at the gates, through which no evacuee could enter without a pass.[32]

While the administration took rapid steps to protect itself, the evacuee leaders were filled with optimism. Quite unaware of the tension and fear prevailing among the center's staff members, they proceeded to publicize and exaggerate the concessions promised by the administration. They also threw their energy into planning a stable and permanent representative body that would be acceptable to the administration. Their idea was to elect a selection committee which would choose nominees for the new body from lists submitted by each block. These nominees would then be subject to final approval by the residents and the administration. After this, the *Daihyo Sha Kai* planned to resign.[33] The plans of the evacuee leaders were shattered, however, as the tensions, created among the residents by the farm situation and among the Caucasian staff by the November 1 incident, culminated in the occupation of Tule Lake by the Army.

The Army moved into Tule Lake with tanks, armored cars, gas, and machine guns on the evening of November 4, 1943, and assumed control of the center. The *Daihyo Sha Kai* was busily at work at the time making plans for the election of a new representative body. The members heard the sounds of tanks and machine guns and were warned by a Kibei youth that the Army had entered the center. Unaware of the seriousness of the matter, however, they merely sent the youth out with instructions to "tell the boys to behave and keep out of trouble." The meeting continued until 2:00 A.M. It was not until later that day that the evacuee leaders learned of the futility of their parliamentary activity.[34]

Although the Army roared into Tule Lake to the rumble of tanks and sounds of gunfire, most of the camp's population lived some distance from the route of entry and were thus unaware that anything untoward had taken place. Accordingly, approximately a thousand workers proceeded as usual to their jobs in the administrative area on the following morning. As they approached the gate, they were met by a cordon of soldiers who told them to return to their homes. However, before the workers could comply with the order, their number was increased by a crowd of curious residents from nearby barracks. Faced by a milling, rapidly growing crowd of evacuees, and unable to disperse it by oral commands, the soldiers released a barrage of tear gas. Some residents reported being kicked by soldiers who refused to listen to their arguments for wanting to enter the area. The would-be workers, bewildered and indignant, fled to their quarters.[35]

This unprovoked attack on the evacuee working staff aggravated the situation. Until this time, only the farm crew was without work. Now the entire evacuee population, except the essential hospital and mess workers, was prevented from working. Moreover, some conservative persons who had not supported the *Daihyo Sha Kai* were also teargassed while attempting to go to work. The people remained bitter for many months after this incident, and for a time they were completely cut off from the administrative area. Passes into the area were denied, and not even telephone calls from the Japanese residents were accepted.[36]

Without Japanese doctors, nurses, typists, warehousemen, police, and garbage, coal, and mess crews, the center could not function. Tule Lake, except for the fact that it was surrounded by barbed wire, was a community much like any other. Its eighteen hundred residents needed to be cared for. Thus, some means had to be found to get the people back to work. On the other hand, the WRA had followed a policy of spreading employment as widely as possible, and, as a result, some work crews had been greatly overstaffed. Such a policy helped the evacuees fight the boredom of camp life, and the sixteen, nineteen, and twenty-one dollars monthly pay, though insufficient, gave them at least some spending money. The work stoppage, however, presented the Army and the administration with an opportunity to drastically cut the number of workers to an efficient level. Consequently, when the *Daihyo Sha Kai* leaders presented the Army with a plan for returning the men to work, they were turned down. Instead, the Army, with the approval of the camp administration, worked out a plan for returning only a limited number to work. This policy was aimed at two objectives: (1) to purge all those who were under suspicion of anti-administration aims or acts from the work crews; and (2) to introduce a more efficient plan for organizing work.[37] The plan met with immediate opposition from the evacuees. A stalemate developed, as even those evacuees who were cleared for employment refused to return to work without their former co-workers.

As relations between the two government agencies and the residents of Tule Lake worsened into ever greater hostility, the evacuees' reliance on Japan for protection increased correspondingly. Japanese interests in the United States were cared for by the Spanish government, whose consul, F. de Amat, made several visits to the camp upon the requests of its residents.[38] His sympathetic attitude was in sharp contrast to the attitudes and actions of the Army and the WRA. This difference was psychologically important in reinforcing the evacuees' dependence upon Japan rather than the United States in their time of need. The evacuee newspaper, the *Tulean Dispatch*, for example, carried articles which gave the impression that Japan would soon intercede and protect the Japanese in Tule Lake.[39]

The leaders of the *Daihyo Sha Kai* made strenuous efforts to ease the tense situation in the center. They attempted to negotiate with the Army and to get the people back to their jobs. At the same time, they urged the people to remain sensible and prudent and not to resort to violence. Parents were asked to caution their children against making insulting remarks to the soldiers. People were told not to congregate in groups of more than five and not to destroy anything in the center.[40]

The Army and the Negotiating Committee carried on discussions for eight days in an effort to restore jobs and return the community to normal. These talks began in a tone of cooperation, but they quickly deteriorated to the point where, on November 12, Colonel Verne Austin, commander of the Army unit in the center, informed the Committee that he doubted its claims of representing the people and that he would no longer recognize it as a medium for negotiations.[41] Nevertheless, the Colonel and the WRA expressed their willingness to join the Negotiating Committee in a mass meeting on the following day, November 13, so that each side could state its position to the people. The real intent of the authorities in agreeing to this meeting was to discredit the Committee before the people.[42]

The *Daihyo Sha Kai* met, however, and voted overwhelmingly to cancel the meeting. The reasons for this action, as later reported to the population in the *Tulean Dispatch* were that the Negotiating Committee felt that there was no report to make to the residents due to the Army's termination of negotiations; the Army did not recognize the Committee as true representatives of the people; and the Army believed that it knew how many workers there should be in each division, and the WRA should choose who the workers would be.[43] In accordance with this decision, members of the *Daihyo Sha Kai* notified the people, at breakfast on November 13, that there would be no mass meeting. No one, however, informed the Army or the WRA of the cancellation.

The Army struck back quickly for this act of passive resistance. It blamed the evacuees' failure to attend on the *Daihyo Sha Kai* and immediately ordered the arrest of members of the Negotiating Committee, other leaders of the *Daihyo Sha Kai*, and prominent members of the farm organization. At the same time, martial law was declared.

With this act, the Army completely destroyed the enthusiasm for democratic action which the residents of Tule Lake had displayed in the election of the *Daihyo Sha Kai*, the only truly representative evacuee organization the segregation center was ever to know. The "disloyal" evacuees had attempted to act like Americans and to create a representative government. Now only distrust and even hatred were felt for the camp administration and, by association, for the government it represented.

1. **Pre-construction site of Tule Lake Relocation Center** shows the isolation and bleakness of the one-square-mile camp that became the home for over 18,000 Japanese Americans. Photograph taken April 23, 1942. Source: National Archives.

2. A lone Nisei crosses a firebreak through mud in Tule Lake created by melting snow. In the background are the tar-paper-covered barracks in which families crowded in twenty-feet-square rooms that often contained cracks in the ceilings and floors and had no running water. Source: National Archives.

3. Guard tower, wire-mesh "man-proof" fence; and gate guard illustrate the concentration camp atmosphere in which the evacuees lived. Despite the fact that Japanese Americans had not been charged with crimes or given hearings, many Americans accepted incarceration as proof of disloyalty. Source: National Archives.

4. Radicals drill in honor of the departure of 171 pro-Japan leaders for the Department of Justice Internment Camp at Santa Fe, New Mexico on January 26, 1945. Similar mass marching exercises were held by male *Hokoku Seinen-dan* and female *Hokoku Joshi Seinen-dan* to impress government hearing officers of the earnestness of their desire for renunciation of citizenship. Source: National Archives.

5. Bugle Corps of the *Hokoku Seinen-dan* perform at the departure of 125 of their number sent to internment at Santa Fe on March 4, 1945. Buglers often played the Japanese national anthem at 5:30 A.M. to awaken militants for drill. Source: National Archives.

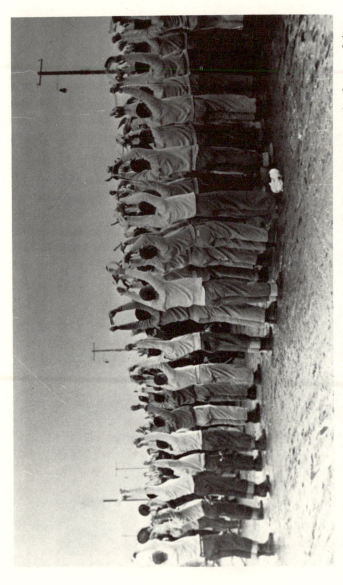

6. **"*Banzai!*" salute to departing radical leaders**—Shouts by young militants were a regular feature of the removal of renunciants and radical leaders from Tule Lake Segregation Center. These demonstrations were accompanied by patriotic songs, bugle blowing, and military drills. Source: National Archives.

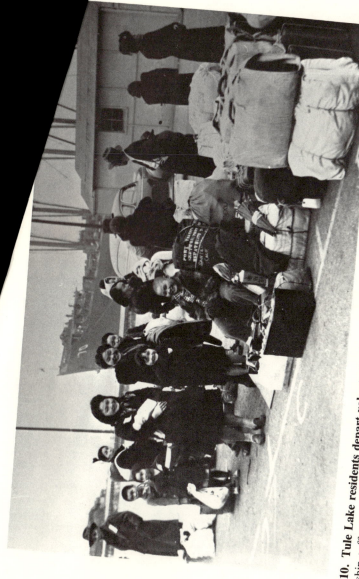

10. Tule Lake residents depart voluntarily for Japan—American citizens too young to renounce their citizenship suffer loss of their native land as alien parents, disillusioned at a future in the United States, get ready to board ship to return to Japan with their children. Source: National Archives.

7. "Lay-down" strikers forcibly removed from Tule Lake—Some of the twenty-five radical leaders were removed from their beds and made to walk in various stages of dress to the Department of Justice train which took them to the internment camp in Santa Fe on June 24, 1945. Source: National Archives.

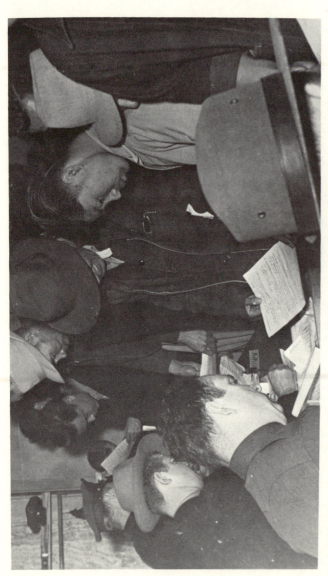

8. Renunciants sign repatriation papers under orders of the Department of Justice. Many who wrote on the forms that they were signing under protest, were forced to tear up their papers and fill out new ones without the protest. The Department of Justice, alone among the government agencies concerned with Tule Lake, was determined to deport all renunciants to Japan. Source: National Archives.

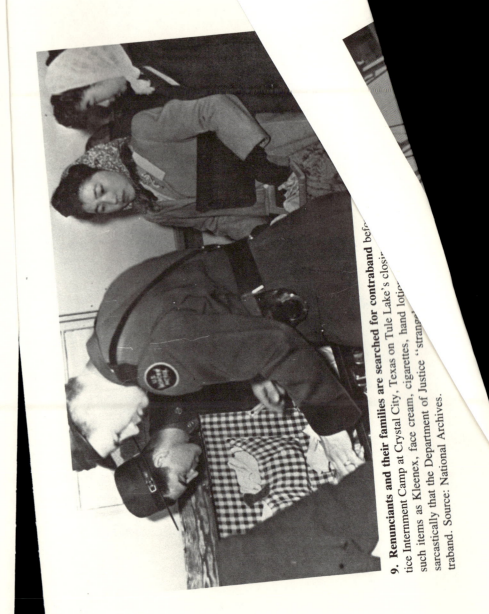

9. Renunciants and their families are searched for contraband before Internment Camp at Crystal City, Texas on Tule Lake's closing. tice such items as Kleenex, face cream, cigarettes, hand lotion, sarcastically that the Department of Justice "strange" traband. Source: National Archives.

5

Martial Law and the Rise of the Radical Underground

The Army took over Tule Lake on November 4, 1943, and declared martial law on November 13. The segregation center was not returned to the control of its civilian administrators until January 15, 1944. The WRA, viewing the period in hindsight after the war, admitted that "the segregation center had become a place of real repression. The peace that its residents had been looking for had receded farther away than ever." The agency belatedly recognized that the situation "arose less from the nature of the people who lived there than from the nature of government supervision and control they experienced." [1]

The period of martial law was one of turmoil, impoverishment, idleness, and uncertainty for the camp's population. The refusal of all but essential employees to work meant that most residents were left without the meager sixteen, nineteen, or twenty-one dollar salaries needed to buy such common necessities as clothing and shoes. Incoming and outgoing telephone and telegraph messages were denied to the inhabitants without military permission, as were all outdoor meetings and gatherings. A curfew kept people indoors between the hours of 7:00 P.M. and 6:00 A.M.[2] Although these restrictions were primarily intended to inhibit agitation among the residents, they also put a stop to dances, ball games, and other forms of amusement.

Some of Tule Lake's residents faced even greater suffering than the general population because of the declaration of martial law. For the leaders of the *Daihyo Sha Kai*, for the alleged instigators of the November "riots," and for a number of other individuals who opposed the administration in one way or another, the period was one of increasingly severe repression, including midnight pickups and incarceration in the infamous "stockade." Confinement of evacuees in this "detention area" became an emotional concern which rapidly replaced unemployment and food problems as the major issue for the ten-month period following its creation on November 4, 1943. Even during the brief period of outward normalcy which returned to Tule Lake in mid–1944, there was an underlying and widespread fear of arrest and detention. By the end of December, 1943, over two hundred evacuees had been confined in the stockade, while the ultimate number was much higher. Some inmates were held for as long as ten months. All were held without hearings, charges, or trials of any kind.

Internment in the stockade proved to be an unnecessarily cruel punishment. Located in an isolated section of the camp, it was guarded by massive sentry towers and search lights. All visits were denied, while mail was censored and sometimes withheld from inmates for long periods. On one occasion, when wives, children, and other relatives and friends began gathering at a fence one hundred yards away from the stockade to wave, the administration denied even this form of communication by erecting beaver-board fences to block their view. The WRA denied that the internees were "prisoners," a term it disliked, and instead referred to the inmates by the euphemism "detainees."[3]

In addition to the creation of the stockade issue, the period of martial law also resulted in the disintegration of the *Daihyo Sha Kai* as a political organization; the development of the Coordinating Committee, an organization aimed at collaborating with the camp administration in carrying out government policy; and the emergence of an anti-administration underground pressure group, called the Resegregationists, dedicated to a separation of the "disloyal" from the "loyal" while awaiting an opportunity to return to Japan to serve the mother country.[4]

The *Daihyo Sha Kai* was mortally wounded by the arrests of its leaders following the November 13 declaration of martial law. Nevertheless, it struggled on for a brief time as several of its leaders, including George Kuratomi, managed to elude the authorities and direct the organization from their place of hiding within the camp. Meanwhile, those members of the *Daihyo Sha Kai* and the Negotiating Committee who remained free formulated a policy for the camp's residents which called for: the continuance of the partial strike; refusal to betray their hidden leaders; and refusal to elect a new representative body. This became known as the "status quo" and was accepted by the great majority of the center's population since they looked to their leaders to act in the best interests of all.[5]

On November 18, the Army and the WRA made an attempt to get the evacuees to give up their hiding leaders. Military and project officials made it clear that they would never recognize the Negotiating Committee. However, they failed to obtain the cooperation of even the most moderate, pro-American residents. The Army then turned to the use of force in its efforts to apprehend the hiding men. On November 26, 1943, it conducted a search, ostensibly for contraband, hidden weapons, and rice from which sake could be made. Both military and WRA personnel were used. The Army formed two teams which worked from each side of the camp towards the center firebreak. A large number of soldiers were used to insure that no resident could slip back into an area that had been searched. Every man, woman, and child was searched at bayonet point. However, only one of the five hidden leaders was found, despite the thoroughness of the search. Approximately ninety other persons were picked up, some merely for lack of Army identification cards. The charges against a majority of these individuals were never stated, and many were kept for months in the stockade.[6]

The Army continued searching evacuee barracks for approximately twelve days and nights. The pressure from the searches, in addition to criticism from within the *Daihyo Sha Kai* and the failure of the Spanish Consul to come to their aid, led the hiding Negotiating Committee members to a decision to surrender.[7] On December 1, 1943, they gave themselves up to officers of the FBI and joined the organization's other leaders in the stockade.

The now leaderless *Daihyo Sha Kai* faced a very grave situation. Although it selected an "Acting Negotiating Committee" to replace the jailed body, the Army continued to refuse to recognize it as representatives of the people. As a result, the *Daihyo Sha Kai* met on December 4 and, in keeping with its democratic character, voted to let Tule Lake's residents decide the future course of action. The voting was by blocks. The options were: (1) to declare a general strike and at the same time enter a hunger strike; (2) by dissolution of the *Daihyo Sha Kai*, select a new body, then request the Army for the release of the two hundred persons held in the stockade; or (3) maintain the "status quo" and the present condition no matter how long, until the authorities give in—in other words, let time solve the problem.[8]

The results, announced the following day by the *Daihyo Sha Kai*, showed: two blocks undecided; three blocks for a general strike; four blocks for dissolution; and fifty-six blocks for continuing the "status quo." The WRA much later correctly interpreted the residents' overwhelming support of the "status quo" as being: a reaction to the curfew; opposition to the patrolling of the center by armed soldiers; opposition to the mere fact of Army control itself; but most of all, the agency saw the vote as a demonstration against the continued incarceration of the men picked up by the military police. The "leaders of the November 1 demonstration were men whom many regarded as their duly elected representatives who had championed their interests against the administration. . . . Consequently, . . . they quickly became symbols around which large numbers of evacuees could rally."[9] To stop the strike without their release would constitute a betrayal.

Meanwhile, the WRA began to find the strict and rigid existence under Army rule almost as uncomfortable as did the evacuees. Some administrators were concerned over the concentration camp atmosphere which the Army's control brought. Moreover, the top civilian administrators found the Army to be personally oppressive. As one staff member put it:

Colonel Meek was kicking Best around. He would come all the way from Fort Douglas [Utah] to do it. . . . Best was here rankling under the situation. Colonel Austin was doing all sorts of things (objectionable to the War Relocation Authority).[10]

The Army agreed that it should return Tule Lake to its civilian administrators. Nevertheless, it did not feel that this could be done until the center returned to what the Army commander considered "normal." This, he believed, would follow: a submissive return to work; the arrest of those responsible for the strike; the dissolution of the *Daihyo Sha Kai*; and a new, genuinely representative body, selected by specifications laid down by the military.[11]

Under these conditions, the best hope of the WRA for ending Army rule was in securing the cooperation of a group of evacuees who would aid in ending the strike and who could then be set up as temporary representatives of the people. Fortunately for project officials, the first signs of a break in the solidarity which the evacuees had displayed against the administration since the establishment of the segregation center began to appear in mid-December. By this date, most of the people in Tule Lake had lost all hope of winning the strike.[12] Accordingly, the administration established an Advisory Council, made up of Caucasian staff members, which began to make overtures to evacuees who might be counted on to favor a policy of accommodation with the authorities. The Council's advances were favorably received by two renegades from the *Daihyo Sha Kai* and by certain officials of the conservative, pro-administration Civic Association and Co-operative Enterprises.[13]

By January 7, 1944, the administration had secured the cooperation of a group of forty men from various evacuee organizations in the project. They called themselves the Divisional Responsible Men. This body, in turn, selected seven men to make plans for a popular referendum on ending the partial strike being carried on as part of the "status quo" program and for a return to work by the center's residents. The seven decided to act without warning to give those supporting the strike no time to organize.

The referendum was scheduled for the evening of January 11, 1944. On the morning of that day, the Army arrested a number of alleged strike supporters. Meanwhile, the collaborationist leaders deluged the center with mimeographed propaganda reminding the residents that the *Daihyo Sha Kai* had failed in its negotiations with the Army and the WRA and that it had not stopped the arrests, which continued to be made daily. For its own part, the committee of seven accommodators pledged to restore employment and to secure the release of men in the stockade.[14]

Voting was by secret ballot, with soldiers present at some polling places. Of 8,713 ballots cast, 4,493 were for abandoning the strike and 4,120 in favor of continuing it. Thus, the decision to return to "normalcy," i.e., conditions before the strike, was won by a plurality of only 473. Since soldiers were stationed at all polling places, overt force was probably not used. Nevertheless, the morning arrests by the Army left the impression that a vote in favor of the strike might lead to arrest and undoubtedly impeded freedom of action by some.

An analysis of the election refutes the contention of the WRA and the collaborationist group that support of the strike was limited to a minority of the center's population. The vote was held after seven weeks of hopeless and wretched resistance, during which all recreational activities had ceased, people had daily faced the very real possibility of arrest, and there was often no money for shoes, clothing, or general welfare. Despite these conditions, 47 percent of the voters favored continuance of the strike, and of those who voted in support of the WRA's plan, most voted to abandon the strike out of fatigue and despair rather than from a spirit of support for a new political faction which would get them jobs and obtain the release of the detainees.[15]

A week after the referendum, the WRA and the Army officially recognized the committee of seven accommodators which had planned the election as a temporary body that would assist in restoring the center to a normal condition. After this was accomplished, the committee was expected to resign in order to make way for an elected body. These seven became known as the Coordinating Committee. Simultaneously, the Army announced the lifting of martial law, withdrew most of the soldiers from the center, and returned the management of the segregation center, except for the stockade, to the WRA.[16]

The members of the Coordinating Committee were moderate men, as had been the leaders of the *Daihyo Sha Kai*. Both desired evacuee government by popularly elected bodies, and the Coordinating Committee looked upon itself as a temporary body whose purpose was to restore normal conditions so that democratic elections could take place. Both organizations desired to settle the camp's problems and to bring harmony to the community. However, here their similarities ended. The Negotiating Committee of the *Daihyo Sha Kai* had been a popularly elected body which had attempted to negotiate with a still-credible project administration. Unfortunately, the events following the November 1 incident brought drastic changes to Tule Lake which the Coordinating Committee now had to face. The hostility between the transferee bloc and the Old Tuleans, and between the "loyals" and the "disloyals," had increased, while the Army and the WRA had become universally distrusted and widely hated. As a result, a policy of collaboration by a pro-administration group which had been "selected" to replace the camp's "elected" representatives was destined for trouble.

Because of these unfavorable circumstances, the Coordinating Committee had to produce results quickly if it were to win the backing of the community. This would require administration support, which the Committee, in assuming its new responsibilities, had the clear understanding it would receive.[17] Unfortunately, it was not always forthcoming. Few members of the Tule Lake administrative staff showed any real concern for the evacuees, and the result was little sympathy, or empathy, for their plight. Moreover, the overall goal of the WRA worked against the plans of the Coordinating Committee. National Director Myer was concerned with making the loyal evacuees in the nine relocation centers acceptable to the American public for relocation into normal "outside" communities. Trouble in the segregation center would once again raise national headlines of "Jap riots" and bring on a rash of congressional and state legislative investigations. Thus, at least an outward appearance of normality was viewed as an essential goal for Tule Lake. Justice to individuals therein was at best a secondary concern.[18] The administration, having lost all contact with the evacuee community during the period of martial law, needed the Coordinating Committee to restore communications. However, future events proved that the administration was willing to support the Committee only when it stayed within the WRA's narrow, preconceived ideas of what was necessary to restore the appearance of normality. Since the WRA never really understood the Tule Lake evacuees, the essential elements of support necessary for a successful program were not forthcoming.

The Coordinating Committee faced a number of other obstacles. One was the development of a radical underground movement which opposed both the administration and the Committee in an intensified effort to resegregate the "loyals" and "disloyals" pending an early move to Japan. For the entire life of the Coordinating Committee, from mid-January until early April, 1944, the two opposing groups strove to win popular support. Throughout this period, neither had much material success. A majority of residents looked upon the radicals as agitators and troublemakers and viewed the Coordinating Committee as *inu* who were collaborating with the unpopular and distrusted administration and as persons who were attempting to replace their imprisoned elected representatives.[19]

The Coordinating Committee announced two goals in its effort to win over this opposition and to return normal conditions to the center: (1) full employment; and (2) "justifiable" release of stockade detainees. The first objective was regarded as essential to the residents, few of whom had worked for over two months, and to the WRA, which needed evacuee personnel to restore community services and to return an appearance of "normalcy" to the center. The second goal was viewed

as essential to the new Committee, since over four thousand persons
had voted to continue striking until the prisoners were freed, and many
who had voted for a return to work agreed with this position. The WRA,
however, had no intention of releasing the leaders of the November
incidents. Administration officials remained diligently on guard against
the slightest symptom of agitation or popular unrest which might return them to what they considered as the nightmare period of the November uprising. Their view was that the release of the leaders and
others whom they regarded as troublemakers or "potential" trouble-
makers would result in new disturbances. Thus, retention in the stockade was seen, incorrectly, as a measure for promoting peace in the
center.[20] This misunderstanding was a result of the complete isolation
of the Caucasian staff from the evacuee community. In the absence of
communication, there was no chance for either side to learn the state
of mind of the other. The Coordinating Committee, with an almost non-
existent base of community support, was not an effective organization
for the necessary liaison.[21]

In spite of these difficulties, the Coordinating Committee achieved
considerable success in securing work for the job-hungry population.
Within a month the center was operating normally, at least on the surface. However, the unemployment problem remained because several
thousand new segregants entered Tule Lake in 1944. By February 29,
1944, approximately one thousand persons were still on the waiting
list for employment.[22] Rather than receiving credit for obtaining thousands of jobs, the Committee found itself severely criticized for not
fulfilling its first promise, that of employment. The second promise,
the "justifiable release" of the stockade detainees, was an impossible
task in the face of the WRA's resistance. As a result, the Committee
was failing in both its announced goals.

By February 3, 1944, the Coordinating Committee felt so insecure
because of its lack of support by camp residents and the government
that it asked the administration's Advisory Council for permission to
hold a popular election to choose a new representative organization.
This request was denied because of both the administration's belief that
it already had reliable men and its fear that an election would restore
"radicals" of the *Daihyo Sha Kai*. Nevertheless, as camp conditions
deteriorated, the Committee continued to push its proposal for dissolution. As a result, on February 18, Project Director Best consented to

its request, and an Arrangements Committee, headed by Taro Watanabe (pseudonym), an elderly Issei transferee, was created to draw up plans for an election. Watanabe's efforts were futile, however, due to both a continued lack of cooperation by the administration and indifference of the residents.[23]

The Coordinating Committee, despite its determination to remain until the election of a new body, soon found itself confronted with circumstances which it felt were too intolerable to accept, and on April 7, 1944, all seven of its members resigned. An important factor in this decision was the growing intensity of community feeling, which had passed from a mood of passive acceptance of the Committee's program in January and February to one of open hostility by the latter half of March. Much of this feeling was created by the Coordinating Committee itself; its use of administration-paid evacuee spies to combat community opposition was partially responsible for the growth of an almost pathological fear of informers, or *"inu"*[24] The seven Committee members were themselves labeled *"inu* par excellence."* Community opposition, however, was only a secondary motive for the resignation. The primary reason was the administration's seeming approval of the emerging radical underground through the granting of a request to circulate a petition for the resegregation of "loyal" and "disloyal" evacuees in Tule Lake.

In mid-January, when the Coordinating Committee came into existence, its concern was for both community acceptance and the destruction of all opposition to its program. The community still supported the imprisoned *Daihyo Sha Kai* leaders. Most persons disliked any organization that would collaborate with the hated administration, but weariness over the hardships and deprivations of martial law and the "status quo" made them willing to give passive acceptance to the Coordinating Committee program for employment and the release of prisoners. By mid-February, community services were returning to normal, and by early March, 1944, the majority of Tule Lake's residents were relieved that the discomforts of the martial law period were largely over. Most people had gone back to work, although a large number were still unemployed. Living conditions in general had improved, even though there was still dissatisfaction in certain areas, with food in particular. Recreational activities were resumed. The people were not satisfied with the center's administration and its treatment of their representatives; however, they had learned the futility of fighting government agencies and wished to avoid activities which might bring on another period of tension and discomfort.[25]

The administration was of a like mind and was well satisfied that conditions were returning to normal. The American schools had been reopened and were well attended. There had been no signs or threats of labor trouble or group action against the administration or any evidence that the underground groups were capable of creating such disturbances. The WRA's optimism was reflected in a statement by Director Myer to the Tule Lake staff on March 17, 1944: "I think the WRA has passed its worse crisis. I feel more confident about Tule Lake than ever before. Things are on the beam now. Everything's going to be all right."[26]

These feelings, however, were not shared by members of the budding underground movement. They would settle for nothing less than complete, physical separation of the "true Japanese," i.e., themselves, from persons loyal to the United States and "fence-sitters" who could not decide upon their national allegiance. About two weeks after Myer made his optimistic statement, the relatively small and still-unpopular underground group threw the center into an uproar, brought about the resignation of the Coordinating Committee, and assumed nominal leadership over almost half of the center's population.[27] That this was accomplished was in large part a result of the post–martial law situation.

During January, February, and March, 1944, the membership of the radical underground groups was extremely small. It consisted primarily of transferees from other centers and the more radical remnants of the *Daihyo Sha Kai*.[28] It probably comprised no more than two or three cliques, each of which had about ten or fifteen reliable members. These cliques eventually joined forces, though when they did so is unknown because of the secrecy of their activities. Above all else, they desired recognition from the Japanese government. They took it upon themselves to define the meaning of the term "true Japanese," which they interpreted as one who had applied for repatriation or expatriation to Japan and wished to be deported on the next exchange ship. Many clique members had enthusiastically participated in the November uprising, although they had not held important leadership positions. These early members conceived of themselves as carrying the torch of the November revolt.[29] However, it is easy to demonstrate that there was little relation between the two movements.

The earlier protest had been characterized by democratic organization and procedures which were directed toward the good of the community as a whole. Important policies were referred to the people, and the leaders were generally regarded as representatives who were to serve the will of the majority. In contrast, the underground cliques set the issue of status [loyal or disloyal] above all else, and saw themselves as the leaders of a particular group of residents whose loyalty was to Japan. Their group, they held, must at all costs and as soon as possible be separated from the contaminating proximity of "loyals" and fence-sitters. These radicals saw camp unity as impossible and separation of the two groups as the only solution. They were unconcerned with improvements in center living conditions. Instead, they preferred to emphasize their willingness to suffer hardships for Japan and their cause. They saw themselves as moral leaders who transcended the necessity of consulting their followers.

Most of the activity of these underground groups was at this time directed at three goals: (1) the release of all of the stockade detainees; (2) the destruction of all political rivals; and (3) the recognition and acceptance of their program of resegregation by the American and Japanese governments.[30] Only the second of these, the destruction of the Coordinating Committee, met with success, thus bringing an end to the influence of the moderate elements in Tule Lake.

During February and March, 1944, the various underground groups and the Coordinating Committee carried on campaigns to win support for their respective positions through appeals to approximately three thousand new transferees from the relocation centers. The underground won over many of the new segregants with propaganda that the root of all of the center's troubles lay in the failure of the administration to clarify the status of segregants, and it implied strongly that further segregation would be the only solution to their problems. Gaining strength and support from these later transferees, the underground cliques soon were able to make an open bid for their program of resegregation.[31]

In the spring of 1944, the underground movement underwent an important change in leadership. During this period, it received considerable strength from the arrival of a number of parolees from Santa Fe, the Department of Justice internment camp for Issei who had been considered "pro-Japanese agitators" in the relocation centers. The most important was Koshiro Yamashita (pseudonym), an educated Issei with degrees from the University of San Francisco and Stanford University. He was a political leader in the Poston Center and had been arrested by the FBI for obstruction to the registration program and complicity in the beating of the national president of the Japanese American Citizens League.[32] Another important leader who joined the underground movement at this time was Stanley Kira (pseudonym), a Kibei who had led a pre-evacuation gang on Terminal Island (California) and had been a powerful gang leader in the Manzanar Center, where he was credited with having instigated much of the violence of December, 1942. These experienced agitators took control of what had been a rather inept underground movement.[33] In February and March, 1944, the radicals had not been regarded with respect by the people of the center. During April, however, their power and influence were greatly increased. They now emerged from the underground and adopted the name *Saikakuri Seigan* ("Appeal for Resegregation") and became known as the Resegregation Group.[34]

During the period from mid-January through April, 1944, the most spectacular achievement of the underground was its establishment of resegregation as one of the major issues in the camp.[35] As early as October 26, 1943, the desirability of such a plan had been proposed by the Negotiating Committee of the *Daihyo Sha Kai*. This was urged on Myer during the November 1, 1943, confrontation when George Kuratomi attributed the unrest in Tule Lake to the lack of separation of "loyals" from "disloyals."[36] During the period of martial law and after, a tendency to attribute the difficulties facing the colony to the failure to resegregate these groups became more and more apparent, along with expressions of loyalty to Japan and denunciation of "fence-sitters."[37] Even persons who were undecided about their loyalties found it necessary for their own protection to find scapegoats who could be denounced as "fence-sitters" or "loyals."[38] Statements of hostility to "loyals," as well as to *inu* and fence-sitters, became common. The feeling was that the "loyals" should be taken out of the center or there would be serious trouble.[39]

Into this atmosphere, the Resegregation Group introduced a petition which sought to clarify the resegregation issue by a positive identification of the "true Japanese," or "disloyals," and separation of these individuals from other persons within Tule Lake. The petition differed significantly from earlier proposals for the separation of residents into "loyal" and "disloyal" groups. The new resegregation plan narrowed the former definition of a "disloyal" person severely. It included only those who had applied for repatriation or expatriation and were willing to embark for Japan at the earliest opportunity. All others, including the "disloyal" who had answered the "loyalty questions" in the negative but had not applied for repatriation or expatriation, the "loyal" family members who had accompanied "disloyal" relatives to Tule Lake, and the one thousand or so outright "loyals" who had remained in the center after the segregation movement, were to be excluded from the newly formed "disloyal," or "true Japanese," organization.[40]

The Resegregationists initiated this proposal with scrupulous legality. Yet, they were careful not to reveal the real sponsors of the plan, because it was their policy to have them work behind the scenes to avoid arrest and confinement in the stockade. Thus, Torakichi Ishikawa (pseudonym), an unimportant Issei member, acted for the group and sent a letter to United States Attorney General Francis Biddle, requesting permission to circulate a petition to be signed by those residents who desired a return to Japan at the earliest opportunity and who, meanwhile, wished to be separated, within Tule Lake, from those not so inclined.[41] This request was forwarded through channels to Assistant Project Director Harry L. Black, who was in charge of the camp during Best's absence.

Black, without informing the Coordinating Committee, gave permission to conduct a survey, but not to circulate a petition. Having won this degree of recognition from the administration, the Resegregation Group disregarded Black's decision and circulated its original petition. Its circulation, between the dates of April 7 and 9, 1944, immediately threw the camp into turmoil. Arguments raged and cases of assault were reported. The rumor spread that failure to sign would mean that one would not be allowed to repatriate or expatriate. Because it seemed to have the administration's sanction, the petition's reference to resegregation within the center was interpreted by some as the first step in another segregation movement. Many did not want to move again, even across the camp. Reaction to the petition was all the more pathetic because most of the residents had not applied for repatriation, and to them the issue of immediate loyalty meant little. What they wanted was to be left alone until the end of the war.[42] The Resegregationists had little sympathy for other points of view, however, and ruthlessly pushed their own program forward.

Approximately sixty-five hundred citizens and aliens signed the petition during the two days of its circulation. This number included the dependents and minor children of the signers, plus in absentia signatures. Persons who had signed the petition were thereafter considered members of the Resegregation Group. Many signers were citizens of the United States, although the leadership clique was almost entirely composed of aliens.[43]

The Resegregation Group felt that its cause had been greatly strengthened by the petition. On April 24, 1944, it sent a copy, with the sixty-five hundred names appended, to the Spanish Embassy in Washington, and on May 30, the organization's leaders followed up by sending a copy to the Spanish Consul in San Francisco. They requested the Consul to expedite the removal of all those who had signed "on the next exchange vessel to Japan." The Resegregationists reiterated their dissatisfaction at having to live among loyal citizens of the United States and emphasized their desire to receive education and discipline "in accordance to the organizations of our mother country."[44]

After submitting their petition to the Spanish Embassy, Resegregationist leaders quietly devoted themselves to matters of organization. The several active proponents of resegregation organized frequent, informal meetings among themselves in order to develop plans for implementing their program. They contained their more violent members until mid-June and waited until August, 1944 to come out in the open with a formal, overtly nationalistic pro-Japanese organization.[45]

The April 7 petition for resegregation had one major side-effect that was not intended but which was welcomed by the radical organization, i.e., the resignation of the Coordinating Committee. To this harassed organization of pro-administration leaders, the recognition of their enemies, the Resegregation Group, was the last straw. Committee members were angered that they had not even been consulted on the question of the circulation of a petition by their opponents. As a last resort, Committee members went over the head of the WRA and complained to the Army that the petition was endangering the peace of the center. They were rebuked by the unit's commanding officer, and their appeal was rejected.

On April 7, the day on which the petition was first circulated, the long-suffering Coordinating Committee resigned in a body. Although it was prevailed upon by the administration to function until the end of the month, its resignation was formally announced in the camp newspaper, the *Newell Star*, on April 13, 1944. After this date, the camp was left without any recognized representative body to act as a liaison between the evacuee community and the government until Tule Lake closed in March, 1946.

In summary, the numerically small Resegregation Group had succeeded in obtaining the nominal leadership of almost half of the population of the center, increased the camp's general insecurity and the tendency to throw the blame for project problems on *inu* and "loyals," and indirectly brought about the resignation of its most important political rival, the Coordinating Committee.

After the temporary excitement of the resegregation petition and the resignation of the Coordinating Committee, the center as a whole experienced a definite lessening of tension which lasted until the middle of June, 1944. The administration also relaxed its previous policy of sternness and caution. Even gossip about *inu* died down. Some people even allowed themselves to become moderately optimistic about the future, remarking that "now Tule Lake is going to become just like the other centers."[46] Nevertheless, the period following the downfall of the Coordinating Committee was marked by a widespread apathy on the part of the residents. The chronic causes of dissatisfaction were still present. The prison-like conditions of camp had only been modified in slight details. On May 7, June Yamaguchi wrote to a friend:

Tule Lake Center continues to be subjected to many trifle discords, unrest, and disharmony, which will probably never end. . . . In spite of many things, Center's social activities continue to function as if there's no trouble whatsoever. Baseball, basketball, dances, shows, *engei kais* (a form of Japanese entertainment), bazaars, and field day of various track games are some of the activities which enliven our almost "dead" spirit.[47]

In this atmosphere, the administration made its first and last effort to establish a representative body elected by the people. The *Newell Star* of May 4, 1944, carried an invitation to the residents to participate in the planning of an election. An Arrangements Committee, which would work with the project director in planning and supervising the election of a body to be known as the Representative Committee, was to be selected by the residents on May 25, 1944. However the *Newell Star* of that date carried the announcement that plans for a permanent representative body would have to be postponed for an indefinite time because of an insufficient response by the residents. According to Best, "The failure of a large number of blocks to hold their meetings and select their nominees serves to defeat the purpose of the organization plan, and indicates that there is not enough popular support in favor of the Representative Committee to warrant a continued effort to carry out the election at the present time."[48] Out of seventy-four blocks in the center, only fifteen had nominated representatives.[49] The WRA was to make no further attempt to sponsor an election for an evacuee body to act as a liaison between the Japanese community and the administration.

There were many reasons for the failure of this belated effort by the administration at establishing an elected representative body. One explanation was the debilitating effects of the stockade issue on the evacuee community. Numerous statements reflected the attitude of the residents on this problem: "I hear so many people say as long as they are obligated to the *Daihyo Sha Kai*, they will refuse to vote until they're released from the stockade."[50] "If we elect more representatives, they will only put more people in the stockade. Everybody said, 'What the heck! We don't want to send any more people to the stockade.'"[51] Other residents, in complaining that the administration had never recognized their representative bodies in the past, stated, "What's the use? We put up representatives once and they wouldn't recognize them."[52] Overall, the administration failed because it no longer had the trust and confidence of the evacuee population, which it had lost through its treatment of the residents' only representatives, the Negotiating Committee of the *Daihyo Sha Kai*. It was now painfully obvious that nothing short of a miracle would produce a situation in which the people would willingly cooperate with the WRA again.

Thus, the period of normalcy, which lasted from March through the middle of June, 1944, was normal in outward appearance only. Many old and new grievances continued under the surface. Only the Resegregationists came out ahead in the period following the end of martial law. They were elated by the failure of the proposed election and expressed satisfaction that the people had remained loyal to their imprisoned representatives. However, the radicals were equally if not more pleased that no new group of rival representatives of the people had been chosen.[53] During the following months, the Resegregationists would grow greatly in numbers, power, prestige, and influence, until they had the entire camp under their domination.

6

Prelude to Renunciation: The Growth of Terrorism and Fear

The *Newell Star*, on May 25, 1944, ended a brief chronological outline of the history of Tule Lake with the note: "March to May [1944]—Return to normalcy."[1] Ironically, an extra edition of the same newspaper appeared later that day carrying the headline: "OKAMOTO DIES FROM GUNSHOT WOUND INFLICTED BY SENTRY." This incident of military violence abruptly ended the period of uneasy calm which had prevailed over the center and introduced an increasingly violent and unstable pattern of life marked by beatings, murder, fanatical pro-Japanese militancy, and finally, mass renunciation of United States citizenship. After six months of this type of existence, Tule Lake reached a state of mass hysteria which was described by the WRA as "a case study in mass neurosis."[2] John Burling of the Department of Justice is said to have jokingly suggested that Project Director Best "should fire all of his staff and replace them with employees who have had some experience in a mental institution."[3]

Throughout the first half of 1944, the leaders of the underground pressure groups had made a conscious effort to restrain their more "hotheaded" members from violence. They hoped to achieve resegregation and removal to Japan through the peaceful tactic of petitions which would demonstrate large-scale support for their goals. When such appeals to the Japanese government, through the Spanish Embassy, and to the United States government failed, they turned to violence to achieve their ends. The leaders confided in Rosalie Hankey (later Wax), a Caucasian sociologist whom they trusted as a "German [i.e., Nazi] Nisei," that they intended to keep Tule Lake in a state of turmoil in order to prove to the authorities in Washington that trouble would not stop until a resegregation of the residents took place.[4]

The first violence, however, came not from the radicals, but from the United States Army, in an incident which was surprisingly well handled, in view of past experience, by both the WRA and the evacuee community. On May 24, an evacuee worker, Shoichi James Okamoto, returning to the center from his assignment outside the area, was shot fatally by a sentry. This incident was even more serious than the death of the farm worker in the October, 1943 truck accident which had precipitated the November 1 confrontation. Added to the tense atmosphere already existing in the evacuee community, the situation was explosive. In this case, however, the administration acted diplomatically. The soldier was arrested. Project Director Best expressed his regret that it had happened, attended the public funeral for the slain worker along with nine thousand evacuees, and delivered a memorial address.

The immediate reaction of the residents to Okamoto's death was shock, intense fear, and anger. Grievance meetings were held throughout the project. However, the sympathetic and fair actions of local and national WRA officials quickly soothed the community's feelings. Furthermore, most persons accepted the shooting as the fault of the soldier and not the administration. The residents expected a "whitewash" and were not surprised when the soldier was acquitted at his court martial, which was held during the first week of July, 1944. The verdict had little impact on the residents generally, since, by this date, developments were beginning to occur which were bringing about serious changes in the temper, mood, and atmosphere of the evacuee community.

On June 12, 1944, Tasaku Hitomi, brother of Yaozo Hitomi, head of the hated pro-administration Cooperative Enterprises, was beaten so severely that he lost his sight for some time and suffered a brain concussion. Although there is no proof of who did the beating, it may be stated with some certainty that this was the beginning of the reign of terror by the now-unleashed "hotheads" of the Resegregationist Group which had been hinted at earlier. On June 13 or 14, a Mr. Moritome, who had objected to the institution of pro-Japanese militaristic exercises in a few of the blocks, was assaulted and suffered a fractured skull; on June 16, a Mr. Kurihara was severely beaten; on June 29, a man named Sumitomo (pseudonym) was waylaid and beaten. Thereafter, the number of assaults increased.

There is a strong probability that the leaders of the Resegregation Group, Kira in particular, engineered the first wave of beatings. The Resegregationists were subject to severe frustrations at this time. They had received no encouragement from either the Spanish Consul or National Director Myer in regard to their petition. Yamashita was convinced that the administration was conniving with the former Coordinating Committee to trick the people into forming a permanent representative body. Whatever the reason, the Resegregationist leaders began to utter a threat which was to become habitual with them; trouble will not stop and there will be no peace until there is resegregation. The Resegregationist leaders realized that if the center became really peaceful there would be no resegregation. Therefore, they were determined to keep Tule Lake in a state of disorder and confusion until they got what they wanted.[5]

Community reaction to the beatings varied from gratification to mild rebukes. The reason for this lack of condemnation was the evacuees' always-present dual fear of being informed upon by *inu* or of being classified as *inu* themselves. Throughout the period of "normalcy," which had been partially characterized by apathy and indifference to administrative proposals and actions, an undercurrent of suspicion toward fellow evacuee collaborators, fence-sitters, and "loyals" had been gaining strength. Most of the Coordinating Committee, many of the Divisional Responsible Men, the Old Tulean clique in general, and a number of transferees who had taken a public stand in favor of cooperation with the administration were being labeled *inu*. The most prominent of these received a special classification as "Public *Inu* Number One," and it was expected that they would become victims of violence.[6] Added to the generally accepted list of *inu* were any persons who dared to speak out against the now-powerful underground movement. The *inu* obsession was so universal that, as a Nisei girl expressed it, "Every place you look you see an *inu*."[7]

Each beating was followed by rumors that the victim had been an *inu*. Such rumors were believed at face value without verification of any kind. During the latter half of June, the beatings were discussed in almost every home and were the main topic of conversation in latrine, laundry, and boiler room. Gruesome details of injuries were repeated and elaborated upon. The evacuee police were helpless to prevent the beatings or to arrest those guilty. They were inherently vulnerable to the *inu* label since they had to carry out administration policies which often clashed with the wishes of the residents. The incompatibility of their duty to collaborate with the administration in enforcing law and order and their obligation as evacuees to observe the unwritten law of withholding damaging information about their fellow evacuees tended to inactivate the police force.[8] As a result of this situation, beatings continued and social disorganization in the community became more and more pronounced.

The series of beatings worked to the benefit of the Resegregationists. The assaults increased the already well-established hostility toward *inu* and enabled the radical leaders to put down any and all opposition by labeling them with that despised term. Fear of violence was also a factor in inhibiting the growth of any effective organized opposition. Because of the general belief that "strong-arm" boys among the Resegregationists had been responsible for the *inu* beatings, residents were reluctant to antagonize the group by reporting its activities. Because of this, the administration failed to obtain concrete evidence as to the source of the terroristic tactics, and the Resegregationists were able to proceed with their program without hindrance.[9]

The violence which had begun in June reached its climax with the murder of Yaozo Hitomi, the general manager of the Cooperative Enterprises, on July 2, 1944. The murderer or murderers were never apprehended, although most persons believed the act was committed by the terroristic gangs working under the Resegregationists.[10] News of the murder produced a general state of panic. It set a pattern of violence over and above the frequent beatings, daily threats, and intimidations which the organized underground was using to dominate the unorganized majority of the camp's people. If Hitomi could be killed, then the same thing could happen to anyone else. There were persons, following the murder, who found their names prominently posted on doors of the latrine with the threatening warning, "You're next!"[11]

The murder completely broke the morale of those evacuees who had openly supported the administration. The *Newell Star* of July 6, 1944, reported that all seventeen members of the Board of Directors of the Cooperative Enterprises had resigned as a result of the slaying. Six other key officials subsequently followed their example. Other minor officials stayed only after being persuaded to do so. Elections were soon held and a new Board of Directors was elected. The new Board included former stockade detainees and others considered to be agitators by the administration. These men were much more acceptable to the people of Tule Lake, however, and reforms were immediately made in the organization which won the support of the community.[12]

One of the most serious repercussions resulting from the Hitomi murder was the resignation of the evacuee police force. Chief of Police Minekichi Shimokon and Assistant Chief Aoyama resigned after anonymous threats were made against them. Then, over a two-week period, members of the 115-man force resigned one by one, because of threats and insults from the residents, until July 19, when the remaining seventy-two resigned en masse.[13] The community was thereby left entirely without protection against the widespread crime and violence in the camp.

For several weeks there were no police in the 18,500 person community except for a handful of Caucasian Internal Security men. Recruitment for the *"inu"* job of policeman would have been impossible if it had not been for a rash of bizarre rumors of rape which caused many residents, particularly women, to fear leaving their apartments at night. This, in addition to administration threats to withhold certain services from uncooperative residents, finally resulted in 60 percent of the blocks agreeing to elect "block wardens" who were to keep order only in their own blocks.[14] The new and reluctant wardens, however, announced that they would serve only so long as they were not asked to work as agents of the administration or to take action in any "political matter." By this they meant that they would not interfere in any of the activities of the Resegregation Group. In this regard it is significant that the Manzanar section of the center where Kira, the underground leader, had the most influence, elected a full corp of wardens who were all members of the radical group.[15] The remaining wardens were commonly viewed as timid, spineless, and all but useless. As a result, the Resegregationists could continue to carry on their activities with impunity and ever more openly.

Within a few weeks after the murder of Hitomi, the mood of the people changed once more. The wave of *inu* hatred declined, gossip about *inu* almost disappeared, and few persons outside of the Resegregation Group used the term to denounce others. First covertly and then overtly many people began to express dissatisfaction with the seemingly unending tension and, as some persons expressed it, the hoodlumism and gangsterism that permeated the center. Some countered the violent activities of the radical "true Japanese" Resegregationists with the claim that the Japanese government sanctioned only peaceful and law-abiding behavior and wanted the residents to live in peace until the end of the war. No one dared, however, to suggest that anyone ought to inform or assist the administration. The murder somehow tended to replace the largely imaginary fear of *inu* with the very real fear of the terroristic gangs belonging to the Resegregationist Group.[16]

In addition to the end of the center's *inu* obsession, the months of June through August, 1944, saw the solution of other issues which had been causes for unrest over the previous year. The removal of Old Tuleans and collaborationist transferees from positions of leadership in the Cooperative Enterprises and their replacement by individuals acceptable to the community eliminated this important source of irritation. Even more important than this, however, was the closing of the stockade and the freeing of its inmates, including the popular Negotiating Committee.

The closing of the stockade had been sought almost constantly by the detainees themselves, by relatives of inmates, and by whatever group was in power or seeking power at any time. After a series of frustrated efforts, this goal was finally achieved when, in August, 1944, San Francisco attorney Wayne M. Collins, a fiery civil libertarian, confronted Myer, Best, Robert Cozzens, and other WRA officials in a stormy meeting and threatened them with habeas corpus proceedings in the United States District Court for imprisoning American citizens without hearings, charges, or trials. Myer yielded to Collins' demands, and Best immediately telephoned Tule Lake and instructed the project attorney to release all of the prisoners from the stockade.[17] The WRA notified the residents of Tule Lake of the closing of the isolation area in the August 31, 1944, issue of the *Newell Star* stating only that "conditions in the center . . . are such that isolation is no longer necessary." With this decision, the issue that had played perhaps the largest part in keeping the center in turmoil for much of the previous ten-month period ceased to exist. The only major source of community unrest now was the increasingly militant and violent program of the Resegregationists.

The primary aim of the radical leaders from the beginning had been resegregation in preparation for eventual removal to Japan. During July, 1944, however, an additional goal appeared which, although subsidiary to the issue of resegregation, would within six months dominate the activities of the Resegregationists and throw the center into the greatest state of turmoil to be experienced by the residents of any center since the original evacuation from the West Coast in 1942. On July 13, 1944, the headline of the *Newell Star* announced: "DENATION-ALIZATION BILL SIGNED; Legislation Enables Citizens to Renounce U. S. Citizenship." From this time on, renunciation was to be given increasing consideration by the underground organization in its drive for control of the community and for resegregation of the "disloyal" and the "loyal."

Renunciation had been discussed in Tule Lake as early as December 13, 1943, when the remnants of the *Daihyo Sha Kai* met with the Spanish Consul and asked that "truly disloyal Nisei" be given the status of Japanese nationals and thus come within the jurisdiction of the protecting Spanish authorities. The plea was rejected by a representative of the United States Department of State, who accompanied the Consul, on the following grounds:

I would like to explain the status of Nisei who have both Japanese and American citizenship. When you are in the United States you are an American citizen. When you are in Japan, you are a Japanese subject. When you are in Japan as a Japanese subject, the American Government does not protect you, and when you are in America as American subjects the Japanese Government does not protect you or in this case the Spanish Government will not protect you. You cannot by saying so throw off your American citizenship. You must do a specific act such as renouncing your citizenship. But you can do it in time of peace, but not in time of war. No American subject can throw off his citizenship.[18]

The question of renunciation remained dormant in Tule Lake for the following seven months, although expressions such as "What's the use of having American citizenship?" were constantly heard.[19] The new law meant that "disloyal" Nisei could now achieve the status of "true Japanese" which the underground group so emphatically stressed.

The denationalization law was the culmination of a movement to strip not only the "disloyal" but all American citizens of Japanese descent of their citizenship. Unsuccessful efforts toward this end had been repeatedly attempted since as early as 1921, when the Controller of the State of California stated this to be the primary objective of the West's anti-Orientalists. In 1943, the Native Sons of the Golden West began to agitate for national legislation to achieve this goal. State Senator Clair Engle and Assemblyman Lloyd Lowry introduced resolutions in the California legislatures which called for the revocation of the citizenship of all Nisei with "dual citizenship" and memorialized Congress to amend the federal Constitution to bar persons of Japanese descent from citizenship.[20]

Throughout 1942, 1943, and early 1944, the nation's Japanese American population was the subject of bitter attacks in the United States Congress. In October, 1943, Representative J. LeRoy Johnson of California introduced a resolution which called for the establishment of a Deportation Commission. It was proposed that all alien Japanese and every citizen of Japanese descent who could not satisfy the government in public hearings that certain "evidence of disloyalty" was in error would be deported to Japan at the end of the war.[21] The bill was ex post facto in that the "evidence" included such acts as "No" answers to the loyalty questions on the Army and WRA registration questionnaires of early 1943.

Sensationalized accounts in the nation's press of the November, 1943 "riots" in Tule Lake turned countrywide attention temporarily toward the purportedly dangerous segregants and made many Americans more receptive to such legislation. The segregation center immediately became the focus of investigations by the California State Senate and the Congressional Dies Committee. Pictures of a threat to the whole nation were conjured up out of the demonstration at Tule Lake. Newspapers everywhere headlined the incidents. There was a stir of excitement from one end of the country to the other, but particularly on the West Coast.[22]

A solution to the problem posed by the "disloyal" Nisei was the goal of at least five bills in Congress during the period from October, 1943 through February, 1944. Congressmen from Texas and Arkansas joined representatives from the West Coast in efforts to deport or denaturalize as many Japanese Americans as possible. The extent to which congressional extremists were prepared to go may be seen in Texas Representative Sam M. Russell's proposal to deprive of his citizenship any American who refused to speak the English language in the United States.[23]

United States Attorney General Biddle was in sympathy with the more moderate attempts to rid the country of the "disloyal" evacuees in Tule Lake. Biddle felt, largely as a result of the November disorders, that the situation that existed in Tule Lake was in desperate need of a solution. He and his advisers in the Justice Department, including Edward Ennis, Director of the Alien Enemy Control Unit, and John L.

Burling, Ennis' Assistant Director, were well aware that a large proportion of the center's population was loyal to the United States. However, they believed that many others were disloyal, particularly among
the two thousand or more Kibei, "some of whom were Japanese by
race, ties of family, ties of friendship, education and language and who
were United States citizens and Americans solely as a matter of place
of birth."[24] It was the opinion of WRA Director Myer at the time of
the November "riots" that "there were one or two thousand men in
Tule Lake who were loyal to Japan."[25] Biddle put the number of
"disloyal" at between fifteen hundred and twenty-five hundred, again
stressing the Kibei as the main source of disloyalty.[26]

It was Biddle's opinion that the constitutionality of detaining American citizens not charged with a crime was extremely doubtful and that
if a writ of habeas corpus were brought and pressed, the detention of
Nisei and Kibei in Tule Lake would likely be declared unconstitutional. On the other hand, he believed that it was not practical to permit the "disloyal" to be at large on the West Coast because of the
adverse public reaction and the possibility of sabotage.[27] Thus, according to Burling, the Renunciation Law "was made for the purpose
of devising a system of controlling the disloyal and riotous elements
at Tule Lake while not doing injury to the Constitution and the tradi-
tions of the Nation."[28]

However necessary it was to solve the problem of the "disloyal"
Nisei, Biddle felt that the four bills then under consideration were either
clearly unconstitutional or at least questionable. He believed that the
solution lay in the "disloyal" Nisei themselves who would, if given
the opportunity, renounce their United States citizenship to show their
fanatical loyalty to Japan and would then seek "repatriation" to Japan
at the earliest opportunity. Since the renunciation would be accomplished voluntarily at the request of the individual, there would be no
violence to the Constitution. The renunciant would thereby become an
alien enemy, subject to legal detention during the war, with probable
deportation after the war.[29] It was further believed in the Department
of Justice that Japanese law provided that a person born in the United
States of parents of Japanese citizenship prior to December 1, 1924,
automatically acquired Japanese citizenship through registration of his
birth by his parents with the Japanese Consul or consular agent. The
Department therefore thought it proper to assume, until the assumption

was rebutted by competent evidence, that those persons of Japanese ancestry who voluntarily gave up their American citizenship and asserted their loyalty to Japan were in fact dual nationals. As such, when their United States citizenship ceased to exist, their Japanese nationality remained, and they were, accordingly, alien enemies under provisions of the Alien Enemies Act of 1798.[30] It is important to note that Biddle, while drafting his proposed bill with the "disloyal" Nisei of Tule Lake in mind, worded the proposal so that it would apply to all American citizens, not solely to Japanese Americans. This gave it some protection against later charges that it was unconstitutional class legislation illegally directed at a single group rather than to Americans in general.

It is significant that the WRA never gave its enthusiastic support to the Renunciation Law, either before or after it became law. The agency was swung over to acceptance only after it became convinced that the Act might have some value in heading off the more sweeping legislation which was then under consideration.[31] The WRA later proved inept in handling the renunciation crisis when it arose, but it was never out of sympathy with the majority of the renunciants whom it believed were acting out of reasons having little or nothing to do with disloyalty to the United States.

On February 2, 1944, the Committee on Immigration and Naturalization gave Biddle's bill preference over the more extreme measures of the anti-Orientalists and sent it to the floor of the House of Representatives where it remained in a comparatively inactive state until June, when it was passed by Congress. On July 1, 1944, it was signed by President Roosevelt as Public Law 405 of the Seventy-eighth Congress, an amendment to the Nationality Act of 1940.

News of the passage of the Renunciation Act reached Tule Lake two weeks later, on July 13, 1944. An article in the *Newell Star* informed residents of the fact and noted that procedures for putting the law into operation were in preparation and would be reported to the people upon completion. This news was not greeted with the enthusiasm which the law's originators had anticipated, however. Although a small number of requests for renunciation forms were received by the Department of Justice by the end of July, very few Nisei were ready, at this time, to take advantage of the new Act.

Nevertheless, the potential for mass renunciation of citizenship did exist. This fact is revealed in an analysis of the "disloyal" portion of Tule Lake's population made for the WRA by one of its evacuee informants. According to this observer:

There are two groups, called "disloyal," which consist of people who have expressed their desire to repatriate or to expatriate to Japan, the majority of these desire to be included at the earliest possible date in an exchange if possible. These two groups do not under any circumstances desire to relocate. Because they fear forced relocation and compulsory draft, they are taking whatever action they believe helpful to prevent such situations. They frequently state that such action on their part is necessary because of inconsistencies in the policies of the U. S. government which they claim to have experienced. They will probably continue to be distrustful of future policies of the U. S. Government. Though both groups have similar ideals in mind, their means of attaining their goals are altogether opposite. These two elements constitute the majority who command the respect of the center, of the two one is radical in its views and actions, while the other is conservative and law-abiding.

Radical Group [i.e., the Resegregationists]. These people show their complete hate and distrust of the U. S. Government by drastic actions which are both detrimental to the other law-abiding Japanese within the center and also undesirable from the point of view of the rules and regulations of the WRA. . . . Although it is the minority group when compared with the "conservative" disloyal groups, the individuals are high-strung and uncontrollable. Their stock remark is that they are the only "true Japanese," although the great majority of the residents hardly agree. The radicals even go to the extent of using force and violence within their own group to hold it intact by putting pressure upon its members. They seem unreasonable and "one-track" and appear to care not in the least for the welfare of their fellow-residents. They further exhibit hostile and disagreeable attitudes which make social functions impossible in many blocks. The majority of the membership in the radical group consists of mild country folk who respond to the pressure of a few extreme leaders.

Conservative Group [i.e., the unorganized "disloyal" majority]. In this group are the people who have requested repatriation or expatriation to Japan. They prefer an exchange, if possible, at the earliest date. . . . Although there is no question of their loyalty to Japan, they feel that the countries involved are at war and that people are sacrificing their lives to protect their respective nations. While many were evacuated from their homes in a sudden action which often resulted in losing practically everything they had, they figure . . . it's too late to do much about the past. Now that they have chosen to become Japanese subjects, they believe it is up to them to comport themselves in peaceful and law-abiding fashion. Being thankful for the shelter and food provided by the Government, and realizing that the tax-paying citizens of this country are being deprived of many luxuries, this group is anything but wilfully antagonistic. . . . But should the attitude of the WRA or the Justice Department change in such a way as to interfere with their possibility of remaining in the center as disloyals waiting for exchange, they will no doubt respond in a manner of utmost hostility to whatever administration exists at that time. These people are complying with every request which is reasonable. . . . But if aroused by unfair treatment, they will certainly respond. If this law-abiding, conservative group is aroused, it would easily enlist the sympathy of the center.[32]

An important development in bringing these two groups of "disloyals" together was the rapid growth in numbers and influence of the Resegregation Group which took place during the latter half of 1944. By the beginning of July, the radicals had developed a powerful and systematically integrated underground organization. Unknown to the administration and to most of the residents, the organization had set up a hierarchy of officials. Representatives were appointed for every block. These were then coordinated under ward representatives, who in turn formed a central committee, called the *Jochi-iin*, or Standing Committee. Ishikawa, a minor Resegregationist official who had signed the earlier petition for resegregation in place of the secretive real leaders, acted in a similar capacity now. While Yamashita and Kira, who were referred to as merely "advisers" to the group, actually controlled the *Jochi-iin*, Ishikawa was made the nominal chairman. This leadership group met regularly and formulated policies, programs, and propaganda which were then passed along to the block representatives. Kira and Yamashita, each of whom had a well-organized group of "strong-arm boys," controlled the meetings.[33]

The resegregationist leaders, although not necessarily their followers, immediately adopted renunciation as a focal point in their policies while continuing their unsuccessful campaign for resegregation. To them renunciation seemed to be the logical culmination of the steps that many Nisei had already taken: first, the "No" at the time of registration; then the decision to go to Tule Lake as a segregant; then the request for expatriation to Japan. These leaders viewed renunciation of citizenship as the final necessary act in the dissolution of ties with the United States in preparation for the ultimate identification with Japan.[34]

The underground was moving more and more into the open. Its leaders, acting largely from behind the scenes or through front organizations, sought to gain a wider following for their cause among the residents. Sometime during July or August, 1944, Kira and Yamashita embarked upon a series of "educational" lectures with this end in mind. These lectures were looked upon favorably by many non-Resegregationists who were interested in preparing themselves and their children for their future homes in Japan. The lectures expounded Japanese political ideology and recounted largely false and exaggerated news items from Radio Tokyo. Japan was convincingly portrayed as winning the war in the Pacific. Japanese losses were explained as being taken on purpose in order to draw the American forces into a trap in which they would be defeated. The speakers expressed their hope that the WRA would give its consent to the formation of organizations which would provide the desired education and discipline needed for their coming life in Japan.[35]

The first of these organizations to be founded was the *Sokoku Kenkyu Seinen-dan* (the Young Men's Association for the Study of the Mother Country). The purpose of this and similar organizations created later was to strengthen the Resegregationists' programs for renunciation, separation of their groups from the "loyal" evacuees, and an early movement to Japan. The fact that the *Sokoku Kenkyu Seinen-dan* was a front for the Resegregationists was carefully concealed from the administration and the camp's residents for well over a month.[36]

In its initial stages, the new organization had an outward appearance of innocence and respectability. Its avowed intention was to prepare its members, who were primarily male Nisei, to be useful citizens of Japan after their expatriation. This was to be accomplished through a series of lectures and classes on the Japanese language, history, and political ideology.[37] The organizational statement of the *Sokoku* strongly implied the desire of its members to renounce their citizenship, while stating three rather innocuous aims: (1) to study Japanese culture; (2) to abide by project regulations and refrain from any involvement in camp politics; and (3) to participate in physical exercises in order to keep in good health.[38] None of these objectives was objectionable to the project's administration, which took the view that preparation for a life in Japan was a natural activity for future Japanese citizens. Within a few weeks of its founding, approximately five hundred Nisei had become *Sokoku* members, and growth was continuous for several months thereafter.

In the beginning, the *Sokoku* won the approval of many non-Resegregationists, including a number of those still loyal to the United States, who believed the contention that the organization was solely educational and non-political in nature. According to one Nisei:

The *Sokuku* [*sic*] is not a pressure group. They just want to study Japanese culture. I know, because I'm a member. That's why I joined. They're not going into politics. I guarantee that they will not start any trouble in here. If I see any trouble coming, I will resign.[39]

To naive residents who believed the organization's claim that it had no political aims, the proposed activities had a strong attraction. Many of the young Nisei who were contemplating expatriation had never been to Japan and had an imperfect knowledge even of the rudiments of the language. It would obviously be of great practical value to them if they learned something of the way of life which they would be expected to pursue in the future. Their Issei parents were wholeheartedly behind such an endeavor, hoping thereby to improve the young people's chances for economic and social acceptance in Japan. At the same time, the pattern of life in Tule Lake was tending more and more to exalt the Japanese way of life and to disparage the American. To enter wholeheartedly into a study of Japanese culture was in conformity with this pattern, while it also provided a defense against being considered "loyal" to America by suspicious residents.[40]

The *Sokoku* soon threw off its innocent appearances, however, and came out openly and aggressively as a militaristic and nationalistic pro-Japanese organization. Japanese language schools were set up as means of indoctrinating their Nisei students with pro-Japanese sentiments in an effort to transform them from Americans into Japanese. Parents were intimidated and coerced by the radicals into enrolling their children in these schools. Students were taught that Japan would control the destinies of the world and that they must renounce their American citizenship and request to be sent to Japan. The most prominent of these schools were the "Greater East Asia Language Schools," which closed only after a number of Resegregationist leaders were sent to Department of Justice internment camps in March, 1945.[41]

The *Sokoku* scheduled frequent lectures for its members. These were given by the alien Resegregationist leaders. Lectures at the earliest meetings dealt with such subjects as Japanese contributions to California. As the weeks passed, however, the speeches took on an increas-

ingly nationalistic tone. Gradually, more and more emphasis was placed
on such topics as the glorification of the war aims of Japan and emperor worship.[42]

The "physical exercises," which had been given as one of the original aims of the *Sokoku*, were made compulsory for members and
gradually became more and more exhibitionistically militaristic. Bugles were purchased and additional militaristic features were included
as weeks went by. The *Sokoku* buglers made it a practice to blow the
"*Kimigayo*," the Japanese national anthem, at about 5:30 A.M. every
day. Then, at 6:00 A.M., members assembled in groups of between
two and three hundred persons, knelt, bowed in the direction of Japan,
rose, and commenced marching in military formation, goose-stepping
and shouting "*Washo-sho! Washo-sho!*," the Japanese equivalent of
"Hip! Hip!" Their heads were shaved, and they wore head bands
stamped with the emblem of the rising sun. Rising sun flags were also
sewn on their coats and sweaters, along with the word "*Ho*," which
was symbolic of "submission to the emperor." This performance was
repeated every morning. On Sundays, all of the smaller groups, including at one time as many as fifteen hundred persons, joined to form
a large marching unit in an area facing the Administration Building.
In addition to the usual drills, special ceremonies were held on the eighth
of each month in commemoration of the Japanese attack on Pearl Harbor.[43] The *Sokoku* and its later-formed companion groups became, in
effect, a kind of private army of the underground leaders.

If project officials were to stop the development of these popular
front organizations of the Resegregationist Group, it would have been
best to have done so during their early stages of growth. Unfortunately
for the administration, however, it found itself inhibited by the fact
that the WRA had originally sanctioned the "pursuance of the Japanese way of life" in the segregation center. Later, when the several
Resegregationist organizations were strongly entrenched, the WRA
hesitated to take action for fear of provoking another riot, the publicity
of which would do the national relocation program enormous harm.[44]
As a result, the increasingly open and militant activities were met with
apparent administration approval, or at least acquiescence, while the
outside world remained ignorant of happenings in Tule Lake because
of the fear of the effects of the harmful publicity on the "loyal" Japanese in the other camps.

During this period, the Resegregationist Group continued its efforts to force WRA approval of a separation of the "loyal" and "disloyal" evacuees. Yamashita, Kira, and other top radical leaders had until now worked more or less secretly through front groups, or less important leaders, for fear of arrest by the authorities. Despite their apprehension, the Resegregationists, in late September, 1944 decided to come out into the open. They now admitted their sponsorship of the *Sokoku*, circulated a new petition requesting resegregation, and began openly to organize two new groups, one for adult aliens and a somewhat altered group for young men. The radical leadership planned to bring social pressure on those who did not want to sign the new petition and to employ violence to contain or to prevent open opposition.[45]

The WRA was fully aware of the pressure tactics of the Resegregationists and knew that coercion was being used to get many of the "Americanized" Nisei to join the "Shaved-heads."[46] As a consequence, the administration made what turned out to be a rather weak attempt at discouraging the Resegregationists by informing their leaders of a July 14 letter from National Director Myer refusing their request for resegregation. The radical leaders managed to turn this information to their own advantage, however, by distributing copies to camp residents with a distorted translation which gave the impression that the Resegregation Group had received official sanction and that plans for a resegregation of the center's population were under consideration.[47]

For obvious reasons, the Resegregation Group leaders began the circulation of their latest petition without attempting to obtain the WRA's permission. It was circulated for at least a two-week period, beginning on September 24, 1944. All residents who desired to return to Japan at the earliest opportunity were requested to sign, including those that had signed the earlier Ishikawa petition. A pamphlet, written in both Japanese and a very awkward English, accompanied the petition and elaborated upon the aims of the Resegregationists. It was stated that since the signers did "not desire to return ever . . . to the State of California" or anywhere else in the United States, they "insist to remain within the center" until repatriated or expatriated. In stressing this point, the Resegregationists played upon the residents' constant fear of being forced to leave camp and resettle in what they believed to be a hostile United States. Rumors stating that the camps were to be closed and the people returned to their former homes greatly intensified the residents' apprehension.[48] The pamphlet also stressed denationalization by pointing out that "whereas, we realize the uselessness of our American Citizenship, and so as soon as and in the event a law of renunciation for citizenship becomes effective, we gladly renounce our citizenships. Therefore, we make clearly our positions by being a real Japanese."[49]

The petition did not cause much excitement among the residents when it was first presented. In marked contrast to their reaction to the first resegregation petition of April, 1944, the people in general did not view the issue of resegregation as exciting or as carrying any moral or ideological implications. By this time, no one except the Resegregationists seemed to be particularly concerned about the polluting presence of "fence-sitters," "loyals," or *inu* in the center.[50] Many persons became irritated by the suggestion that they commit themselves to renunciation of citizenship and an immediate return to Japan, and they expressed the wish that Resegregationist "agitators" and pro-Japanese "superpatriots" leave them alone.[51] A substantial majority of the residents disapproved the petition and resented the pressure being applied by its circulators.[52]

The Resegregationists were determined to go ahead, however, "even if the people squawk." They were not afraid to use social pressure, threats, and physical violence; and such means were openly used. Rumors were spread that the Department of Justice would soon take over the camp and only proven "disloyals" who had signed the petition would be allowed to remain within the protection of the center. Nisei were told that they would be drafted if they did not sign the petition and join the *Sokoku*. It was claimed that adults who did not sign were not "true Japanese." Morning exercises were set up for children, and the children of non-signers were not allowed to participate, thereby shaming them before their friends. The Buddhist priest who headed the *Sokoku* tried to spread fear throughout the camp by letting it be known that his group included "a number of hired killers."[53]

Such tactics were extremely effective. Very few individuals dared to criticize the Resegregation Group or its petition openly. Kira and his gang moved promptly to silence residents who were brave enough to do so. One elderly Nisei who publicly exhorted a group of Nisei to behave themselves, telling them that the violence and "hooliganism" of the Resegregationists were incompatible with the high ideals of Japan, was brutally beaten a short time later with clubs and a hammer.[54] This and similar cases of violence brought a number of residents to sign the petition despite their opposition. As a result of the Resegregationists' efforts, the petition eventually was signed by over half of the center's residents, or approximately ten thousand persons.

All those who signed the resegregation petition were claimed as members by the Resegregation Group, even though the organization's active membership probably did not exceed 2,500 persons.[55] Thus, by October, 1944, the radicals totally dominated the camp, although a very substantial proportion of the residents silently disapproved of their activities.[56] As a result, the Resegregationists became more and more openly exhibitionistic and arrogant. A staff office, covered with Japanese flags and patriotic mottoes, was secured in the residential area. A printed sign informed members that any person speaking English in the office would be fined at the rate of one cent a word. This was an expensive punishment for an impoverished people. Publication of mimeographed weekly and monthly newspapers was also begun to promote the group's activities. The Resegregationists now resorted even more openly to violence. At an October 21, 1944, meeting of the *Sokoku*, Kira quoted a Japanese proverb which, in English translation, stated that "to help the cause, we must kill those who stand in its way." This was interpreted by the assembled Nisei as a threat of violence to those persons who opposed the policies of the Resegregation Group.[57]

As a result, many residents feared that they were in immediate danger of physical violence if they opposed the Resegregationists or their program. One of Kira's more violent lieutenants bragged of how he and his gang terrorized or planned to terrorize the organization's opposition. On one occasion, he proposed a "grand plan" to have his "boys" beat up twelve *inu* in one night and thereby prove to the "people in Washington" that Project Director Best was incompetent. Yamashita vetoed the plan, however, out of fear that it would result in his own arrest.[58] The general fear of physical harm was greatly increased by the widespread belief that the Resegregationists operated a spy system which reported on opposition to their policies.[59]

In November, the radical leaders moved to formally organize the older Resegregationists who, up to this time, had only been loosely organized as the *Saikakuri Seigan*, an association paralleling the young men's *Sokoku*. At the *Jochi-iin* meeting on November 10, the predominantly Issei leadership adopted a plan to form a dues-paying organization called the *Sokuji Kikoku Hoshi-dan*, usually referred to as the *Hoshi-dan*. The purpose of this reorganized body was expressed in its name, which in translation meant the "Organization to Return Immediately to the Homeland to Serve." Membership was limited to those who had signed the resegregation petition and were willing "to sacrifice life and property in order to serve" Japan. The renamed alien group continued its control over the Nisei organization, i.e., the *Sokoku*, through its guidance of the latter's officers.[60]

At about the same time, the *Sokoku* changed its name to the *Hokoku Seinen-dan* which was usually shortened in use to *Hokoku* (the Young Men's Organization to Serve Our Mother Country). This new name reflected a change in the stated purpose of the organization from the study of Japanese culture to the service of Japan. The Resegregationists explained the name change signified that the period of cultural preparation had been completed and the young men were now ready to serve the Mother Country.[61]

The citizen *Hokoku* and alien *Hoshi-dan* leaders were now ready to push Nisei members toward renunciation of citizenship as a symbol of complete rejection of the United States and identification with Japan. Pressure for a wider acceptance of renunciation was stepped up by an intensification of the nationalistic activities, which increased and became more strictly regimented. The number of buglers multiplied, and bugling was indulged in more loudly and frequently. Morning exercises became more elaborate. The short-clipped *bōzu* haircut, in imitation of that required of Japanese soldiers, was made mandatory for members to set them off from dissenters.[62] Members tried to induce their children to leave the American schools and to concentrate on Japanese studies. Young women relatives of members of the two organizations began to wear longer skirts, braid their hair in pigtails, and adopt the dress customary in Japan for working in the fields.

Rumors were also spread concerning the rewards for renouncing and the penalties for failing to do so. It was said that those who did not renounce would be drafted into the Army; that non-renunciants would be ineligible for expatriation to Japan and could not therefore accompany repatriating parents; that the Department of Justice would take over the administration of Tule Lake on January 15, 1945, and that after that date applications for renunciation would not be accepted, and non-renunciants would be forced to resettle. People who believed the rumors of a victorious Japan felt that renunciation would be looked upon favorably by the Japanese government upon arrival in that country.[63]

In spite of the proselytizing activities of the leaders and the spread of rumors favorable to their program, the Resegregationists failed to win the bulk of the population over to their view of the benefits or necessity of renunciation. Until December, 1944, a substantial majority of the citizens were not markedly interested in renunciation and did not welcome the law giving them the opportunity.[64]

In contrast with the average Nisei, however, the radical leaders were enthusiastic. They believed that the segregation center would soon be transferred to the Department of Justice and that the "loyal" residents would be removed to other centers. The radicals hoped that an early and enthusiastic eagerness to renounce their citizenship would cause their group to be recognized by the Department as persons worthy of remaining in the center.[65] Thus, their goal of resegregation prior to deportation to Japan would finally be achieved.

The stage was now set for renunciation on a large scale. The Renunciation Act had been passed and needed only to have the details worked out by the Department of Justice. The Resegregation Group provided a small, but enthusiastic, nucleus to give the initial push for denationalization; while the conservative majority of the population, which was either indifferent or antagonistic to renunciation, was ready to accept it or any other path that might save them from forced relocation in a hostile United States or endanger their goal of security in Japan. The month of December, 1944 would supply the impetus necessary to swing much of the population over to the Resegregationists' radical goal of renunciation of United States citizenship.

7

Renunciation of Citizenship

During a period of three months, from December, 1944 into March, 1945, more than six thousand persons of Japanese descent filed applications for renunciation of their United States citizenship. The December 17, 1944, announcement of forced resettlement in the hostile "outside" brought to a head an accumulation of grievances. Faced with prospects of violence and economic impoverishment in West Coast communities, the residents of Tule Lake fought to remain within the security of their concentration camp homes. The only weapon at their disposal was renunciation of citizenship. The reasons for renouncing were many, but few had anything to do with loyalty or disloyalty either to Japan or the United States. Even those who did "denounce" their American citizenship out of "loyalty" to Japan more than likely developed that "loyalty" as a result of the injustices resulting from the evacuation, rather than from any love for Japan. The number of Nisei desiring to protect themselves and their families from both real and imaginary dangers overwhelmed the Department of Justice hearing team sent to Tule Lake to implement the Renunciation Act. The Department was handicapped in its administration of the Act because of its outdated legal concept of "coercion" and its rigid interpretation of the renunciation law. Despite a desire to do justice to United States nationals of Japanese descent, the government agency stood by helplessly until 5,589 Americans were without citizenship.

The Renunciation Act made denaturalization a relatively simple task. The statute required only that a person, during time of war, appear before any official named by the United States Attorney General and sign a designated form. If the Attorney General then found the renunciation would not be harmful to the national defense, the applicant became a stateless person. The Attorney General and his advisers considered making renunciation procedures that easy, setting up simple forms that could be executed rapidly in the presence of any competently trained government clerk. The overzealousness of the Resegregationists in pursuing renunciation, however, gave the Attorney General second thoughts and resulted in more stringent regulations.[1] As soon as the radical leaders became aware of the new law, they encouraged their followers to take advantage of it. By the end of July, a small number of letters and group petitions were sent to the Department of Justice in Washington asking permission to renounce. The Attorney General doubted the validity of some of these requests, however, because of the ease with which signatures could be coerced or forged. Consequently, it was decided that steps should be taken to insure that no person renounced his citizenship unless he desired to do so.[2]

The revised regulations, completed in October, 1944, contained safeguards which the Attorney General believed would prevent involuntary renunciations. In order to renounce, an applicant was required to write to the Department of Justice in Washington, D. C. Forms would then be sent which were to be completed by the prospective renunciant and returned, with a certified copy of his birth certificate, to the Department. This was to be followed by a private hearing before a government examiner. The final decision was then to be made by the Attorney General, whose judgment was to be based on the hearing officer's recommendation and on a determination of whether or not the individual's renunciation was contrary to the interests of national defense.[3]

The Resegregationists, however, tried to bypass even this theoretically foolproof procedure. During October, 1944, the Department of Justice sent a number of application forms to Tule Lake in response to requests for permission to renounce. Once these forms had been received, the *Sokoku* attempted to speed up the process of renunciation by typing several hundred copies for distribution to its members. By the end of the month, a large number of these unauthorized forms had been received by the Department, which noted that all were nearly identical in wording and seemed to have been prepared by the same typist.[4] This, plus concern that coercion might have been used to secure signatures, led the Department of Justice to send Assistant Attorney General Burling to Tule Lake to investigate the situation.[5]

The radical leaders were well prepared to make full use of Burling's presence in the camp to impress the Department of Justice with their desire for resegregation and renunciation. Burling interviewed sixty two Resegregationists concerning both their desire to renounce and the typewritten forms. The uniformity of their answers indicated considerable coaching and practice had taken place prior to the meetings. Virtually every one indicated a desire to go to Japan and expressed the hope that Japan would win the war.[6] The radical organizations further attempted to impress the Department of Justice representative with the intensity of their desires by holding their noisy bugling and drilling exercises as close to his residence as possible.

Through observation and reports from project personnel, Burling learned about the Resegregationist organizations, their behind-the-scenes advisers and strategists, and their use of terrorist "goon" squads.[7] He found that these organizations were entirely open and that they had an office assigned to them by the camp's administration. The Department of Justice representative took a critical attitude toward the War Relocation Authority for permitting persons under its charge to prepare themselves for service in the Japanese Army. Burling's solution to the problem was to identify the radical leaders and solicit their renunciations. Once he had accomplished this, he reasoned, they would be alien enemies subject to removal to one of the Department's alien internment camps. He apparently believed that removal of the leaders would allow the remaining residents to make their own decisions concerning repatriation, expatriation, or relocation.[8]

This decision demonstrated the Department of Justice's lack of understanding of the prevailing situation in Tule Lake. Some of the most respected alien members of the West Coast's Japanese community had been arrested since the beginning of the war and imprisoned in the Department's alien internment camps. As a result, there was no loss of dignity or prestige in being interned in the same camps as their influential pre-war leaders. Furthermore, transfer of "disloyals" to a separate center amounted in effect to resegregation, which meant the attainment of a long-sought goal. Thus, the Department of Justice's idea of "punishment" was looked upon as a reward by the Resegregationists and was eagerly sought. The Department's plan, then, was destined to fail in breaking up the organizations and in halting renunciation. On the contrary, it actually encouraged both.

Prior to December 17, 1944, the Department's plan for restoring normal conditions to the segregation center through imprisonment of the radical leaders might have succeeded. During late November and early December, the Resegregationists had been in a brief period of decline, during which several small evacuee groups came out in open opposition. The result was a weakening of the influence and prestige of the radicals. Some members of the *Hokoku* became frightened or disillusioned. When Burling called in the leaders of the radical organizations soon after his arrival in early December, there was a general feeling of approval among the non-Resegregationist residents, who believed that the Department of Justice was going to arrest and remove a bad element from the community.[9]

This period was also notable for a general lack of enthusiasm for renunciation, except among the leaders of the Resegregation organizations and their hard-core followers. In order to offset this reluctance to renounce, the Resegregationists attempted to encourage renunciation through a variety of rumors which threatened the security of non-renunciants.[10] Nevertheless, few citizens wanted to renounce, as evidenced by the small number of applications received by the Department of Justice before mid-December. It has been estimated that only six hundred were received, although over six thousand persons eventually applied.[11]

This reluctance to renounce changed so dramatically after December 17, however, that the flood of applications to the Department of Justice in Washington caused a temporary breakdown of the Tule Lake post office. Two unpopular administrative decisions announced on this date caused community sentiment to shift from antagonism or indifference to the Resegregationists to active support of their renunciation program. The first decision, made by the Western Defense Command, rescinded the orders which had excluded persons of Japanese descent from the West Coast since 1942. This ruling was almost certainly prompted by knowledge that a pending Supreme Court case involving the detention of a loyal Nisei in Tule Lake might free citizens of Japanese descent from confinement in the WRA centers. The second decision, announced later that day by the WRA, informed evacuees that all relocation centers, including Tule Lake, would close within a year. The expected Supreme Court ruling, *Ex parte* Endo, was handed down on December 18, 1944. It found that protection against sabotage and espionage did not permit the detention of a citizen whose loyalty to the United States was conceded by the WRA, nor was his freedom to be restricted by conditional release. As a result, the WRA and Army had little choice but to begin releasing most of the citizen inmates of the centers and to reopen the West Coast to resettlement by citizens of Japanese descent. It is ironic that a judicial ruling favorable to the Japanese American population in general actually helped supply the impetus for pushing so many others toward renunciation of citizenship.

The Army's decision to reopen the West Coast to resettlement by persons of Japanese descent was a traumatic experience for the residents of all relocation centers, but particularly for those at Tule Lake. Tuleans, because of their fear of the "outside," believed they had a safe haven in the concentration camp. Three years of confinement in relocation centers, including one under conditions of extreme tension and hardship in the segregation center, caused Tule Lake's residents to be "predisposed to fall into mass anxiety and mass hysteria." Such conditions, according to Rosalie Hankey (Wax), made Tuleans less capable of "logical or well-considered action." [12] As a result, their reaction to the news of the lifting of the exclusion of persons of Japanese descent from the West Coast was a mixture of surprise, anxiety, doubt, and shock.

An extra edition of the *Newell Star* informed residents that the Army's proclamation was to become effective at midnight, January 2, 1945. Residents of all relocation centers, including Tule Lake, were to be divided into two groups: (1) those free to resettle anywhere in the United States, and (2) "those who have definitely indicated that they are not loyal to the U. S. or are considered as potentially dangerous to the military security." The latter group's exclusion was to continue. [13]

The WRA's decision to force resettlement of all persons classified by the Army as "free to move" was transmitted to the residents in a mimeographed statement by Myer on the same day as the announcement ending exclusion. Residents were told that all relocation centers were to be closed within a period of six months to one year after the revocation of exclusion orders. This unwelcome news was followed immediately by Project Director Best's announcement that Tule Lake had assumed the position of both a relocation and a segregation center. Those whom the Army designated as free to resettle were now considered to have the same status as residents of a relocation center. [14]

Thus, Tule Lake residents were informed by the Army that most of them were presumably free to leave, by the project director that those free to leave had the same status as residents of relocation centers, and by the national director of the WRA that all projects would be closed within a year. These declarations imperiled the security of thousands of residents who, at the price of being branded "disloyal," believed that they had attained a war-duration refuge in the segregation center. Forced resettlement for all and induction into the armed forces for young men of draft age now loomed, if not as certainties, at least as disturbing probabilities.[15]

The West Coast's hostile reactions to returning persons of Japanese ancestry were known to the residents of Tule Lake and were magnified by rumors. Just before rescission of the exclusion orders, residents were reading and hearing reports such as the following, which served to intensify their fears of leaving the safety of their concentration camp homes:

President Roosevelt, Western Defense Command and the War Department yesterday were "strongly" urged by the [California] State Senate's Committee on Japanese Resettlement "not to permit the return of Japanese to the Pacific Coast, and particularly California for the duration of the war. . . . To allow the Japanese to return during the war is inadvisable because it would cause riots, turmoil, bloodshed and endanger the war effort.[16]

These warnings of potentially hostile actions were followed by numerous acts of actual violence, accounts of which were read by the incarcerated Japanese: "At Auburn [California], approximately 300 residents signed a petition . . . agreeing not to do business or fraternize with returning Japanese"; "An unoccupied house at the Yamasaki nursery was destroyed by fire on the night of January 3, the third building owned . . . by persons of Japanese ancestry to burn in Placer County in the last six weeks"; "[Sumio] Doi . . . report[ed] that several carloads of persons had parked on his property. Shots were being fired at the house, he said, in an effort to keep him and his family indoors."[17]

Each new story and rumor intensified the determination of the residents not to leave the security of Tule Lake, no matter what the cost. They were willing to use any means available to avoid resettlement. Numerous statements reflect this new determination to remain within the barbed-wire confinement of the segregation center: "Reading the papers and considering all the other facts, the people have a feeling of not wanting to return to the Pacific Coast"; "They say the Army will back us up. But that's only against mob-violence, and not against what an individual might do"; "What do they want us to do? Go back to California and get filled full of lead? I'm going to sit here and watch." [18] Such reports and rumors continued for many months. As late as May 8, 1945, a Nisei exclaimed, "Yeah, you're free all right if you go out. You've got civil rights. Civil rights to have your head cut off! They're even trying to take poor Doi's land away from him now." [19] Thus, the residents were slowly driven to acceptance of the *Hokoku* program as the only solution of their problem.

Immediately following the announcements by the WRA and the Western Defense Command, most Tuleans refused to believe that they themselves might be forced to leave Tule Lake. They expressed the opinion that they would continue to be excluded from the West Coast states because the Army would classify them as disloyal to the United States. Tuleans further assumed that exclusion would mean their continued detention at Tule Lake or some other segregation center. [20]

An Army team of twenty men arrived in Tule Lake a few days after the announcement ending exclusion and began holding hearings to determine which residents were to be free to leave the camp. Reports quickly spread that irrespective of statements made or answers given, exclusion orders denying settlement on the West Coast were freely issued to those called for hearings. Individuals receiving such orders were expected to leave the camp to resettle in areas east of the Pacific Coast states. [21] Within a few days after the start of the hearings, it thus became apparent that segregant status was no guarantee of continued residence at Tule Lake. Moreover, the fact that only males were given hearings implied that the military draft, which had been suspended for Tule Lake residents in July, 1944, was once more imminent. [22]

On December 24, 1944, a Nisei girl expressed a growing concern among the evacuees regarding the Army's exclusion hearings. In spite of pro-Japanese statements to hearing officers, those who made them, she reported, were not given detention orders. A Nisei boy stated that in his hearing the soldier had asked him if he wanted to renounce his citizenship. "So I said I was going to renounce, because I figured that then I could stay in Tule Lake." Another report told of a young citizen who, after informing the soldier of both his loyalty to Japan and his application for expatriation, was nonetheless handed a permit to leave the camp.[23] On December 19, a Kibei said "Four men in my block were called by the Army. They asked them questions like 'do you want to go out or do you want to renounce your citizenship?' " Concerned about such questions, Project Director Best asked the hearing officers for clarification. They told him that they had been ordered to inquire about renunciation in order to determine each evacuee's exclusion status, and they asked about resettlement "just to be human."[24] The effect of combining the two questions in the exclusion hearings, however, was to influence the apprehensive and frightened Nisei into renouncing their citizenship in hope of avoiding forced resettlement.

Citizenship for those in Tule Lake who possessed it was coming to have less and less meaning. As an Issei expressed it, "If you're a *Hakujin* [Caucasian], you take this matter of soiling your loyalty record seriously and would never do anything to [soil] it. But if you're a Jap and nobody believed your loyalty in this country anyway, you'll think about your family first."[25] Citizenship thus became a tool to be used for individual and family security, to avoid the draft, or to remain in the safety of Tule Lake or some other segregation center. If to renounce citizenship would help secure these things, there was a rapidly growing tendency to do so.

Even the alien parents of the Nisei sought to take advantage of their children's American nationality in order to protect family unity and security. As one Issei stated, "We're going to have [our children] renounce their citizenship just to stay here."[26] Thus, just as had occurred during the 1943 registration crisis, parental pressure became a strong influence on the decisions of the young. In both situations, the preponderant reasons for apparent acts of disloyalty were family security, maintenance of family unity, and avoidance of the draft.

During the winter of 1944–45, Tule Lake was suffering from mass hysteria and verging on panic. A number of factors within and outside the camp combined to bring this condition about: the announcements of December 17; intimidation and violence by the Resegregationist organizations; uncertainty over possible separation from family members and reinstitution of the draft; fear of forced resettlement and the economic impoverishment that might follow in the hostile "outside"; awareness that the evacuee police force was too weak to protect the community; knowledge that the camp administration had allowed the Resegregationists and their terrorist groups to grow and flourish; and rampant rumors. A common joke of the period had the camp taken from the WRA and placed under the Public Health Service to be run as a form of giant mental institution.[27] A psychiatrist, Dr. John Alden, explained that the pressures on evacuees were so great during this period that the normal and natural reaction of an individual would be to go along with the opinion of the group, even with the opinion of the most vocal members of the group, whether or not this constituted a majority opinion. In fact, only the queer or mentally deranged individual would hold opinions at marked variance from his surrounding community. Therefore, the belief in renunciation of citizenship, continued detention, and escape to the security of Japan were natural developments of the hysterical state of mind that prevailed in Tule Lake after December 17, 1944.[28]

The belief that continued residence in Tule Lake could best be maintained through renunciation of citizenship made rapid progress following the December 17 announcements. This belief revived the declining Resegregationist organizations. It was known that Burling had recommended to the Attorney General the immediate acceptance of applications for renunciation from *Hokoku* leaders. The *Hokoku's* position was further strengthened on December 27, when seventy Resegregationist leaders were moved to the Department of Justice's detention camp at Santa Fe, New Mexico, for internment as undesirable enemy aliens. This "punishment" was interpreted by many Tule Lake residents as a reward: the *Hokoku* leaders had applied to renounce; they were given priority in hearings; their requests for renunciation were accepted; and they were to be resegregated. The Resegregationists alone were being removed to the haven of an internment camp from which both resettlement and military induction were "impossible."[29]

The removal was accomplished with an impressive display of force as forty armed guards accompanied the seventy unresisting men. The Resegregationist organizations participated en masse in a spectacular farewell demonstration. The young members marched up to the gate, stood in formation, sang patriotic songs, blew bugles, and shouted "*Banzai!*" as their leaders left for internment.[30]

Immediately after the send-off, representatives of the Resegregationists met and selected a new slate of officers to replace their interned leaders. Under this new leadership all restraint was discarded. Increased pressures were put on the residents by means of an intensification of militantly nationalistic activities, coercive and terroristic tactics against dissenters, and extensive propaganda. Resegregationists stepped up their bugling, goose-stepping, morning drills, and *Washo-sho* chants. Participants often numbered more than fifteen hundred daily.[31] Elderly people and little children sometimes marched with the boys so that, as one resident expressed, "even the old ladies are running around in slacks yelling '*Washo-sho*.' "[32]

The Resegregationists looked upon renunciation and internment with pride. They taunted nonmembers by telling them that those remaining in Tule Lake would be "kicked around," while interned members were "safe and sound." The *Hokoku* and *Hoshi-dan* circulated rumors that individuals who had not renounced their citizenship by January 20 would either be "kicked out of camp" or drafted.[33] When *Hokoku* members received notices from Washington approving their applications, they waved them ostentatiously in front of their friends and neighbors and exhorted them to send in their own applications without delay. They elaborated upon the advantages of renunciation and internment: families of internees would be reunited and resegregation would be accomplished, while the "loyals and fence-sitters" would be forced to resettle.[34] These tactics, reinforced as they were by fears of relocation and the draft, drove residents day by day nearer renunciation. Whereas only six hundred persons had applied for renunciation by December 17, 1944, the date of the rescission of exclusion orders, the total rose to twelve hundred by the end of the month, and to forty-six hundred by January 31, 1945. Thus, by the end of January, half of the citizens in Tule Lake had applied for renunciation. After this date, the rate declined, although over fifteen hundred additional applications brought the final total to over six thousand.[35]

The large number of applications greatly disturbed both the WRA and the Department of Justice, neither of which had anticipated more than two thousand renunciations. However, efforts to stem the tide were defeated by a lack of cooperation between the two agencies. Burling believed that the WRA was mainly responsible for the mass renunciation because of its announcement that all centers would close by January 1, 1946.[36] He therefore attempted to relieve the evacuees' anxiety over forced resettlement by requesting national officials of the WRA to designate Tule Lake as a "refuge center" from which no one would be forced to resettle for the duration of the war. Burling approached Project Director Best with the problem, and both agreed to write Washington to ask that the center closing order be rescinded.[37] Best warned National Director Myer that many citizens feared returning to what they believed to be hostile American communities and were renouncing solely in hope of remaining in the center.[38] Myer, however, refused to yield in the matter of forced resettlement or to exempt Tule Lake from the WRA's plan to close all of its centers. His only concession was to agree to allow persons in Tule Lake who desired to do so to remain there or in some similar center until January 1, 1946.[39]

It was the consensus of the Tule Lake administrative staff, on the other hand, that the holding of the renunciation hearings at the time chosen by the Department of Justice was the principal cause of the renunciations. Project Attorney Louis M. Noyes charged that residents of the segregation center were psychologically unprepared for the hearings. The sudden lifting of the exclusion orders, he reasoned, enabled the Resegregationists to stampede them into believing that renunciation of citizenship was the only security they had against family separation and the draft.[40] Noyes and many other government officials came to the conclusion that the hysteria created by the December 17 announcements made conscious and free decisions in the citizenship hearings impossible.[41] Requests by the WRA and members of the Tule Lake administration that the hearings be cancelled were ignored by Burling and the Department of Justice.[42]

A difference of opinion in regard to the status of the renunciants added to the conflict between the two agencies and made cooperation in solving the renunciation problem difficult. The Department of Justice believed that all renunciants would be expatriated to Japan, by force if necessary. This belief was communicated to WRA Director Myer early in the program, and he and his subordinates strongly disapproved of it, feeling that it would be possible and desirable to relocate renunciants in the United States at an early date. This and other differences between the WRA and the Department of Justice gave rise to the former agency's disapproval of the renunciation program generally.[43] Apparently as a result of this conflict, the WRA, as of January, 1945, was determined to maintain a hands-off policy in regard to the Department of Justice's renunciation program.[44]

Burling and the Department of Justice, nevertheless, were determined to continue the hearings. Burling was a humanitarian, however, who made every effort to conduct fair hearings. He felt the evacuees had been treated unjustly in their removal from the West Coast, and he tried to impart this feeling to his hearing officers during the long train ride from Washington, D. C. to California in early January, 1945. He told them: there was no evidence of sabotage or espionage by any person of Japanese ancestry either at Pearl Harbor or thereafter; negative answers to the loyalty questions during the 1943 registration did not necessarily indicate disloyalty but might have been due to confusion or resentment over evacuation; the entire evacuation had been a tragic mistake brought on by a wave of public hysteria; and segregation in Tule Lake did not necessarily indicate loyalty to Japan but rather, in most cases, resulted from other factors, such as resentment at treatment given to American citizens by their own government, a desire to keep the family together, and hope of avoiding the draft.[45]

Burling also informed hearing team members of the strong pro-Japanese pressure groups in the center and stressed that each officer should be particularly diligent in endeavoring to detect any sign of coercion, since coercion would make a renunciation invalid. On this point, however, Burling showed a lack of understanding of the pressures existing on the residents of Tule Lake and displayed a distorted knowledge of actual conditions in the center. He would accept only a strictly legal definition of coercion, i.e., a renunciation "would be coerced and hence void [only] if it were done under imminent or immediate threat of physical injury to one's self or to a member of one's family." Burling disregarded the enormous social pressures that numerous WRA staff members informed him existed in Tule Lake. Instead, he steadfastly stood by this narrow legal concept of coercion which, as he said, "had been understood in the law for centuries."[46]

Burling acknowledged that the rush toward renunciation was "illogical and unreasoned," that many of the men marching in makeshift Japanese uniforms had been loyal Americans before the war, and that "the asserted loyalty to Japan was often a kind of hysteria." However, it was determined in Washington that the excitement in the segregation center was not of a character, such as insanity, for example, which could be given legal effect.[47] Burling admitted further that beatings and threats of violence existed within the center. These were not interpreted as signs of coercion, however, since they were attributed to "struggles for political leadership" that "did not relate to private behavior." The murder of Hitomi, moreover, was considered to have been the result of improper relations with another man's wife, rather than part of the general wave of terrorism designed to stifle opposition to the Resegregationists and renunciation.[48]

Burling regretted that many persons loyal to the United States were renouncing, but it was the viewpoint of the Department of Justice that everyone had a right to renounce during wartime, and the Department had a duty to provide hearings and renunciation forms for those who desired them. Thus, the only valid consideration of a hearing officer in determining the acceptability of a request for renunciation was that the applicant understood what he was doing, wished to do it, and was not coerced.[49]

The Department of Justice's hearing team arrived in Tule Lake on January 11, 1945, soon after the Army's exclusion hearings had ended. A special office building in the administrative area, as well as two Caucasian interpreters, were made available. No person of Japanese descent other than the individual applicant was permitted in the hearing room. It was believed that the renunciant would thereby be free of coercion and state his true intentions without fear that his decision would be reported back to others in the camp. Each hearing lasted from a few minutes to more than an hour. The practice was for the hearing officer to obtain the necessary statistical data, to show the evacuee his application for permission to renounce in order that the signature thereon could be verified, and then to ask the applicant why he had signed it and if he had done so of his own free will. There followed a period of questioning, generally very brief, designed to explore the reason for renunciation, in order to determine the existence of coercion and the applicant's understanding of what he was doing. Once this was done, he was given the final form to sign.

According to Burling, each applicant was also told that if he signed the renunciation document, he would forever cease to be an American citizen and that in all probability he would be sent to Japan at the close of the war. Furthermore, he would most likely never be allowed to return to the United States.[50] The Department's claim that applicants were actually told of the irrevocability of renunciation and the plans for deportation was sharply denied later by the renunciants, however, through their attorney, Wayne Collins.[51] Moreover, the administrative practice of allowing, and even encouraging, changes in answers to the military registration questionnaire in 1943 led to a widespread belief among Tuleans that a "disloyal" status could be later transformed at will to a "loyal" status.[52] Thus, even if such statements as Burling alleged were made during the hearings, a prospective renunciant, judging from past experience, might tend to ignore them.

As noted, the camp was in a condition of extreme turmoil during the winter of 1944–45. On January 1, 1945, ten days before the renunciation hearings opened, the *Newell Star* carried messages from both the national and project directors of the WRA repeating the unwanted news that residents on the Army's exclusion list were now free to return to their former homes and resume civilian lives without restriction. On January 5, Myer, in a pamphlet circulated throughout the center, reaffirmed his determination that the agency's prime objective was to close the relocation centers and restore their residents to private life in normal communities.[53] Such announcements served only to increase the fears of the people and to reinforce their determination to resist forced resettlement through any means available, which at that time meant primarily renunciation of citizenship. As a result, expressions of anxiety and fear increased in number and in force. Many residents complained that they had been given no specific information by the WRA as to who was going to be allowed to remain in Tule Lake. One apprehensive Nisei exclaimed:

I don't know what's going to happen to us! It's very confusing. I think everybody feels that. They don't know what's what yet. In the first place why do they want to kick us out? It's their fault we came here. They can't say "We'll give you 25 dollars and coach fare. Get out by such and such a day." Since the people here have been in camp three years, their funds are exhausted. It's all right for people who can afford.

This same individual then asked the question that virtually every citizen in camp was asking: "Can people be thrown out even if they renounce their citizenship?"[54] The answer, if one were to believe the Resegregationists, was "No."

Meanwhile, the new leaders of the Resegregationist organizations stepped up their pressures on both residents and the administration for quick renunciation. They continued to circulate rumors designed to both push undecided citizens into renouncing and urge alien parents to exert influence on their children to do likewise. A number of remarks reflect the variety of rumors then circulating: "I think the *Hoshi-dan* undoubtedly has started the rumor that by renouncing citizenship the people will be allowed to stay here at Tule Lake"; "They say all those persons who have not renounced . . . will be kicked out of camp"; "They say . . . [that persons who are not interned in Department of

Justice camps] are going to be kicked out while . . . [persons who are interned] will be safe and sound."[55] Such statements were not only widely circulated but taken as factual. In addition to social pressures and rumors, the Resegregationist organizations continued to threaten opponents of their program with violence. Many people found themselves compelled to become at least nominal members of these organizations in order to protect themselves and their families from physical harm.

Camp authorities were constantly informed of the various pressures exerted on inhabitants. However, government efforts to prohibit such activities were insignificant or non-existent until well into March, 1945, after the damage had been done to the citizenship of well over five thousand Nisei and Kibei in Tule Lake. In January, 1945, a loyal Issei, Masami Sasaki, and the Nisei project Legal Aid Counsel, Tetsujiro Nakamura, informed Project Attorney Noyes of the radical activities, but they were told that these were problems for the Department of Justice, not the WRA.[56] As a result, a number of evacuees who might have resisted renunciation if offered significant protection from harm renounced for reasons of self-protection.

On January 18, 1945, Assistant Attorney General Burling, acting for the Attorney General, attempted to put a stop to Resegregationist activities by means of an open letter to Masao Sakamoto, Chairman of *Sokuji Kikoku Hoshi-dan* and to Tsutomu Higashi, Chairman of the *Hokoku Seinen-dan*. In this letter, copies of which were publicly posted, Burling ridiculed the leaders and questioned their sincerity and loyalty to Japan. He informed them that residents loyal to Japan might continue to live in the center in peace. These persons did not, however, have a right to engage in pro-Japanese demonstrations, wear semi-military uniforms, or publish pro-Japanese newspapers. The Resegregationists were warned that efforts to convert American citizens to their cause were treasonous and that their activities were "intolerable" and, therefore, must cease.[57] Many residents were relieved that the government was finally taking action against the radicals. According to one, "Many of the people think he did the right thing. . . . The Department of Justice means business. The people are kind of happy."[58]

Burling's letter proved to be a threat only, however, as the Department of Justice relied solely on internment as a punitive measure against the radicals and made no move whatsoever to prohibit coercive activities and militaristic demonstrations within the center. Rather than abate, radical activities continued to increase in intensity and flagrancy until sometime in July, 1945, when the last of the renunciation hearings were held. A week after Burling's command that the Resegregationists' "intolerable activities" should cease, it was reported that the *Hokoku* was "going about the camp coercing signatures to a statement of loyalty to the organization." That fear of the leaders was much in evidence within the membership is indicated in the statement of a Kibei, who told that a friend was in fear of physical violence because his orders for internment in the Santa Fe detention center had been cancelled.[59] Thus, despite Burling's threat, neither the violence nor the pressure from the Resegregationists on the camp's residents had declined.

Besides continuing their campaign of rumors, intimidation, and violence, the Resegregationists applied pressure directly on Burling and his hearing officers to accept their renunciations and to remove them to internment.[60] Immediately upon learning the location of Burling's living quarters, the *Hokoku* began to hold its Sunday demonstrations, complete with uniforms, drills, and corp of bugles, at the point of the fence nearest his room. In addition, in mid-January, 1945, the organization supplied the Assistant Attorney General with a list of its members.

The Department of Justice answered the Resegregationists' activities by resuming its policy of transferring radical leaders to its alien internment camps. *Hokoku* leaders were given priority in hearings, and their applications were given quick approval so that they could be separated as rapidly as possible from the regular membership. Consequently, the second group of officers to leave Tule Lake was removed to Santa Fe on January 26, 1945, just one month after the first shipment.[61] The 171 men received a spectacular farewell, similar to that of December 27. At 5:30 in the morning, the *Hokoku* loudly blew its bugles, and the young members who were not being interned drilled and then faced the fence near the gate. As each truck of internees left the center, a farewell shout of "*Banzai!*" arose.[62]

Faced with the loss of their leaders a second time, the members met and elected a third complete slate of officers. In addition, the defiant Resegregationists informed the Department of Justice that they would continue doing so after every new shipment. This ability to continue replacing leaders made the Department realize that the organizations had broad support and were not the work of a few fanatics. Burling, therefore, after consultation by telephone with his superiors in Washington, decided that the entire membership of the *Hokoku* should be removed.[63] All *Hokoku* members were thus given priority in hearings, a fact which naturally enhanced their numbers and influence in a community that was rushing in desperation to renounce. During the weeks that followed, all those named on the *Hokoku* membership list were called for hearings. Virtually every one appeared before the hearing officers with his head shaved and wearing a white sweatshirt with the Japanese Rising Sun emblem embroidered on the breast.

About 650 *Hokoku* and *Hoshi-dan* members were removed on February 11. On this occasion, the president of the *Hokoku* called an emergency meeting of its members. The young men assembled at the call of bugles, and each one accepted personal notice of internment. On March 4, 1945, the Department completed its program of internment when 125 more men were sent to the Santa Fe camp. By this time, all the leaders and members who had been on the list given to the Department of Justice had been removed. In addition, several sets of leaders of the alien *Hoshi-dan*, the writers for the Resegregationist newspaper, the teachers of the Greater East Asia School and a number of other Japanese language schools, and several Buddhist priests had also been interned.[64]

The decline in applications for renunciation and in militaristic activities which the Department of Justice hoped would follow these large-scale internments did not materialize. Since only persons eighteen years of age or over could renounce and be interned, their places were taken by younger boys who had remained in camp and now blew the bugles and drilled. Similarly, since no women were removed, the women's organization, the *Hokoku Joshi Seinen-dan*, which had been organized January 8, joined the boys in their drilling exercises. Moreover, citizens who had applied for renunciation prior to the removal of the leaders continued to persist in completing the renunciation procedures.

Many people continued to believe that they had to convince the hearing officers of their loyalty to Japan in order to have their applications approved.[65] As early as January 19, residents were being told to "answer in a radical way" so that their citizenship would be taken away.[66] The Resegregationist organizations had learned the procedures of the hearings after the first few interviews with Burling in December, 1944. With this knowledge, they were able to establish what Assistant Project Director Black referred to as a "College of Renunciation Knowledge'' and carefully coached those called for hearings on the questions that were to be asked and the answers that were to be given. The Resegregationists had definite ideas on the impression that should be made on the hearing officers, and they taught prospective renunciants how to act when their turns came.[67]

Burling himself admitted that it was frequently impossible to conduct a frank and free examination of a renunciant's state of mind and that it became useless for hearing officers to ask many of the questions because the answers had become stereotyped. As an example, if a prospective renunciant were asked his opinion of the Japanese Emperor, he would almost always leap to his feet, stand at rigid attention, and assert that he regarded the Emperor as the Living God. Similarly, substantially every prospective renunciant who was asked if he believed Japan would win the war answered affirmatively and said that he hoped for that result.[68] Despite this obvious combination of coaching and irrational behavior, hearing team officers believed that the vast majority of the renunciants had legally fulfilled the requirement of the Renunciation Act: they understood the law, desired renunciation, and were not coerced. The Attorney General agreed with his hearing officers and accepted the renunciations, feeling that the Act, which he himself had devised, did not give him the authority to reject an application when it met the previously mentioned qualifications and when a threat to the national defense was not involved. In the Department's view, the renunciants could not be considered dangerous since they were not being released either in the United States or in Japan until the end of the war.[69]

When the Department of Justice completed its two and one-half months of hearings on March 17, 1945, it had heard approximately six thousand applicants.[70] Of this number, 5,589 renunciations were accepted by the Attorney General, 5,461 from Tule Lake and 128 others scattered widely among eight other relocation centers.[71] In Tule Lake, seven out of every ten citizens age eighteen and above gave up their citizenship. Approximately 1,343 Tulean citizens of comparable ages who did not renounce were able to avoid the effects of the mass hysteria. Most of them either lived in remote blocks where the pressure groups were inactive, had been moved into the fenced-off hospital area by the authorities, worked in the administrative area during the day where they avoided the pressures of camp, or were persons clever enough to make the pressure groups believe they had renounced.[72]

That the Department of Justice erred in accepting the great majority of applications was to be emphatically demonstrated in court decisions over the following twenty-three years. The Department's obvious mistake was in the narrowness of its interpretation of coercion, which the Attorney General limited solely to violence or threats of violence directly to the individual applicant or his family. Had this definition been broadened and the Department's understanding of the atmosphere existing in Tule Lake been clearer, the total number of renunciations would certainly have been far lower than it turned out to be.

Forced relocation and the draft, the most frequently mentioned causes for the large-scale denationalization of citizens in Tule Lake, were but the most obvious reasons for renunciation. Several persons close to the problem subsequently offered their own evaluations of the situation. Burling fell back on the old Kibei theory of disloyalty which had been rejected by the WRA while it was considering proposals for segregation in 1942 and 1943. He saw "the most obvious" motive for renunciation as a "genuine disaffection for the United States and loyalty to Japan." He felt this was particularly true among the "2,000 or more Kibei," among whom "sentiments of loyalty to the country [to] which they were bound [i.e., Japan], both by ancestral ties and by cultural and educational ties, sprang up." [73] From the point of view of numbers, however, Burling saw the "most significant cause of renunciation" as the announcement that the center was to be closed within one year. Lesser reasons given by the hearing team head were: the draft; family loyalty; the desirability of establishing a pro-Japanese record prior to removal to Japan; fear of violence outside the center; determination to remain by the publicly adopted negative answer to Question Twenty-Eight on the registration questionnaire; and the "irrational mass hysteria" existing throughout most of the hearing period. [74]

Perhaps the most knowledgeable Caucasian in Tule Lake was Rosalie Hankey (Wax), the graduate student employed by the University of California to observe the effects of evacuation and incarceration on the evacuees in the segregation center. She viewed the renunciation of citizenship as a cumulative process which she traced back to the 1942 evacuation. This included the stigma of disloyalty resulting from the registration and segregation processes; the pressures of the Resegregationists; the failure of the government to stop or punish the pressure groups; the demoralizing effect of four years in the centers; and beatings of evacuees by Caucasian personnel—in short, "for almost four years, their experience had been of a nature calculated to make them lose faith in America and blight their conception of the value of American citizenship."[75]

Beyond this accumulation of grievances, however, Hankey felt that the most immediate and "tragic" causes were the events which followed the December 17, 1944, announcement lifting exclusion from the West Coast: the panic resulting from administration announcements of the closing of the center; evacuee interpretation of questions asked at the Army hearings; the shipments to internment; and the widespread rumors. These produced a state of mind which, according to her, was comparable "to a crowd of persons who believed that they are about to be bombed, rush to shelters, and finds there officials whose statements they interpret as 'Renounce your citizenship or you cannot enter.' "[76]

In addition to these conclusions, Hankey listed: fear of grave economic hardship on the outside; fear of physical violence from hostile citizens of Caucasian ancestry; fear of family separation; fear that non-renunciants would be drafted; and tremendous parental and familial pressures.[77]

Besides such opinions from Caucasian "outsiders," the renunciants themselves recorded their own reasons for renunciation in numerous letters written to the Department of Justice, the American Civil Liberties Union (ACLU), and various attorneys. The most frequent explanation dealt with the pressure tactics of the *Hokoku* and *Hoshi-dan* in forcing members and nonmembers alike to renounce. Equally important in particular cases were: bitterness over evacuation and racial prejudice; ostracism of non-renunciants by friends and neighbors; pressures exerted by spouses and parents; fear of forced resettlement; and frustration over inability to prevent the events that brought them to renounce.[78]

A statistical study of the renunciants is of further significance in determining motivations for discarding American citizenship. In regard to family security, Tuleans viewed renunciation by any member as protection for the whole family from forced resettlement. Consequently, 73 percent of all Tulean families had at least one renunciant. However, renunciation was generally an "all or none matter." In 80 percent of the families where one person renounced, everyone eligible to renounce did so. The most striking characteristic of the renunciant group was its youth.[79]

Fear of the draft is indicated by the fact that 77 percent of all Tule Lake males renounced, while only 59 percent of all females did so. Furthermore, the predominance of transferees among the renunciants shows that their initial tendency to join the camp's protest faction carried through into the renunciation movement. Seventy-eight percent of the transferees renounced, but only 49 percent of the Old Tuleans did likewise. That membership in the Resegregationist organizations played a prominent part is indicated by the fact that 91 percent of the *Hokoku* and *Joshi-dan* renounced, but only 59 percent of the nonmembers did so.[80]

The fact that one group of renunciants was larger than another should not draw attention from the fact that renunciation was a collective phenomenon involving all classes of the Tule Lake population. No block had less than 34 percent of its citizens to renounce, while in sixty-eight of the total seventy-four blocks at least 50 percent of the citizens chose denationalization. Even among the Old Tuleans, as resistant as they were to pressure group tactics, the lowest proportion renouncing in any one block was 21 percent.[81]

With mass renunciation of citizenship by Nisei and Kibei, the cycle which began with evacuation was complete. Their parents had lost their hard-won foothold in the economic structure of America. The children themselves had been deprived of rights which indoctrination in American schools had led them to believe inviolable. Charged with no offense, but victims of military and governmental misconception, they had suffered confinement behind barbed wire. They had been stigmatized as disloyal on grounds often far removed from any criterion of political allegiance. They had been at the mercy of administrative agencies working at cross-purposes. They had yielded to parental compulsion in order to hold the family intact. They had been intimidated by the ruthless tactics of pressure groups in camp. They had become terrified by reports of the continuing hostility of the American public, and they had finally renounced their irreparably depreciated American citizenship.

8

Reaction against Renunciation: The Retreat from "Disloyalty"

The year (1945) began with a fanatical movement to discard all things American, including citizenship and country. During the first three months, the radical pro-Japanese minority had manipulated the fear and anxiety of the community over two unpopular administrative and military decisions to win undisputed leadership and domination over all but a small number of Tule Lake's population. The project administration counterattacked in March, and by July, a mass reaction against renunciation began which almost equalled the renunciation movement itself by the end of the year. The camp swung back to an orientation toward America and away from Japan. The great majority chose to rebuild their lives in the United States. And for the more than thirty-five hundred renunciants who remained in this country and for many who left it for Japan, a long, hard, uphill struggle began in the federal courts which was finally to end, after twenty-three years, in a hard-won victory for all but a handful of the 5,589 renunciants.

The Department of Justice's efforts to stem the tide of renunciation and to stop the militant activities of the Resegregationists were a complete failure. The WRA belatedly, therefore, decided that it must act to break the power of the radical organizations. Several tactics were used. The least successful and most unfair of them was the reinstitution of the Department's policy of shipments to internment, which had been discontinued on March 4. Project officials obtained a list of members in a raid on the offices of the organization.[1] With the information obtained, the WRA made arrangements with the Department of Justice for transferring some of the most ardent Issei and renunciant members of the societies from Tule Lake to the Department's internment camps near Bismarck, North Dakota, and Santa Fe, New Mexico. Between December, 1944 and the end of summer, 1945, the two agencies removed approximately twelve hundred renunciants.[2] Since forced resettlement was still feared by most residents, these removals had no more effect on the evacuee community than had the earlier movements.

On March 15, only two days prior to the completion of the renunciation hearings by the Department of Justice, the WRA took its first effective steps to destroy the Resegregationist organizations. A set of Special Project Regulations was formulated by the project administration which prohibited the social, cultural, and militaristic activities that it felt were promoting Japanese nationalistic attitudes. These regulations interdicted marching, parades, bugling, wearing Japanese nationalistic emblems, public ceremonies, attendance at organizational meetings, coercing youths to take part in organizational meetings, speeches, and so on.[3] The prestige of the organizations diminished, and many evacuees notified the authorities of their withdrawal from the pressure groups. There was no slackening of resistance to the ultimatum on the part of the remnants of the radical organizations, however. Their activities continued and their influence remained strong.[4]

Following dozens of court trials of violators of the Special Project Regulations, the administration took steps to divide and further weaken the militant Resegregationists. Members were offered a choice of three "logical alternatives," or "propositions." Proposition Number One was to cease all prohibited activities and remain at Tule Lake without further family separation. Proposition Number Two was to cease violations of the regulations while the WRA arranged an internment trip for eligible males. Proposition Number Three was to continue the pattern of defiance and take the consequences.

The first proposal had little influence. Members split over acceptance of the second and third propositions, however, and this division destroyed the unity which had been the main asset of the organizations. Those who accepted Proposition Number Two quit morning drill and, without fanfare, left the project during June and July, 1945. The more radical members who had chosen Proposition Number Three remained in Tule Lake, except for their top leadership which was forcibly ejected.[5] From that time, the organizations continued to dwindle in size, although their presence in the camp remained a source of fear for a number of residents.

With the decline of the Resegregationists and their influence on the center's population, the residents increasingly turned away from the desire to go to Japan and looked instead toward a future in the United States. Tule Lake's evacuee community dramatically reversed its character. Contacts between the evacuees and the administration, which had been lost for a year, redeveloped. The Japanese language schools not only began to cooperate with officials of the camp's American school system, but willingly curtailed activities and curricula as the latter system grew in enrollment. In other activities, Japanese movies gave way to the familiar Hollywood type, the project director was invited to throw out the first ball of the baseball season, and shaved heads and braids gave way to the usual American hair styles. Renunciants, in some instances, attempted to join the Army before final victory was assured. Nisei soldiers on leave were feted in the blocks. Resettlers, who earlier had to sneak out of camp, were now given farewell dinners. The administration also began to loosen restrictions on the residents, and shopping passes were issued.[6] Except for the 4,406 Tule Lake evacuees who sailed for Japan, the remaining 14,000 residents chose to continue their lives in America, despite past hardships and future uncertainties.

Conditions favoring resettlement greatly increased during the latter half of 1945. On September 4, following Japan's surrender, the Western Defense Command rescinded all individual exclusion and detention orders. Only renunciants and "segregated parolees" remained under detention. All other evacuees were free to resettle. Although bizarre rumors still circulated in camp concerning the dangers of relocation, the great majority wanted to resettle in America. Hardships remained, but the physical dangers, which had proved very real to persons of Japanese descent who were in the vanguard of the returnees during late 1944 and early 1945, had begun to taper off by April, 1945 and showed signs of disappearing entirely by August.[7] Individual and legislative discrimination against the returning Japanese was still present, but the trend was toward acceptance. The greatest immediate hardships faced were an extreme shortage of housing and problems of beginning life again on meager resources.

On October 18, the WRA announced that February 1, 1946, would be the closing date for Tule Lake and that all persons eligible would have to leave the center by then. Those who refused to designate a place in which they wished to resettle would be returned to the point from which they were originally evacuated and released. On October 10, 1945, the Department of Justice assumed control of the camp, and from that date relocation was speeded. Whereas only 140 Tuleans resettled during the first half of the year, the population began to decline at a rate of 2,000 per month after August 1, 1945. By January 31, 1946, the project held only 5,045 persons, consisting only of evacuees under detention and their families.[8]

Most of the renunciants also wished to resettle in the United States. The first significant move from within the evacuee community in opposition to renunciation and a future in Japan came in early February, 1945, while Resegregationist power was still at its height. Tetsujiro Nakamura, a non-renunciant Nisei and the camp's Legal Aid Counsel, and five loyal aliens, Zenshiro Okubo, the chief of the block managers, Jutaro Narumi, Kaoru Takahashi, and Masami Sasaki and his wife, met in secret in Sasaki's one-room apartment to organize a group in opposition to the pressure group's propaganda, influence, and disloyal activities. Because of the personal danger, they had to talk to other residents in secret in their efforts to sway them against the Resegregationists and renunciation.[9] In March, 1945, these men attempted to enlarge their activities and turned for help to the JACL. This organization, however, refused cooperation, as it did in every case involving the renunciants and the "disloyal" at Tule Lake.[10]

That the efforts of such persons to prevent renunciation were generally unsuccessful is shown by the fact that approximately six thousand Nisei and Kibei had appeared before hearing officers to cast off their United States citizenship by the completion of the renunciation hearings on March 17, 1945. Many of the Caucasian staff and others who witnessed the renunciation phenomenon realized that most of the renunciants did not understand the consequences of their actions or did not really wish to renounce. Rosalie Hankey (Wax) was one of these sympathetic individuals. During the renunciation panic she advised the hearing officers that the great majority were not renouncing their citizenship out of loyalty to Japan. Moreover, Hankey was convinced that a great many did not appreciate the gravity of their act and later would attempt to get their citizenship back. This was not the first time that they had been given a hearing which they were assured was very grave and which later signified little. "Indeed, at the time of segregation they were assured by the WRA that they would be allowed to remain in the Center until the end of the war."[11] According to the residents of the segregation center, if the government had reversed its position on such a serious matter as that, it was only to be expected that the decisions of the hearing officers and the Attorney General were not necessarily permanent.

Toward the end of the renunciation hearings and soon after they were over, renunciants began to realize their mistake and sought aid in undoing the harm done to their future in the United States. A number of young people secretly visited the Reverend Thomas W. Grubbs, a Caucasian Christian minister in Tule Lake, to ask what could be done and to confess they had not really wanted to renounce their citizenship. Grubbs advised them to write the Department of Justice. He actually wrote many of the letters and received replies in order to conceal these activities from alien parents, pressure groups, and block managers.[12] Project Attorney Noyes reported similar experiences from renunciants who visited his office once they came "out of their psychotic state." After the hearing officers departed for Washington, his office was deluged with inquiries from renunciants who wanted to "renounce their renunciations of citizenship." Noyes referred such requests to the Alien Enemy Control Unit of the Department of Justice.[13] Burling recognized that renunciants received aid from others in Tule Lake and charged that letters to his department from renunciants showed evidence of having been written with the aid of War Relocation Authority personnel.[14]

Such pleas for help were generally ineffective. The Attorney General began approving applications for renunciation soon after completion of the hearings on March 17, 1945. Prior to this date, only eighty-four persons had been denaturalized as a result of the Renunciation Law. Between March 22 and May 5, however, 5,049 approvals were made.[15] Notices were sent to renunciants, by form letter from Assistant Attorney General Herbert Wechsler, stating simply, "You are no longer a citizen of the United States . . . nor are you entitled to any of the rights and privileges of such citizenship."[16]

As soon as the renunciants received their alien status, the Department of Justice issued detention orders to the WRA to hold them in the center. The renunciants themselves were not informed, however, of the fact that they were now prisoners ineligible for release or resettlement in the United States. The Department justified keeping this information secret on the grounds that the certainty of detention for those who renounced would only encourage further renunciations from other evacuees who wanted to avoid forced resettlement. The renunciants were told that they were prohibited from leaving Tule Lake only after they applied for permission to resettle.[17]

The number of renunciants who wished to leave Tule Lake to start life anew in normal American communities began to grow rapidly even before Japan's surrender on August 14, 1945. The war news no doubt played some part in their decision.[18] However, the flood of letters sent to the Department of Justice and other agencies pleading with officials to allow them to withdraw their applications for renunciation and asking permission to resettle spoke not of war, but of hysteria and temporary insanity, among other things. The renunciants' letters told pitiful stories relating the reasons for their renunciations and begged for relief from the hardships caused by their hasty actions.

The Department of Justice's answer to all such requests was a flat refusal, claiming sympathy, but standing rigidly by its legal position. Most were answered with form letters informing renunciants that "under the law, neither the Attorney General nor any other official of the Government has any authority whatsoever to permit you to reconsider your action in renouncing United States nationality." Permission to resettle was likewise denied. The only glimmer of hope was that "your letter will be made part of your file . . . in the event that your case is re-examined at a later date."[19]

Renunciants who wished to remain in the United States were faced with an even more serious problem than loss of citizenship in the Department of Justice's plan to deport them to Japan. This move was made possible when President Harry S Truman, on July 14, 1945, promulgated Proclamation Number 2655, under authority of the Alien Enemy Act of 1798, which states:

All alien enemies now or hereafter interned within the continental limits of the United States . . . who shall be deemed by the Attorney General to be dangerous to the public peace and safety of the United States because they have adhered to . . . enemy governments . . . shall be subject upon the order of the Attorney General to removal from the United States and may be required to depart therefrom.[20]

The proclamation was apparently requested by the Attorney General and was valid only during wartime, since the Alien Enemy Act provided that "whenever there is a declared war . . . and the President makes public proclamation of the event, all natives, citizens, denizens, or subjects of the hostile nation . . . who shall be within the United States and not actually naturalized, shall be liable to be apprehended, restrained, secured, and removed as alien enemies."[21]

In order to use this proclamation, the renunciants, who had been informed in 1943 that segregation was not a punishment and in 1945 had been told in their "Notice of Approval of Renunciation" only that they were "no longer a citizen of the United States," were suddenly designated "enemy aliens" who were "dangerous to the public peace and safety" of the country and thereby subject to deportation. Thus when Japan surrendered unconditionally on August 14, it gave up any right to protest the dumping of thousands of additional destitute persons in the war-torn and defeated country.

The renunciants were not officially informed of the Department's deportation plans for some time, although Representative Samuel Dickstein of New York unofficially stated on August 25, 1945, that they would be removed to Japan within two months "or as soon as shipping is available."[22] During July, August, and September, most of the renunciants grew increasingly anxious to avoid removal to Japan, to cancel their renunciations of citizenship, and to be freed from internment.[23]

The renunciants' anxiety began to subside, however, soon after attorney Wayne Collins started to take an interest in the situation.[24] His participation in their case was the most significant occurrence in the twenty-three-year struggle against deportation and for restoration of citizenship. In Collins, the evacuees had the friend they needed. He was almost violent in his determination to stop the government's efforts against the renunciants. He became a virtual commuter between San Francisco, Tule Lake, Bismarck, North Dakota, Santa Fe, New Mexico, and Crystal City, Texas. During the early years he did not take a single vacation, confessing, "I was frightened stiff that if I was not able to be in my office every day early and late that the government might attempt to remove all of them to Japan."[25] Some of his clients called him a "brave man," while others, including Nisei and the Department of Justice, said that he was a "fanatic" and a "maniac."[26]

Collins was probably the first person outside of Tule Lake, the Department of Justice, and the WRA to learn that renunciations of United States citizenship had taken place en masse within the center.[27] The government agencies involved were not anxious to have this knowledge spread, because they feared adverse publicity for the relocation program. Collins first became aware of the situation in July, 1945, while investigating the possibility of litigation over the Special Project Regulations which had been instituted on March 16, 1945, to combat the militant Resegregationist organizations.

The regulations had resulted in numerous arrests and trials of members of the radical organizations, some of whom were minors. Such persons were tried by the project director, who had formulated the rules and then acted as judge in carrying them out. Individuals brought before him were denied trial by jury, representation by counsel, the right to subpoena witnesses, and all other elements of due process. The WRA insisted that "the action . . . is not a judicial proceeding, but is an administrative disciplinary proceeding." The agency compared it to the authority of "a warden to discipline prisoners who misbehave." The ACLU of Northern California, however, protested that the segregants at Tule Lake were not prisoners because they had never been convicted of any offense. Furthermore, the administrative officers did not, the Union charged, "have the right to arrogate to themselves the powers of judicial officers." [28]

The Union notified the project administration that it would request the United States District Court to order the release of five young members of the Resegregationist organizations, fifteen to seventeen years of age, who had been sentenced to from 120 to 370 days in jail for "blowing bugles and wearing nationalistic insignia on their sweat shirts." [29] When it became evident that the United States District Court and the United States Attorney in San Francisco might be overwhelmed with suits brought by other persons in the Tule Lake stockade, Judge A. F. St. Sure, attorney Clarence E. Rust, and United States Attorney F. J. Hennessey asked Collins to visit Tule Lake to try to resolve the situation. Collins was chosen for the task because he was known in the segregation center as a result of his involvement in the *Korematsu, Hirabayashi, Yasui,* and *Endo* cases and in the earlier closing of the camp's stockade in 1944. [30] The attorney's visit, in late July, 1945, combined with the threat of litigation in the District Court, proved successful and resulted in the freeing of the young prisoners and the permanent closing of the stockade.

As noted, the real significance of Collins' visit was his discovery of the mass renunciation of citizenship in the center. While preparing to leave the project, the attorney was informed by Project Director Best and Project Attorney Noyes that a number of the camp's residents had heard that a lawyer was present and that they wished to consult with him. The group, consisting of the alien parents of several renunciants, met privately with Collins in Noyes' office and told him that their children and thousands of other American nationals of Japanese descent had renounced their citizenship.[31] Collins' reaction was one of disbelief. He had not heard of the Renunciation Law that now made it possible to renounce during time of war, and he exclaimed, "That's ridiculous! You can no more resign citizenship in time of war than you can resign from the human race."[32]

The Issei parents, and a number of renunciant children who entered the room later, wanted to know if anything could be done to restore citizenship to the renunciants and prevent deportation to Japan. Collins concluded that the Renunciation Law was unconstitutional. He advised the renunciants present to write to Attorney General Tom Clark and inform him of the conditions under which their renunciations were made and assert that the renunciations were unconstitutional and void because of governmental duress and coercion from within the community itself. Collins then wrote several identical sample forms requesting cancellation of renunciations of citizenship and instructed the renunciants to send them to the Secretary of State, Secretary of the Interior, Director of the WRA, project director, and other government officials. He believed such letters were necessary as preliminary steps to the initiation of any law suits. Collins' letter was widely copied and circulated throughout Tule Lake and other camps in which renunciants were interned. The San Francisco attorney did not accept any renunciants as clients at this time but instead advised them to seek immediate aid from their own or other attorneys of their choice.[33]

Throughout August and September, 1945, those renunciants interested in the restoration of their citizenship and the avoidance of deportation began to organize. Previous to this time, most of them had demonstrated little interest in taking legal steps to regain their citizenship rights. However, during August, events occurred that encouraged a substantial number to join together and pledge to act as a group and to contribute to a common litigation fund for use if and when it became necessary to initiate court action.[34] On August 14, Japan surrendered. With this event, and the spread of rumors that the government intended a general removal of renunciants to Japan, the view of the residents toward legal action suddenly changed. They became filled with anxiety, and a general hysterical condition developed in Tule Lake and in other internment camps in which renunciants were held. The internees decided that something must be done quickly, or they might find themselves on board Army transports bound for Japan.[35] Consequently, many of them, although they suffered from the feeling that they had done something shameful, in Collins' words, "stood up on their hind legs and began to fight."[36]

During August and September, many renunciants, acting both individually and in groups, sought to retain attorneys from throughout the country, but without success. Apparently, all contacted objected to representing internees of Japanese ancestry who had renounced their American citizenship, had been branded as disloyal and subversive, and were being detained as alien enemies. Only Collins was agreeable to working with the renunciants, and he made several trips to Tule Lake to advise them. Nevertheless, he continued to urge them to contact and hire other lawyers. Then, according to Collins, if they all filed suits against the government, "Christ, there will be hell popping all over the country . . . and they can't get away with removal."[37]

During July, August, and September, 1945, the growing movement to go to court in order to prevent deportation, to win freedom from confinement, and to restore citizenship encountered opposition from block managers, most of whom were aliens, and many alien parents. Many of these people despaired of reestablishing themselves in the United States and now wished to return to Japan with their children. The anticipated lawsuits would jeopardize what they had dreamed of for two years or more. Moreover, many Issei were convinced that deportation was only a matter of time, and they wanted to take their children with them. They therefore opposed any action in the courts and hoped for Collins' failure, for if he lost, all renunciants would be removed to Japan.[38]

Despite this Issei opposition, those renunciants and other residents who chose to remain in the United States formally began, shortly after V-J Day, September 2, 1945, to organize to carry out their plans. The Tule Lake Defense Committee which resulted was democratically elected in a manner similar to that of the *Daihyo Sha Kai* in 1943.[39] The residents in each block who were interested in restoring their citizenship and freedom elected a block representative to be a member of the defense committee. These men in turn selected from their group a committee of ward representatives. Finally, the ward representatives elected from their group an Executive Committee of five persons. The Tule Lake Defense Committee, thus formed, met to discuss their problems and possible solutions. Interviews with many attorneys who had been consulted and advice of both the ACLU of Northern California and Collins assured the Committee that success would be difficult. Nevertheless, it was agreed, in September, that the effort should continue and that Collins would be hired as the sole attorney.[40]

Virtually the only other aid, in addition to that of Collins, received by the renunciants at this time came from the ACLU of Northern California, with which their attorney had a long association, and of whose Executive Board he was a member. Collins, however, chose to handle the cases alone, with the nominal support of the Northern California ACLU. He refused to be limited by the ACLU rules, informing the organization that, "I am not going to raise just a civil liberties issue. I'm going to raise any God damn issue that is possible: governmental duress, private duress, the illegality of this, that, and the other thing, statutory construction, and so forth." He believed that this was essential, because "you never know what the Supreme Court is going to do. They pass up the main question every damn time they possibly can."[41]

One of the major questions to be settled was the form court action might take. First thoughts were given to individual suits or perhaps a single test case. However, these ideas were soon discarded as impractical because of the great variety of circumstances that led to the host of renunciations. A single suit would not protect renunciants whose citizenship had been surrendered for reasons other than those under litigation. Moreover, litigation involving one, or even several persons, would not prevent the deportation of all other renunciants while the suits were in court. The only possible method of protecting all renunciants was through one or more mass suits including as many of them as cared to join.[42]

To gain time for preparation, Collins sought to slow down any plans or actions of the Department of Justice. Therefore, throughout the latter part of 1945 and early 1946, he set out to create as much confusion within the Department as possible. As he himself put it, "When you throw a monkey wrench into the machine, you want the whole God damn machinery to come to an end."[43] Perhaps the most visible wrench was a virtual deluge of letters to the Department and other agencies of government. Upon Collins' advice, the renunciants, in August, 1945, began to multigraph and/or mimeograph the form letter he had prepared requesting cancellation of renunciation applications.[44] Individuals as well as relatives and Caucasian friends of the renunciants were asked to write. Every time the government made a new move against the renunciants, new letters and form letters flooded pertinent agencies.

Prior to October, 1945, there had been intimations, reports, and rumors concerning removal of the renunciants to Japan. However, there had been no official word from the agency responsible for this task. In consequence, renunciants were uncertain of their fate and could make no definite plans for their future. The WRA tried to impress upon the Department of Justice the importance of clarifying the status of the people in Tule Lake as rapidly as possible, but the Department chose to let the situation rest for several weeks before acting.[45] During October, however, the Department began to take action on the long-anticipated removals. On October 10, Tule Lake was transferred from the control of the WRA to that of the Department of Justice. Because the Department operated only internment camps, the status of the renunciants quickly changed from that of "detention" to "internment." Two days earlier the agency had begun fingerprinting, photographing, and registering the renunciants as aliens, informing them that they were now "native American aliens."

On the day the Department of Justice assumed control of Tule Lake, it announced that on and after November 15, 1945, "all persons whose applications to renounce citizenship have been accepted by the Attorney General of the United States, will be repatriated to Japan, together with their families, whether citizens or aliens, who desire to accompany them."[46] Consideration was not given to the reasons for renouncing or to the desire to remain in the United States or settle in Japan.

Although there was little opposition in the country at large to the Department's announcement for ridding the United States of this "disloyal" element, a small number of individuals, groups, and agencies spoke out against the plan. On October 25, the Portland (Oregon) Citizens Committee to Aid Relocation wrote to Attorney General Clark urging that, in order "to avoid a wholesale miscarriage of justice and to prevent innumerable personal and family tragedies, a rehearing be granted each of the persons involved who desires one."[47] The WRA tried several times unsuccessfully to persuade the Department of Justice that such a step would result in a grave injustice to thousands of basically blameless people.[48] On November 1, Secretary of the Interior Ickes urgently recommended to the Attorney General that individual hearings be given, since "the deportation of the renunciants could in many cases be called seriously into question on the grounds of legality, justice, and plain decency."[49]

In addition to such pleas, Collins, with the backing of the ACLU of Northern California, introduced litigation to prevent the Department of Justice from carrying out its plan. On November 13, 1945, only two days before the first ship was to sail loaded with both willing and unwilling renunciants and aliens, he filed four suits in the United States District Court in San Francisco. These suits, which will be discussed more fully in the following chapter, asked that specified renunciants be set at liberty; that the deportation orders be cancelled; that the applications for renunciation be declared void; and that the plaintiffs be declared nationals of the United States. Many renunciants refused to join the suits immediately because they feared the government would brook no further defiance, even in this legal form, and would blame any coercion on various rank and file followers of the Resegregationist organizations who, although members, were actually innocent of any wrongdoing.[50]

The renunciants were successful in their efforts to prevent involuntary deportations. Collins obtained a court order in the habeas corpus proceedings which forbade removal until a decision had been reached. Thus, the Department of Justice found itself in a dilemma. It could not carry out its mass deportation plan, and it did not want to release renunciants within the United States. Yet, keeping the camps open for the two to four years of legal proceedings might require the expenditure of millions of dollars annually.[51]

The Department of Justice found a solution to this problem in what appeared as a magnanimous acceptance of the pleas for individual hearings made by Ickes, the WRA, and others; and at the same time it avoided the necessity of keeping the internment camps open for years to come. The change in policy was announced to the renunciants on December 10, 1945, in an extra edition of the *Newell Star*: deportation, or so-called "mitigation," hearings (similar to those normally held in cases of deportation of aliens to discover whether undue hardship would be occasioned by the move) would be held for all renunciants who did not wish to go to Japan, as well as for aliens who had been interned and were then at Tule Lake under special segregation or parole orders. Aliens or renunciants who did not ask for a hearing, those who expressed a desire to be sent to Japan, and those aliens and renunciants removed from Tule Lake during the renunciation hearings would be sent to Japan.[52]

Hearings were held between January 7 and April 1, 1946, in all of the Department of Justice camps in which renunciants were interned. Since a large number of renunciants and interned aliens had applied for removal to Japan, or had already left, there were only about 3,300 renunciants remaining in Tule Lake in January, 1946 when the hearings began, plus a small number elsewhere. Of these, 3,161 in the former segregation center and twenty-five in the internment camps at Bismarck and Santa Fe applied for a hearing. Only 107 renunciants at Tule Lake failed to do so.[53]

On New Year's Day, Department of Justice Attorney Charles Rothstein arrived in Tule Lake to head a hearing team of fifteen persons, including some who had been with Burling during the renunciation hearings. The Department stated that any renunciant who could prove he was the victim of duress at the time of renunciation would be freed from detention, although citizenship would not be restored. In addition, hardship cases, such as a renunciant who could establish that immediate family members depended upon him for support, would be given consideration and probably released from detention. However, no special consideration was given to persons who were minors at the time they renounced.[54]

The Department of Justice took the position that the hearings were an "act of grace" and that it could conduct them to suit its own purposes.[55] Individual hearings lasted anywhere from ten minutes to two hours. The renunciants were denied counsel, the right to be represented or advised by an attorney, or to have any legal advice whatsoever but could bring a "friend" as an observer.[56] This practice was often discouraged by the hearing officers, however, many of whom became annoyed when this was done. On one occasion, at least, a hearing officer barred the "friend" and, on another, frightened the subject into excluding the "friend." Witnesses were allowed to testify for the renunciants, but by the time of the hearings, over fifteen hundred Tule Lake residents had already relocated, thereby making this provision virtually meaningless. Moreover, the government discouraged the calling of witnesses by telling people they did not need them.[57] The hearing officers questioned the renunciants from dossiers in their possession but denied the individuals concerned access to the material contained therein.[58] A few of the government examiners were kind and sympathetic, but most were reported to be brusque, overbearing individuals who browbeat their subjects with unfair cross-examinations. As a result, many renunciants were frightened and confused, while most lacked the legal skill and knowledge to prepare their own cases.[59]

On February 12, 1946, after slightly over half (1,800) of the applicants had been granted hearings, the Department of Justice announced that 449 renunciants had been rejected by the Hearing Board and would be deported.[60] There were no additions to this figure despite the fact that another thousand hearings were conducted.[61] The failure to add to the names on the list as further hearings were held caused Collins to charge the government with bad faith. He believed that this proved the 449 renunciants had been chosen arbitrarily and that continuation of the hearings was only for the purpose of giving an appearance of fairness and legality to the proceedings.[62]

Many of the rejected renunciants refused to accept the Hearing Board's findings and sought rehearings. Encouraged by Collins and the Tule Lake Defense Committee, the letter-writing campaign was revived. Individual and form letters were again sent to Department of Justice officials from Tule Lake, Bismarck, and Santa Fe, protesting the denial of due process. Inclusion on the deportation list prompted a number of detainees to join the other renunciants in mass habeas corpus and equity suits.[63]

The number of renunciants on the list for deportation was reduced from 449 to 406 by the time Tule Lake closed on March 28, 1946. Some removal orders had to be revoked upon discovery that not all renunciants were dual nationals and thus not Japanese citizens under the laws of Japan.[64] This number was further lessened even as the trains pulled out of Tule Lake to transfer the 406, and their forty-three family members, to internment at Crystal City, Texas, and Seabrook Farms, in Bridgton, New Jersey. At least fifty notices of release from detention were received during the twenty-four hours before the last train left for Crystal City on March 20. Releases continued to be made as the train stopped in San Francisco and Los Angeles. With the Bismarck camp closing in March, and Santa Fe shortly afterwards, all remaining renunciants were detained at Crystal City and Bridgton to await the outcome of Collins' mass habeas corpus suit.[65]

Renunciants cleared by the mitigation hearings were informed they were expected to resettle as quickly as possible. The *Newell Star* announced on February 15, 1946, a new "five-day rule" for completion of relocation plans for all Tule Lake residents no longer under detention or removal orders. Of the 3,186 renunciants who appeared for hearings, 2,780 were given unconditional releases to resettle anywhere in the United States.[66] On March 28, 1946, the Tule Lake camp finally closed its gates.

The former residents of Tule Lake were scattered throughout the United States and Japan. In both countries the renunciants faced serious difficulties. Those who resettled in the United States, particularly in the West, during 1946, benefited from their late appearance. The violence which had met the first returnees had disappeared, and many Caucasian leaders, for the first time, publicly urged acceptance of persons of Japanese descent, particularly citizen Nisei. However, renunciants were now considered "aliens ineligible to citizenship" and faced the same legal and economic discriminations as their Issei parents. As aliens, they were unable to practice in many of the professions. The establishment of any business by alien Japanese, including renunciants, became a risky and difficult venture.[67] The alien land laws of various Western states prevented aliens ineligible for citizenship from owning land. The State of California reactivated this relatively dormant legislation during the war and vigorously instituted escheat (i.e., the reversion of property to the state from persons ineligible to own it) proceedings against Japanese aliens until 1952, when the California Supreme Court in Fujii v. California banned such action. Collins was specifically informed by the California Attorney General's office that if any renunciant attempted to acquire land, the state would institute escheat proceedings.[68] Collins therefore advised each renunciant not to purchase or lease agricultural, commercial, or residential land or buildings in California or any other state which had alien land laws.[69] In addition to land law restrictions, renunciants were: compelled to register as aliens and carry alien registration certificates; ineligible to vote or hold public office; required to pay non-resident fees to attend the University of California; denied civil service positions; not allowed to travel abroad and re-enter the United States without filling out a special affidavit; and ineligible for old age pensions in states which provided such benefits for citizens only.

Approximately eight thousand people of Japanese descent left for

Japan either during or immediately after the war. Some had failed to adjust to life in this country; some had become economically impoverished because of the long years of internment; some were bitter and frustrated over their treatment; and others went to Japan to accompany parents or other aging relatives, although they would have preferred to remain in the United States. Of the 6,200 persons removed to Japan from Tule Lake and the Department of Justice internment camps, 1,800 to 2,000 were renunciants. Out of the 4,406 shipped from Tule Lake alone, 1,767 were American citizens who had not renounced, including over 1,000 under ten years of age and another 679 teen-agers who were accompanying parents. Only forty-nine United States citizens age twenty or over left for Japan from Tule Lake.[70]

The Issei and Nisei who returned to Japan in late 1945 and early 1946 found conditions far worse than those who had chosen to resettle in the United States. Japan had just lost a war. Houses, buildings, and factories had been devastated. Food had to be supplied from outside the islands. Every major city except Kyoto had been subjected to the American bombing and fire raids. Because of the severe food shortage, the Japanese government continued wartime rationing which allowed each person one-third the calories served as a minimum to American soldiers. Unemployment was also widespread. The December 15, 1945 issue of the Los Angeles–based Japanese American newspaper, the *Pacific Citizen*, described the hardships faced by the first arrivals from Tule Lake and the Department of Justice internment camps. They found that people in Japan considered them "suckers" for having left the United States. The repatriates and expatriates complained about the food and were told they were lucky to get it, that thousands were starving in Japan. Messages were sent back to the remaining renunciants pleading with them to forget about Japan and to remain in the United States.[71]

The first few years in Japan were unbearable. The ability to speak English helped the renunciants to get jobs with the American occupation forces. However, in September, 1947, a directive cancelled the government jobs of the renunciants. Some of the expatriates considered this act to be the final rejection by the United States.[72] Even many Issei were shocked at the changes in their "cherished land." Sons and daughters reported that their parents could "almost shoot themselves for having been duped to leave America."[73]

Conditions eventually improved for many of the repatriates and expatriates from the United States. However, many others never adjusted to life in Japan. Gladys Ishida, a Nisei graduate student in sociology from the University of Michigan, spent a year studying twenty-seven renunciants in Yokohama Prefecture, Japan. She found that the Kibei renunciants, because of their early education in Japan, were entirely satisfied with their new life and were accepted by the Japanese people. Their mannerisms were Japanese; they did not brag about life in America; they had forgotten the little English they knew; and they showed a tendency to conform. According to Ishida, the Kibei did not "lament the loss of their American citizenship, but considered it gone forever." [74]

The Nisei, however, were restless in Japan and wanted to go back to the United States. They still celebrated American customs, ate Western food when they could, had more informal manners, and spoke of the Japanese, whom they did not understand, as "nationals." [75] As a result, many of them joined Collins' mass suits and were receptive to other attorneys who sought to represent them in the American courts. Collins corresponded with his clients and warned them to avoid acts that would endanger the restoration of their citizenship, should the mass suits be successful. Thus, renunciants desiring restoration of American citizenship and return to the United States were denied the right to vote, hold office, perform certain jobs, and other privileges that otherwise were open to them as dual nationals and citizens of Japan. These Nisei renunciants were American by culture and Japanese by citizenship. Now they wanted only the opportunity to be American in both once again. It was for this purpose that Collins and the Tule Lake Defense Committee were working.

9

The Renunciation Cases: The Restoration of Citizenship

The mass suits for the cancellation of renunciation of citizenship and the prevention of forced removal to Japan, which were initiated on November 13, 1945, remained in the courts for twenty-three years. The key figure in this long struggle was Wayne M. Collins, attorney for the renunciants. The San Francisco lawyer persisted through periods of victory and defeat and in the face of opposition from the Department of Justice and from the national office of the ACLU, particularly through its Los Angeles representative, A. L. Wirin, whose victory for three renunciants threatened the chances for success of thousands of others. At the end of this period, all but a handful of the 5,589 Japanese Americans who renounced in 1944–45 had their citizenship restored, while not a single renunciant had been forcibly deported.

As discussed in the previous chapter, Collins had at first urged each renunciant to hire his own attorney who would then file a suit in his behalf. However, this was later seen to be impractical because only those persons involved in such suits would be protected. The remaining renunciants would continue to be subject to detention and deportation while these individual cases were in court. Thus, success in a single case would not necessarily benefit the others. Collins therefore decided to institute mass suits in which all could join to protect the rights of the entire group. Such action offered several benefits: (1) a common defense fund, obtained by contributions to the Tule Lake Defense Committee and maintained by Collins, which would enable the poorest renunciant to seek redress in the courts; (2) the largest possible number of renunciants could obtain the benefits of the suits, including delay or prevention of deportation and perhaps freedom from detention; and (3) the avoidance of a multiplicity of suits which would tie up the federal courts for years. The massing of plaintiffs further enabled Collins to treat the proceedings as a class action, because all of the renunciants constituted a group whose complaint arose out of a common series of occurrences and also because the points of litigation and questions of law involved were common to each of them.

Collins' basic argument was that all evacuees, particularly those in Tule Lake, were victims of duress by the United States government which made the renunciations invalid. An incidental argument was that the duress was two-fold: (1) government duress which, in turn, induced coercion by a small group of aliens and citizens who had been informed that they could live as Japanese and would be removed to Japan; and (2) these then pressured others to join them. Specifically, Collins contended that the government was aware of the pro-Japanese pressure groups in the center and condoned them by failing to stop their radical activities; arrest and prosecute the leaders and active members; invoke the federal sedition, espionage, or other criminal laws against them; and segregate or isolate such elements from the loyal residents of the center.[1] Even the more radical members of these organizations suffered from duress by the government which, according to Collins, made their renunciations invalid. Such duress took many forms, including: evacuation from their homes without hearings while German and Italian nationals remained free; four years of internment, including two under the oppressive conditions existing in Tule Lake; the discharge of Nisei from the Army and their subsequent IV-C "alien" classification by the Selective Service; imprisonment in a stockade without hearings, charges, or trials; and the failure of the government to protect those under its care from coercion and violence. "In consequence," the renunciants' attorney concluded, "every renunciation was the direct product of governmental duress" and "was not the product of free will."[2]

The immediate and major threat to the renunciants in Tule Lake and the Department of Justice internment camps in November, 1945 was the impending forcible deportation of the entire group to Japan, scheduled to begin on November 15 of that year. Such removal had not been contemplated by Attorney General Biddle, who had been the author of the Renunciation Law. The former Attorney General had viewed the Act primarily as a means of providing detention for certain "disloyal,'' and therefore dangerous, American citizens who might otherwise be released within the United States during wartime.[3] This early objective of internment changed to deportation under Tom Clark, Biddle's successor in the Department of Justice. Clark had always been a hard-liner on the question of the West Coast's Japanese. As a Department of Justice attorney, he had worked with General DeWitt at the time of the evacuation, had carried out the various evacuation orders, and had, in fact, chosen the site upon which Tule Lake was constructed.[4] The new Attorney General therefore decided that even though the fighting with Japan had stopped, the renunciants were "dangerous" persons and should not be allowed to remain in the United States.

Clark, however, had not counted on such determined resistance as he met in the renunciants' attorney. Faced with the immediate removal of his clients to Japan, Collins, with great urgency, filed four suits against the government on November 13, 1945, only two days before the Army transports were due to sail. The first two suits, Abo v. Williams and Furuya v. Williams were applications for writs of habeas corpus requesting freedom from internment and prevention of deportation. Because the two suits were similar in all details, they were consolidated and tried together. At the same time Collins also filed two suits in equity, Abo v. Clark and Furuya v. Clark. These sought to cancel the renunciations and have each plaintiff declared a citizen of the United States. Like the habeas corpus proceedings, these were also tried together. Collins' purpose in the mass suits was to aid any and all renunciants who desired restoration of citizenship and resettlement in the United States. However, only those who applied to him directly or through the Tule Lake Defense Committee were included in the suits. Originally only 987 of the 5,589 renunciants joined the mass suits. This number continued to increase, however, until 4,754 persons were counted as plaintiffs.

The habeas corpus proceedings were considered more important than the suits in equity, because freedom from detention and deportation took precedence over restoration of citizenship. This view was shared by the United States District Court in San Francisco, which was scheduled to conduct the trial.[5] Those renunciants who joined in the litigation were protected by a series of court orders which prevented their removal from the jurisdiction of the District Court.[6] Thus blocked in its removal plans, the Department of Justice announced, on December 10, 1945, that "mitigation" hearings would be held, beginning in January, 1946, for renunciants who wished to remain within the United States. Because such hearings had a direct bearing on the habeas corpus cases, Judge A. F. St. Sure agreed to delay action pending their outcome.[7] The Court, by an order dated March 14, 1946, permitted the 449 renunciants who received unfavorable verdicts in the hearings to be moved to internment camps in Santa Fe, New Mexico, Crystal City, Texas, and Bridgton, New Jersey.[8] A short time later, the Tule Lake and Santa Fe camps were closed.

On September 23, 1946, ten months after the initiation of litigation by the renunciants, the government filed its answers to the habeas corpus suits. It claimed that the petitioners were detained because they were dual nationals who renounced their United States citizenship and thereby became Japanese nationals subject to detention and removal as alien enemies under provisions of the Alien Enemies Act of 1798, Presidential Proclamations 2525 and 2655, and to the regulations of the Attorney General promulgated thereunder. As a result, it was maintained that the detention was lawful and writs should be denied.[9] The Department conceded, however, to many of Collins' contentions. It admitted that the Resegregationists misrepresented the government's renunciation program and attempted to get the residents of Tule Lake to renounce their citizenship. Furthermore, it agreed that alien parents attempted to persuade their citizen children to renounce and that many of the renunciants were minors at the time of renunciation. Nevertheless, the Department continued to maintain that the renunciants "were not . . . coerced or led by any form of duress to renounce, . . . but . . . were voluntary and active participants . . . with full knowledge of the nature and consequences of their act."[10]

The following month, on October 14, 1946, Collins made a motion to the Court that the renunciants be awarded the requested writ of habeas corpus. The Department of Justice countered, and the Court ruled that its judgment would be made primarily on the basis of affidavits and briefs of the parties concerned. Before a decision could be reached, however, Judge St. Sure became seriously ill and, on February 20, 1947, the motions were transferred to Judge Louis Goodman for consideration. On June 30, 1947, one year and a half after the initiation of the suits, the District Court announced that the writs would be granted. Goodman ordered that all renunciants should be freed from internment and that none could be removed involuntarily to Japan. The 331 renunciants detained in the camps in Texas and New Jersey were thus freed after being held for five years by their government.[11]

Judge Goodman had long been familiar with the conditions of duress that had existed in Tule Lake and was sympathetic towards the camp's residents. In Kuwabara v. the United States, in which he had presided, he noted the absence of an atmosphere conducive to free will in the center. Goodman now reiterated this view in regard to the renunciants faced with deportation. His opinion rejected the Department of Justice's concept of dual citizenship which claimed that renunciation within the United States made each automatically a citizen of Japan. He ruled instead that possession of Japanese citizenship by renunciants did not make them aliens until they had voluntarily left the United States. As a result, the District Court judge denied the Department's contention that, under the Alien Enemy Act (which was the basis for the planned removals), a renunciant might be deported.[12]

Goodman issued the writs of habeas corpus on August 11, 1947. Two days later, all detained renunciants were ordered released to their attorney pending final outcome of appeals taken by the Attorney General. On September 6, the 138 litigants in the habeas corpus proceedings were released to Collins and were then allowed to resettle. Another 164 detained renunciants who had not joined the litigation because they had been transferred from the jurisdiction of the Court were paroled to Collins and likewise returned to their homes.[13] A few renunciants had been released prior to this, following the June 30 decision. The government agreed to bear the cost of transporting the group from the internment camps in New Jersey and Texas to their former homes on the West Coast.[14]

On January 17, 1951, William Denman, Chief Judge of the United States Court of Appeals for the Ninth Circuit, reversed the 1947 decision and returned the cases to the District Court for further proceedings for all who had been adults at the time of their renunciations and were still under removal orders. The earlier judgments were affirmed for persons who had been minors at the time of renunciation. Three hundred and two renunciants, against whom removal orders were still outstanding, were affected by this decision.

Denman agreed that renunciation did not automatically make each person a citizen of Japan, as the government had maintained, unless the laws of Japan accepted them as such. The government's efforts to prove that Japanese laws confirmed the dual citizenship of the renunciants were denied as hearsay, since they were based on unverified statements regarding Japanese statutes. Therefore, the matter of whether or not Japanese law conferred Japanese citizenship on individual renunciants was returned to the District Court and was to be decided in separate hearings for each renunciant in the case. According to the Chief Judge, "It well may be shown that each before renunciation sought Japanese citizenship or that he afterwards claimed it" and that "a person so permitted to renounce American citizenship may assert his Japanese citizenship in the United States" if evidence shows that Japanese law permits a person residing in the United States to claim such citizenship. The applicability of such Japanese law was to be determined for each applicant by the trial court.[15]

The Appeals Court also denied Collins' argument that the Renunciation Law was invalid and discriminatory class legislation because its background and application showed that the right to renounce would be claimed only by citizens of Japanese descent. Denman denied the statute was invalid merely because Congress had a particular group in mind when it legalized renunciation. The Court further denied that the law was discriminatorily applied because the right to renounce had not been systematically or arbitrarily refused to citizens of other than Japanese ancestry.[16] Collins appealed to the Supreme Court but was denied certiorari in October, 1951. Thus, the cases were returned for individual hearings in the District Court in order to allow the government opportunity to present evidence against each renunciant separately.

The threat of removal to the remaining 302 renunciants who were still under deportation orders ended on April 28, 1952, when the treaty of peace between the United States and Japan became effective. After that date it was no longer possible for the American government to deport stateless persons into that country without permission. In addition, the end of the war made the Alien Enemy Act of 1798, under whose authority the deportation orders were issued, inoperative. On April 30, Acting Attorney General Philip B. Perlman signed individual orders cancelling the outstanding removal orders against each renunciant.[17] Collins' custody of the 302 who had been under threat of deportation likewise came to an end, thereby ending the uncertainty of continued life in the United States. With the reason for the petitions ended, Collins, on May 2, 1952, terminated the two habeas corpus suits begun in November, 1945 and concentrated his energies on the restoration of citizenship to the renunciants in the equity suits. Until this was accomplished, all renunciants, while possessing freedom of movement, were denied the right to depart from the United States and re-enter, the right to vote, to hold public office, to enter public service, and all the other rights that flowed from national citizenship.

The Department of Justice displayed a determined resistance to the mass equity suits since their initiation in November, 1945, which was not shared by other federal agencies concerned with the Tule Lake renunciants. Even before the suits were filed, top officials of the WRA and the Department of the Interior had urged leniency toward the former citizens. After litigation began, Department of Justice lawyers were informed that the secretaries of the Interior and State departments, and other defendants named by Collins, were opposed to contesting the suits. On December 10, 1946, Dillon Myer and Raymond Best were removed as defendants, leaving only the Department of Justice in opposition to the renunciants.[18]

The District Court's decision to give priority to the habeas corpus proceedings resulted in a delay of over two years, until April, 1948, for a ruling in the equity cases. On that date, however, the renunciants won an apparent victory as Judge Goodman accepted completely Collins' charges of governmental duress. Goodman held to the common practice of abstaining from deciding constitutional questions unless required to do so by the record of a particular case and declined to rule on the constitutionality of the Renunciation Law, which had been challenged in the suits. Such a decision was considered unnecessary because affidavits presented as evidence by both Collins and the Department of Justice were in agreement as to "the combination of factors which lead to the execution of the renunciations." What disagreement there was concerned the relative importance of the various causes of renunciation upon the plaintiffs. The factors cited by Goodman included: indoctrination of the young and threats by the Resegregationist organizations; pressure by alien parents to prevent family breakup and avoid draft induction; fear of hostility outside of Tule Lake; fear of reprisals in Japan; and mass hysteria induced by the experiences since evacuation. Such factors, singly or in combination, rendered any act of renunciation incompetent.[19]

Goodman charged the government had erred in accepting most of the renunciations and must be prompt and decisive in correcting its mistakes. He therefore issued an interlocutory decree cancelling the renunciations and declaring the plaintiffs citizens of the United States. However, because it was recognized that certain plaintiffs might indeed have renounced freely and voluntarily, Judge Goodman ordered the Department of Justice be given ninety days "to file a designation" of such plaintiffs it might wish to pursue further. Designated plaintiffs would be subject to further hearings in the District Court. Others would be restored to citizenship.[20]

The ninety days were extended to ten months because the Department of Justice won repeated delays to prepare its evidence. Both sides used their time well. Because all renunciants in Tule Lake had suffered the same conditions as the successful plaintiffs in the equity cases, hundreds and perhaps thousands sought to be included as plaintiffs during the months between Goodman's opinion and the final decree. At Collins' request, the Court ordered the inclusion of additional plaintiffs on sixty different occasions between the initiation of the cases and the interlocutory decree of April 28, 1948. Following this, the renunciants' attorney was granted the inclusion of plaintiffs on six additional dates prior to the final decree.[21] As a result, the number of renunciants included in the mass suits rose from 987 on November 13, 1945, to 2,300 on April 28, 1948, and to 4,315 ten months later.[22] Collins received requests in almost every mail from renunciants desiring the benefits of the District Court victory.

The Department of Justice continued to pursue its hard line, determined to challenge the bid of each renunciant who sought restoration of citizenship. Under the guise of checking its files for evidence against individual renunciants believed to have renounced freely and voluntarily, it sought continued extensions of time, ostensibly to designate such plaintiffs concerning whom it desired to present further evidence. After three extensions, the Department filed its designations on February 25, 1949. Rather than citing particular individuals, as the District Court had suggested, the Department listed all 4,410 plaintiffs, which it simply divided into various classifications. Included were eight persons admitted by the government to have been medical cases who had been mentally incompetent at the time they renounced.

The designations created twenty-two classes, or groups, of renunciants, each of which was purportedly guilty of certain offenses serious enough to deny restoration of citizenship. It was the government's contention that the trial of a single designee from each group would ordinarily suffice.[23] In effect, the Department attempted to create twenty-two mass class actions for the one already decided by the District Court. Against each class, the Department claimed evidence which would prove or tend to prove that each designee renounced freely and without duress, coercion, intimidation, fraud, or undue influence. That much of the "evidence" was exceedingly weak may be seen from the fact that classes five and fifteen would deny restoration to 1,335 renunciants solely because they had applied for expatriation or voluntarily returned to Japan.[24]

The Department's action was in direct contravention to the instructions of Judge Goodman, who had clearly indicated the Court was not interested in classification of plaintiffs but merely wished a simple listing of persons believed not entitled to the restoration of citizenship. He emphasized that these should be compiled in good faith for the purpose of serving the interests of justice. Goodman especially urged that careful judgment be exercised so as not to overburden the Court with a large number of unnecessary cases.[25] The Department answered that the Attorney General felt he could not properly concede that the renunciations of any of the designated plaintiffs were involuntary as a matter of fact or law.[26]

Collins immediately challenged the Department's attempt to list all of the plaintiffs in its designations as not being in good faith. He saw it as a violation of an agreement entered into between himself, the Department of Justice attorneys, and the judge on October 10, 1947. This provided that the suits should be decided on the evidence thus presented, with the exception that the Court could order additional evidence if necessary.[27] Because Goodman had not requested new evidence but had merely permitted the government to list certain renunciants against whom additional evidence might be offered, Collins charged that the Attorney General was attempting to subvert the District Court judge's order.

Judge Goodman agreed with Collins and ordered the Department's designations stricken from the records. It was the view of the Court that the Department's offers of proof covered matters which had already been decided in favor of the renunciants and failed to carry out the Court's instructions.[28] Therefore, on April 12, 1949, Goodman entered his Final Decree in favor of all the renunciants, declaring their renunciations *void ab initio* and that each was entitled to the complete exercise of United States nationality and citizenship.

While the mass suits were meeting success in the federal District

Court in San Francisco, ultimate victory in the higher courts was being
threatened by sources outside the government. From the beginning, the
only active support received by the renunciants had come from Collins, who acted with the nominal support of the ACLU of Northern
California. The former citizens had been rejected by the JACL, which
had never wavered in its support of the United States government and
was embarrassed by "disloyalty" from within the Japanese community. This lack of support from an expected ally neither helped nor
hindered the renunciants' cause. However, this cannot be said for the
opposition received from the national office of the ACLU, an organization from which aid might have been expected.

Strained relations developed between the national office of the ACLU
and its Northern California branch during the early years of World War
II. The Union's headquarters opposed the San Francisco chapter's
challenge of the authority of the military to exclude the Japanese from
the West Coast. The opposition of the national office resulted from a
Union policy which limited aid to persons accused or suspected of disloyalty solely to due process questions. Ernest Besig, director of the
California organization, and Collins maintained that exclusion was a
racial matter and refused to drop the case until it reached the United
States Supreme Court and was decided in Korematsu v. the United
States. Relations grew worse as the national headquarters and Roger
Baldwin, the ACLU's founder and national director, continued to op-
pose other cases of the Northern California branch.[29]

Beginning in 1945, the national office of the ACLU put pressure on
the Northern California branch to halt representation of the renunciants. As a result, Collins broke all relations with Baldwin and the
national Union, which then went through Besig in an attempt to either
stop or control the mass suits.[30] One form of pressure applied on the
local office was a new regulation that no ACLU attorney could accept
a fee for appearing in any civil liberties case. This was particularly
directed at Collins, who under the new rule would have to refuse all
fees for over twenty years of litigation. The San Francisco organization agreed to abide by ACLU policy in regard to the renunciation matter
and promised not to take any new cases without the national office's
consent. It continued, nevertheless, to give favorable publicity to the
mass suits. Collins, however, was "too much of a lone wolf" to surrender to the New York office's wishes and continued to pursue the

struggle on his own. He became so immersed in the renunciants' cause that for years he maintained virtually a one-case office.[31]

The ACLU's national headquarters continued its attempts to undercut Collins' efforts to aid the renunciants. The basic disagreement between Collins and Baldwin was the San Franciscan's charges of governmental duress as the primary cause of the renunciations. Baldwin was a close friend of many leaders in the Roosevelt administration, including WRA Director Myer, Myer's superior, Secretary of the Interior Harold Ickes, and Edward Ennis, head of the Alien Enemies Control Unit of the Department of Justice and a member of the ACLU. Collins steadfastly contended that Baldwin conspired to protect the administration from charges of guilt in the mass renunciation crisis by means of the institution of individual cases charging community duress only and ignoring all government responsibility.[32]

A. L. Wirin, counsel for the Southern California branch of the ACLU and an associate of Baldwin's, was the vehicle for representing the national office's position. Wirin, like Collins, had a long career in representing persons of Japanese descent on the West Coast. In 1942, he had been attorney for the Congress of Industrial Organizations (CIO) but resigned in order to handle Japanese evacuation cases.[33] Throughout the war and thereafter he was closely associated with the JACL and its head, Saburo Kido. Acting sometimes privately and sometimes for the ACLU, Wirin fought many battles for Issei and Nisei rights. In 1948, the Los Angeles attorney argued the case of Fred Oyama, in which the United States Supreme Court ruled that the Alien Land Law of California could not deprive United States citizens of Japanese descent of land purchased in their names by their alien parents. Among his other efforts to help persons of Japanese descent during and after World War II, Wirin: represented Issei efforts to win United States citizenship; successfully challenged California's efforts to prevent Issei from obtaining commercial fishing licenses; represented Nisei "strandees," who were caught in Japan in 1949 and were prevented from returning to the United States after the conclusion of the war; and defended Nisei who refused to be drafted into the military while confined in WRA camps.[34]

Wirin's reputation as a civil libertarian and a champion of Japanese American rights was not entirely accepted, however, by the residents of Tule Lake and members of the ACLU of Northern California. San

Francisco Union leaders questioned his motives and charged him with numerous unethical practices. Besig, describing Wirin as a "slippery" individual, criticized him for privately accepting civil liberties cases in order to get money and publicity while at the same time accepting an annual salary from the ACLU of Southern California.[35] The San Francisco Union director further protested to the national office that the Los Angeles counsel was "invading" the territory of the local branch.[36] Wirin's popularity within the segregation center suffered from his association with the JACL, an organization which refused its aid during the renunciation hearings and whose president, Saburo Kido, had predicted the failure of any court suits. Wirin was further hurt by reports of his having given testimony before the Congressional Dickstein Committee in 1945 stating that all renunciants should be deported to Japan.[37] The national office of the ACLU worked hard, through Wirin, to secure plaintiffs in Tule Lake but was forced to admit, in its July, 1946 annual report, that "all of the renunciants who were willing to file suits preferred to work through private lawyers already engaged."

Collins developed an intense hostility toward Wirin as a result of the latter's questionable practices in Tule Lake and the Department of Justice internment camps.[38] In apparent violation of legal ethics, the Los Angeles attorney had openly advertised for cases in the *Rocky Shimpo*, a Japanese language newspaper. Fees of $250 per person were asked despite the fact that he was paid an annual salary by the ACLU for handling civil liberties cases.[39] From October, 1945 through March, 1946, Wirin and his associate J. B. Tietz attempted by various means to represent renunciants in the internment camp. Wirin made it a practice to urge the internees to set up defense committees to collect money to finance his operations.[40] A "Defense Committee," separate from the Tule Lake Defense Committee, was established in October, 1945, purportedly by a small group of renunciants, but actually by Wirin and Tietz, for this purpose.[41] An effort was also made, in February, 1946, to establish a "Trust Committee" in Tule Lake in order to collect defense funds to be used by Wirin and Tietz.[42] Such activities were highly unsuccessful as they resulted in only three clients from Tule Lake compared to over four thousand in Collins' mass suits.

The three clients thus secured, however, were sufficient to enable Wirin to institute legal proceedings which seriously threatened the success of the mass suits. The Los Angeles attorney initiated two suits. The first sought restoration of citizenship for three Nisei who renounced while in Tule Lake and for one who had renounced at the age of eighteen while in the Manzanar relocation center. This case, Inouye v. Clark, was won in the United States District Court in Los Angeles on September 18, 1947, but lost on appeal to the United States Court of Appeals in San Francisco on a technicality.[43]

The second suit, Acheson v. Murakami, was initiated in the same District Court on July 6, 1948, two months after Judge Goodman had given his preliminary opinion cancelling the renunciations of plaintiffs in the mass suits in San Francisco. For this reason, it was viewed by Collins as an attempt by Wirin and the national office of the ACLU to bypass his cases and win a ruling that was more favorable to the government. The *Murakami* suit involved the same three Tule Lake renunciants who had been in the *Inouye* case. During May and June, 1948, they had applied for passports and been turned down because it was held that they were no longer citizens of the United States. The three thereupon sued the Secretary of State for restoration of citizenship, using arguments that conditions in Tule Lake had made free and intelligent decisions impossible. On August 27, 1948, more than seven months before Judge Goodman's final judgment in the San Francisco court, Judge William C. Mathes declared the renunciations of Wirin's three plaintiffs void and ordered the Secretary of State to treat them as citizens of the United States. The government appealed to the Ninth Circuit Court of Appeals in San Francisco and, on August 26, 1949, Wirin succeeded in bypassing the still-to-be-heard mass suits in that court, as Judge William Denman upheld the lower court's opinion.

"Publicity handouts" inaccurately suggested that the *Murakami* decision would determine the rights of all renunciants.[44] Denman's scathing denunciation of the "unnecessarily cruel and inhuman treatment" of Japanese at the Tule Lake center apparently showed sympathy for the plight of all Japanese Americans and implied that such would be the case. Denman, in rendering his decision in favor of the three renunciants, took into consideration the fact that "some four thousand similar cases [in the mass suits] who are seeking identical relief" were still to be heard by the Court and gave extensive attention to those "uncontested underlying facts, certain to have their effect upon the minds of the mass of deportees [i.e., renunciants] incarcerated at Tule Lake."[45] All of Tule Lake's renunciants were held to have suffered equally: (1) the "racial" evacuation, the "repeated recitals" of which in the "crowded dust filled halls and cells of the Tule Lake Center" had "their effect upon the psychology of those contemplating the value of an American citizenship"; and (2) the "incarceration" at Tule Lake and "its effects upon the minds of our fellow citizens as to the value of their citizenship."[46]

However, despite the sympathy displayed for the overwhelming majority of renunciants, Wirin's victory in the federal courts was a set back for the renunciants' cause. The major damage was done by Wirin's separate treatment of each of the three individuals in his suit, which practice was followed by the Court in rendering its opinion. This procedure, if carried over into the mass suits, would result in thousands of separate hearings which would tie up the District Court and delay restoration of citizenship for years to many renunciants and would prevent restoration to countless others who might fail to satisfy the Court individually. The mass suits were further damaged by Denman's acceptance of community duress by pro-Japanese pressure groups as the reason for renunciation, while governmental duress as charged by Collins was largely ignored.[47] Members of the Resegregationist organizations, who had been considered victims of governmental duress due to the evacuation and other events, now found themselves charged with responsibility for coercing renunciations and were in danger of losing when the mass suits reached the Court of Appeals.[48]

Collins viewed the *Murakami* decision as the end result of a conspiracy by Baldwin and Wirin "to relieve the WRA, the Justice Department and government agents from any charge of responsibility for the vicious renunciation program."[49] Credence is given Collins' charges of efforts to "white-wash" the government's guilt for the renunciation crisis by the support given Wirin by high-ranking officials in the Tule Lake administration. Assistant Project Director Black, Project Attorney Noyes, and several other officials provided affidavits in support of the theory of duress by pressure groups as opposed to governmental duress. The *ACLU News* (of Northern California) reported that "observers" believed the Los Angeles cases were supported by the government, because they relieved its agencies of responsibility for the renunciations.[50]

The government thus had received an opinion that it could support and chose not to appeal the *Murakami* decision to the Supreme Court. The arguments of community duress were acceptable because they avoided criticism of government agencies, particularly of the Department of Justice, while the policy of having individual hearings for each renunciant, as practiced in these cases, would provide the Department an opportunity to challenge the restoration of citizenship to each and every renunciant, thereby making sure that no "disloyal" Nisei could claim American nationality. On October 26, 1949, Assistant Attorney General H. Graham Morison announced that the appellate court decision would be "accepted and applied in all future cases" where the facts were close to those described in the *Murakami* decision.[51]

The Justice Department's appeal of Collins' mass suits for restoration of citizenship was finally heard in the Ninth Circuit Court of Appeals beginning in May, 1950, more than eight months after that court had rendered its decision in the *Murakami* case. Still another eight months later, on January 11, 1951, that court partially reversed the District Court's ruling that restored citizenship to the renunciants in the mass suits. The earlier decision was affirmed in part for the 899 Nisei in the suits who had been under twenty-one years of age at the time of renunciation.[52] Citizenship was likewise restored to eight persons who had been declared mentally incompetent and to fifty-eight renunciants whom the Department of Justice had opposed in court solely for the reason that "they went to Tule Lake to be with family members."[53] This the Court regarded as insufficient evidence for contesting restoration of citizenship. However, for the remaining three thousand adult renunciants, Denman ordered that their cases be returned to the District Court in order to give the Department of Justice an opportunity to present evidence against each, in individual hearings, which he felt might prove that the individual had renounced of his own free will and not from coercion, intimidation, or other such circumstances.

According to Denman, the return to the District Court was ordered because that court had erred in not accepting the Department of Justice's "designations." It was his opinion that the evidence contained therein was sufficient in some cases to overcome Collins' assertion that each plaintiff had renounced under coercion or duress. Denman ordered that the Department should have an opportunity to present this evidence. However, it was further ruled that the former residents of Tule Lake were to have as part of their proof of coercion "the oppressiveness of [conditions during their] imprisonment by . . . government officials." This created a "rebuttable presumption" that their acts of renunciation were involuntary, i.e., the Department was required to produce evidence that would rebut the effects of experiences in the segregation center on individual renunciants in order to prevent restoration of citizenship.[54]

Collins blamed the appellate court decision directly on Wirin and the *Murakami* case. The San Francisco attorney informed his unsuccessful clients that "it is unfortunate that the *Murakami* case arose. Except for the decisions therein branding so many Nisei and Kibei [particularly members of the Resegregationist organizations or persons educated in Japan] with the charge of disloyalty it is likely that the Court of Appeals in the mass suits would have affirmed Judge Goodman's decision in its entirety without permitting a reopening of the cases for any individual hearings."[55] Thus, the mass suits, which had apparently been well on their way to a successful conclusion, were stymied and in effect broken up into thousands of individual cases. The *Murakami* case had influenced a sympathetic Court of Appeals into accepting the Attorney General's efforts to challenge the renunciants on an individual basis, thereby prolonging the suffering of thousands who would ultimately regain their rights.

The success of the *Murakami* case, however, was not the sole reason for the reversal suffered by the mass suits in the Court of Appeals. The renunciation cases, involving the possibility of disloyalty to the United States, reached the Court at an inopportune time for a favorable hearing. During the late 1940s and early 1950s, the Cold War crisis and concern over the Communist movement, inflamed by the *Hiss*, *Gouzenko*, *Rosenberg*, and *Gubitchev* cases, and by Senator Joseph McCarthy's unsubstantiated charges of Communists within the American government, made Americans hypersensitive to questions involving national security. The Department of Justice had stressed the issue of loyalty in opposing restoration of citizenship, even though former Attorney General Biddle and Burling had refused to consider disloyalty as a valid criterion for accepting or rejecting applications at the time of the renunciation hearings. The reversal of the Department's stand on the issue reflected the growing concern of the nation's citizens. Judge Denman revealed the Court's concern over the issue in his written opinion which noted the "certainty" that many of the 4,315 plaintiffs were disloyal to the United States. Because of the Cold War with the Communist countries and the current hot war in Korea, Denman believed that the federal courts should be vigilant that the massing of so many plaintiffs in two suits did not conceal any "enemy minded renunciants.[56] The remaining adult plaintiffs thus became innocent victims of America's postwar "loyalty" hysteria and saw their uncertain citizenship status prolonged indefinitely by the Court.[57] The Department of Justice was not satisfied with the restoration of citizenship granted to the minor renunciants and challenged Denman's opinion by appealing unsuccessfully to the Supreme Court.

Collins likewise sought to reverse the ruling but was denied a rehearing by the appellate court on February 27, 1951, and by the United States Supreme Court, which on October 8 of that year refused to review the case. It is ironic that Tom Clark, who had assisted General DeWitt in the evacuation of the West Coast Japanese from their homes, had selected the location upon which Tule Lake was constructed, and who had been the Attorney General that had opposed the mass suits when they were initiated in November, 1945, was a member of the court which now declined to hear the cases. Clark, however, excused himself and did not take part in the decision. Collins, in defeat, had little satisfaction in Denman's slight recognition of governmental duress in the Court of Appeals opinion. The renunciants' attorney was now left with the seemingly endless task of helping his clients through continuous hearings to clear up their status under the requirement that each must prove that he had been coerced by persons or groups in the camp.

The mass equity suits for restoration of citizenship returned to the District Court in San Francisco on May 29, 1952, after their unsuccessful struggle in the higher courts. Almost immediately, the Department of Justice, which had also failed in an appeal to the Supreme Court of Judge Denman's ruling, sought to defeat the renunciants' efforts by filing a motion to dismiss the cases. Judge Goodman refused, however, and instead granted Collins' motion to join one hundred and sixty additional renunciants as parties in the suit.[58] These were the first of more than four hundred renunciants who decided to join the mass suits following their return to the lower court.

Faced with a protracted series of hearings in the District Court, lawyers for the Attorney General met with Collins throughout 1952 and 1953 in an effort to avoid such a situation. On October 16, 1953, Collins wrote to the Tule Lake Defense Committee that he had come to an agreement, after a conference in Washington with Assistant Attorney General Warren E. Burger and Department of Justice attorney Enoch E. Ellison, for an administrative clearance procedure which would avoid court trials for many of the renunciants.[59] According to the system established by the two sides, Collins was to send several copies of affidavits to each renunciant, who would fill them out and return them to him for examination. A copy was then forwarded to the Department of Justice to be checked against its own files and those of the WRA and the FBI. If the Department's attorneys were satisfied from the contents of the affidavit that a renunciant had renounced as a result of coercion or duress and there was nothing adverse in his records, the Department would withdraw its offers of proof, which had been presented in its "designations," and agree not to oppose restoration of citizenship to that individual. A judgment would then be entered in favor of the renunciant in the District Court cancelling the application for renunciation and the Attorney General's approval of the application and declaring him to have been, *ab initio*, a citizen of the United States.[60] In the event the Department's lawyers denied a plaintiff administrative clearance, his affidavit, according to the agreement, was to be returned to Collins, who would then proceed to trial in the District Court.

This administrative procedure was not all that Collins had hoped for. The Department of Justice did not give credit for the cancellation of renunciation to Collins, to whom the credit belonged, but to Wirin and the *Murakami* case. This was revealed in the form letters sent by the Department informing the United States Attorney in San Francisco of its acceptance of individual affidavits: "We have examined the affidavit, together with pertinent Government files and are of the opinion that the case of the subject affiant may be considered as coming within the ruling of the Court of Appeals in the *Murakami* case."[61]

The administrative clearance procedures at first moved slowly. The Department of Justice rejected more affidavits than it approved. An examination of the bases for refusal to permit restoration of citizenship reveals that the Department followed a narrow and rigid rule for acceptance of affidavits. In a typical example, the Department based its rejection on the following factors: residence in Japan from 1927 to 1931; negative answers to the loyalty questions on the Army-WRA registration questionnaire; and speaking in favor of a Japanese victory during the renunciation hearings.[62] Such reasoning showed the same determination to prevent restoration of citizenship as was demonstrated by the Department in 1949 when it sought to defeat Judge Goodman's ruling by naming every renunciant in the mass suits even though they had been judged, in the main, to be loyal American citizens. The Justice Department continued to ignore Judge Goodman's ruling that each of these items was the result of duress or coercion and used them as grounds for opposing restoration.

In Collins, however, the government had an equally determined adversary. He prepared his clients extensively. In order to insure that the affidavit forms would be filled out correctly, his clients were exhaustively briefed on the background of the evacuation, the segregation center, and the renunciation hearings through various types of printed materials. In addition, each person was asked to complete a twenty-nine-page questionnaire of 109 multi-part questions against which the affidavits could be checked before sending them on to the Department of Justice.[63] When the Department began rejecting the majority of affidavits, Collins answered by sending them back to Washington for reconsideration. Some were returned four and five times before the Department agreed to approve them.[64] A review of the rejected affidavits was reluctantly agreed upon after the initial administrative policy had been established. As a result, the affidavit system of restoring citizenship proved to be increasingly successful. From 1955 through 1959, numerous approvals were made by the Department.[65] By April, 1957, some 2,600 persons had been cleared through the mass suits, while another eight hundred affidavits were still pending in the Department of Justice, including three hundred which had been formerly denied administrative clearance. At the current rate of approvals, Collins expected some three hundred additional affidavits to be cleared within the following thirty to sixty days.[66] An optimistic Tule Lake Defense Committee announced, on December 21, 1955, that it was suspending operations and closing its office "in view of the progress made in the administrative program."[67]

The trend toward restoration of citizenship was speeded in August, 1956, when the Department of Justice announced a new "liberalized" policy in regard to the renunciation cases. The Department admitted that many of those whom it had opposed in the courts had renounced because of the "coercive influences" of fanatic pro-Japanese in Tule Lake. It was announced to the press that the government's opposition to 157 suits then pending in California courts was withdrawn and action in at least one thousand other cases would be permitted to be decided in favor of the repentant Nisei. The new criteria upon which the Department based restoration of citizenship required that a renunciant had to demonstrate loyalty to the United States by showing that: (1) he took a first step toward restitution while at Tule Lake; (2) he then served or offered to serve in the American armed forces; (3) he be able to satisfy the Department that he renounced through fear or apprehension; or (4) in the case of wives, they were coerced and acted in unison with their husbands.[68] Assistant Attorney General George C. Doub personally informed Collins that 80 percent of the renunciants "should succeed in recovering U. S. citizenship" under the new policy.[69]

Two years later, the Department announced that its liberalized program for the restoration of citizenship had come to a successful conclusion. Of the 5,589 persons whose applications for renunciation were accepted, 5,409 had asked to have their citizenship returned, and in 4,978 cases, their requests were granted. This figure includes 1,327 of those who had expatriated to Japan during 1945 and 1946, while 347 of these had been denied restitution. According to Doub, "The only applications which we have denied are those where reliable evidence of disloyalty to the United States was found."[70] On May 20, 1959, ceremonies were held in Attorney General William P. Rogers' office which marked the completion of the program. The guest of honor was Eugene V. Rostow, Dean of the Yale Law School and author of the article, "Our Worst Wartime Mistake," which was highly critical of the government's World War II Japanese American policy.

Collins was not so easily pleased, however, as he rejected the Department of Justice's criteria for restoration and fought on for the unfortunate few who had been excluded from the government's belated amnesty. Although the majority of cases had been won, the mass suits continued for another nine years. Ironically, when the case of the last plaintiff was brought forward on March 6, 1968, the renunciant changed his mind and withdrew from the suit.[71] After this date, although Collins handled the cases of several renunciants who had not been included in the mass suits, the litigation instituted more than twenty-two years earlier was finally and officially ended. Of the residue who had remained outside the suits, a small number had been handled by other attorneys, some had died, and a few decided to stay in Japan.[72] Thanks to Collins, the renunciants had successfully endured the years of hardship and rejection by their own people and government to become productive members of the West Coast's favored and prosperous "model minority."

The conclusion of the mass suits ended the final chapter in the long history of social, legislative, and legal discrimination against the Japanese population of the Western states. Denial of their Bill of Rights guarantees was a major crisis in American constitutional history. Whether similar denials could be attempted is always a possibility under our constitutional system. Despite the growth in awareness of civil rights guarantees since mid-century and the present belief that neither Japanese Americans, nor any other group, are in danger of a recurrence of the events of the war years, it is presumptuous to assert that the national conscience has been cleansed of such impurities as victimized West Coast Japanese during the 1940s. Their removal and incarceration, the acceptance of the Renunciation Act by the federal courts, and the passage of legislation of questionable constitutionality in the postwar years all continue to pose threats to Bill of Rights guarantees.

The constitutionality of forcibly evacuating American citizens was accepted by the United States Supreme Court in 1944 in Korematsu v. the United States. The danger of this for the future was recognized in a dissenting opinion by Justice Robert M. Jackson: "The principle [of transporting American citizens] lies like a loaded weapon ready for the hand of any authority that can bring forward a plausible claim of urgent need." Within six years of Justice Jackson's warning, Congress provided, over President Truman's veto, such a "loaded weapon" with the Emergency Detention Act of 1950. This law empowered the President, in a self-declared "internal security emergency" such as invasion, insurrection, or war, to apprehend and hold in detention camps persons whom the government suspected might engage in espionage or sabotage. Because of protests of minority groups and other concerned persons, the law was repealed in 1971. The act's constitutionality has never been tested, however, and future Congresses are free to react to other real or imagined emergencies with similar legislation to "protect" the country at the expense of its citizens. Perhaps as great a threat to the future security of Americans is the fact that the constitutionality of the Renunciation Act of 1944 has never been ruled upon by the Supreme Court. Collins saw the danger of this and argued the unconstitutionality of depriving native-born Americans of their citizenship. The government cannot, the renunciants' counsel claimed, "deprive the Constitution of the citizens which constitute its support." Therefore, he concluded, Congress cannot authorize the renunciation of citizenship or the exclusion of the citizens of the nation because this would "destroy not only the grant of the Fourteenth Amendment but impair the foundation of the Constitution itself."[73] Collins' argument, however, was disregarded by the district and circuit courts which handled the renunciation cases. This failure to determine the constitutionality of the government's efforts to deprive Americans of their citizenship and deport such persons forcefully from the land of their birth leaves the nationality status of future groups of unwanted minorities or individuals in danger of similar unjust treatment at the hands of the government.

APPENDIX ONE

The Case against the Renunciants: The Position of the Department of Justice on the Renunciation Law, the Renunciation Process, the Renunciants, and the Restoration of Citizenship

Edward J. Ennis, Director
DEPARTMENT OF JUSTICE
Alien Enemy Control Unit
Washington 25
August 22, 1945

AIR MAIL

Ernest Besig, Esq.
Director, American Civil Liberties Union
Northern California Branch
216 Pine Street
San Francisco 4, California

Dear Mr. Besig:

I have for reply your two letters of August 7, 1945 and your letter of August 11, 1945 relating to the detention as alien enemies of persons of Japanese ancestry who were formerly United States citizens but who renounced their citizenship. . . . I shall also refer to your letter to the Attorney General of July 24, 1945. It is evident from all of these communications that you are not familiar with the considerations of policy which led this department to recommend the enactment of the amendment to the Nationality Act permitting voluntary renunciation of citizenship nor with the subsequent problems and considerations associated with the administration of the new status. Because of your interest in this important public question I shall furnish you with a statement concerning the Act and concerning the legal questions which you now raise.

In the fall of 1943, following the disorders at Tule Lake on the first and fourth of November, a great deal of thought was given to the entire problem presented at Tule Lake by persons of Japanese ancestry, both citizens and aliens, who freely asserted their loyalty to Japan. It was found that there was at Tule Lake an inner group numbering well over a thousand young American citizens who were militantly loyal to Japan and who asserted the hope to return to Japan to fight for the Emperor and the desire to make all possible trouble for the United States. As a practical matter, it clearly would not hve [sic] been possible to expel this group from the camp and to permit its members to be at large on the West Coast. As a legal matter, however, since they were born in the United States, there was no doubt that they were United States citizens, whatever their loyalty might be. It was Attorney General Biddle's opinion that the constitutionality of detaining American citizens not charged with crime on the ground that they had been administratively determined to be disloyal was, to say the least, extremely doubtful. He thought it not unlikely that, if a writ of habeas corpus were brought and pressed, such detention would be held unconstitutional. If there was ever a case where the practical necessity of the situation was such, however, that the court might be driven to diminish the historic liberties of American citizens by permitting such detention a habeas corpus case brought on behalf of avowedly disloyal persons of Japanese ancestry during the war most certainly would have been that case.

The answer to the apparent dilemma appeared to lie in the fact that the very degree of disloyalty which prevailed among the fanatical group at Tule Lake would in all probability induce the members of the group to renounce their citizenship if given an opportunity to do so. This it was believed would permit the detention of that group which clearly had to be detained in the real and demonstrable interests of national safety while at the same time avoiding the detention of American citizens. I believe that it was Mr. Biddle's view that such a program would serve the purposes both of national defense and of safeguarding civil liberties.

Accordingly the Attorney General recommended an amendment to the Nationality Law to permit a citizen voluntarily to renounce his citizenship. Because it appeared that during the war some renunciation of citizenship, not necessarily associated with the problems of Japanese-Americans, might be injurious to national defense, it was recommended that the right to renounce citizenship be limited by the power of the Attorney General to reject the renunciation if he found it contrary to the interests of national defense. The legislation was enacted by Congress in the form recommended by the Attorney General, and now every American citizen in time of war has an absolute right to renounce his citizenship limited only by the power of the Attorney General to disapprove it if the Attorney General finds the renunciation contrary to the interests of national defense. Neither the Attorney General nor any one else has any authority or discretion to reject renunciation of citizenship on any other ground.

It is also to be observed that at the time of the Attorney General's recommendation of this legislation to Congress there had been introduced in Congress at least a dozen bills providing for some form of involuntary loss of citizenship such as on the basis of a negative answer to question 28 of the so-called Loyalty Questionnaire of February 1943 or on the basis of any written or spoken statement of disloyalty to the United States. The danger which such legislation presents to civil liberties is apparent and it is believed that the enactment of the voluntary renunciation of citizenship bill was effective in preventing the passage of involuntary expatriation bills.

Precisely because it was foreseen that pressure might be brought to bear on citizens at Tule Lake to renounce and because it was feared that duress in the legal sense might be employed, every practicable measure was taken to make sure that each renunciant was not under immediate duress and understood the legal consequences of his act. Under the statute it would have been possible and easy to have appointed a group of clerks at Tule Lake and to permit those desiring renunciation merely to file past and sign a renunciation form. Instead, the Attorney General promulgated regulations requiring each person desiring renunciation individually to write to the Department asking for an application form. The application form itself then had to be sent to Washington and subsequently an individual hearing was held.

Inasmuch as the only issues which the Hearing Officers could legally consider were (1) whether the applicant understood the nature and consequences of his act and was voluntarily renouncing his citizenship, and (2) whether the renunciation would be detrimental to the interests of national defense, the hearings went far beyond what was legally necessary. They were under the general supervision of my assistant John L. Burling who has been working on problems concerning the Japanese-American group since several months before the evacuation and who is keenly sensitive to the civil liberties aspects of the problem. He conducted the first hearings himself and set up the pattern. All of the Hearing Officers were sent out from the Department in washington [*sic*] and were either attorneys or other professionals of high standing. They were all given instruction as to the background of the evacuation and as to the group at Tule Lake. The form of the hearings themselves went as far as possible toward minimizing the possibility of duress. Each applicant was heard alone in a closed room with no other person of Japanese ancestry present. This necessitated the use of Caucasian interpreters which was difficult from the standpoint of personnel. A full stenographic transcript was made of each hearing and each hearing continued until the Hearing Officer was satisfied that applicant understood that the signing of the paper would constitute and [*sic*] abandonment of all rights as an American citizen and until he was satisfied that the applicant desired to sign the renunciation form. In endeavoring to make sure that the renunciation was voluntary the Hearing Officers frequently asked questions such as concerning the applicant's experiences and loyalties before the outbreak of the war, his reasons for not considering himself an American and his attitudes toward Japan and the Japanese Emperor. In almost every case the applicant responded with a determined effort to paint himself as being fanatically loyal to Japan and as believing that the Emperor Hirohito is the living god, for whom he would willingly die. Since the applicant was alone, except for the Government officials, during the course of these hearings, it would have been possible for him, in the event that he feared injury if he did not renounce his citizenship, to have told the Hearing Officer and for him to have left the hearing without signing the renunciation form and without his failure to renounce being known to any person of Japanese ancestry except himself. On several occasions this was done.

It is true that the number of renunciations was several times larger than the number anticipated. I do not, however, attribute this to the existence of a great number of persons who did not desire to renounce their citizenship but who were forced to do so because of fear of reprisal. I do attribute it to a great wave of pro-Japanese feeling which reached its high point in the late autumn of 1944 and the early months of 1945. At the time the hearings were started there were two organizations at Tule Lake having very large memberships which were openly carrying on pro-Japanese activities. One of these, the Hokoku Seinen Dan, was made up of young men. Nearly two thousand of these men were getting up in the morning, putting on a kind of uniform which included a rising sun embroidered on a sweatshirt and were marching in military formation and taking part in Japanese patriotic observances. These rites were accompanied by a well-trained bugle corps. Members of this organization shaved their heads so that they might more closely resemble Japanese soldiers. The purpose of this organization was to train those men so that they would be ready to fight in the Japanese Army if they should be returned to Japan. Their elders were less noisy but equally fervent. Their organization openly published a Japanese language paper containing Japanese propaganda. A Greater East Asia School was flourishing.

What stimulated this wave of pro-Japanese feeling is a matter for conjecture and need not be gone into here. Its existence, however, is beyond dispute. It appears furthermore that at least to some extent the number of renunciations was also increased by the opinion, which may or may not have been correct,

among citizen-residents of the Tule Lake Center that renunciation was necessary to avoid compulsory relocation before the end of the year 1945. In any
event, whether the residents of Tule Lake Center renounced because they felt
loyal to Japan and thought that the renunciation of American citizenship would
serve as an indication of allegiance to the Emperor upon their return, or whether
they renounced because they believed that this would make sure that they would
be kept in detention during the war, or whether they renounced because they
wanted to be in the same legal status as their parents or brothers, the fact is
pretty clearly established that they understood what renunciation meant and
that they wanted to go through the process. Whether they were wise or intelligent in making the decision, is, of course, another matter entirely. I am satisfied, however, that in substantially every case the renunciation was accomplished as an exercise of the renunciant's free will.

The situation in which the various persons who have written to your organ-
isation asking your assistance in helping them restore their citizenship is that
of persons who voluntarily made a change in their legal status and who now
regret their action. As I have written several of these people, I have sympathy
for them; but I am at a loss to understand how the Department's policy can be
criticized. It is difficult to see in general why any citizen should not have the
right to renounce his citizenship if he wishes to do so and it is also difficult to
see what the Government should do in such cases beyond making sure that the
act is understood and is not coerced. I do not perceive how any Government
official could be asked to go further and to undertake to decide for the particular applicant that, notwithstanding his professed desire to renounce his citizenship, renunciation would not be in accord with his best interests.

It must be admitted that it is unfortunate that as a result of their own folly
some 5,000 American citizens have thrown their citizenship away. On the other
hand, it must be admitted that important public benefits have also been achieved
as a result of the renunciation program. Following the decision of the Supreme
Court in *Ex parte Endo*, the constitutionality of the detention of American citizens on the ground of disloyalty became even more dubious and at the same
time it would have been, as a practical matter, impossible to release the 2,000
young men in the Hokoku Seinen Dan who asserted their desire to die fighting
for the Emperor of Japan and who were already organized in semi-military
formations. Due to the renunciation program, however, the problem was never
posed, and in fact, shortly before he left office Attorney General Biddle informed the War Department that he did not believe that the detention of American citizens on the ground of disloyalty was then constitutional and the War
Department and the Western Defense Command accepted his opinion and removed all citizens from the detention lists. Military officials have made it clear
that the renunciation program was an important factor in leading them to accept this view. Had the Japanese war gone on longer the importance of this

victory for civil liberties would, of course, have been greater, but even as it is every American citizen of Japanese ancestry (except those involved in criminal proceedings) was free of detention for sometime prior to the cessation of hostilities.

Coming to the specific criticism raised by your letters, I have already dealt to some extent with the question of pressure and renunciation. I have no doubt that there were many cases in which pressure was put on citizen children by alien parents. In every case, however, the child was given full opportunity to make a statement in the absence of his parents and, if he decided to do as his parents wished, it was his own choice and there was no means by which the law could step in and forbid him to do so. The hearings were in no sense perfunctory and were far more careful than was necessary as a technical legal matter to determine whether the subject was acting in immediate fear of bodily injury and since the renunciant in every case was alone at the time of the hearing and could not have been in immediate danger of any sort of physical injury from another person of Japanese ancestry.

As I have indicated, the Attorney General is without authority to disapprove renunciations unless he finds that such disapproval would be contrary to the interests of national defense. There is no case arising at Tule Lake in which the interests of national defense would be injured by approval of the renunciation. It follows, therefore, that the Attorney General is, as a matter of law, required to approve the renunciations (I am not discussing the somewhat difficult question of whether a renunciant may withdraw his renunciation prior to the Attorney General's approval) unless he should find it to have been involuntary.

It is the present intention of this Department to keep in detention all renunciants. . . . The authority under which this detention is ordered is to be found in Section 21 of Title 50 of the United States Code and the Presidential Proclamation of December 7, 1941, delegating to the Attorney General the power to detain aliens of enemy nationality. . . .

Since the Tule Lake Center is maintained by another department of the Government, the Attorney General has not sent an order to the Department of the Interior but has accomplished the same purpose by authorizing a letter to be written to the Department of the Interior requesting that the Department detain renunciants whose names appear on lists supplied to it. The name of every renunciant at Tule Lake appears on such lists.

Individual renunciants have not been informed that they are to be detained because the War Relocation Authority, I believe correctly, feared that if it became generally known in War Relocation Authority Centers that every renunciant would be detained that might lead to a fresh wave of renunciation in other Centers by persons who were loyal to the United States but who, because of economic fears, were unwilling to leave the Centers and who might renounce their citizenship as a means of insuring their continued detention in a camp. For this reason only such renunciants at Tule Lake as have indicated a desire to leave have been told that they are in detention. For the reason just given I feel that you would be performing a grave disservice and would be inviting thousands of additional renunciants if you were to inform your clients that the order is a general one.

Coming to the question of whether some of these renunciants are stateless, as you suggest, or are nationals of Japan, you are correct in believing that this Department is of the opinion that every renunciant may be presumed to be a Japanese national. The basis of this presumption is that under Japanese law a child born in the United States of Japanese citizen parents may himself acquire Japanese citizenship. Prior to a date in 1924 citizenship automatically attached to the child unless the parents went to the Japanese consulate and filled out a form rejecting it on behalf of the child. After that date Japanese citizenship attached to the child if the parents registered his birth with the Japanese Consulate. The question of which American-born have Japanese Citizenship, therefore, is a question of fact depending upon formalities before the Japanese Consuls. The records of the Consulates, however, have been destroyed and no evidence as to this question of fact would appear to be available except perhaps in some cases the testimony of the parents. The authorities are clear, however, that if an alien is detained as an alien enemy under Section 21, Title 50, U.S.C. the burden of persuasion is upon him to prove that he is not relying upon the legal circumstance that the renunciant is unable to sustain the burden of persuasion but relies upon the additional evidence of the subject's adherence to Japan in time of war. In almost every case the subjects told Hearing Officers that they were dual nationals or that they considered themselves as being Japanese. For example, . . . (name withheld by author), who you state advised you that he has never held dual citizenship made these responses in the course of the hearing:

Q. Why don't you hold your citizenship?

A. Well, I can't have both at one time.

Q. Why not?

A. No, I think I have to make up my mind one way or the other.

Q. Don't you think it would be better if you held on to your citizenship and then went to Japan and if you didn't like it, come back?

A. I don't think they will stand for that either, because I am pretty sure they want me to be definite and I don't think this country would want a person like me if I weren't definite.

Q. Why don't you retain your citizenship?

A. If I go back, it is the only way I have to be definite you know. I appreciate all the help you people are giving me.

Q. Do you understand if you give up your citizenship and go to Japan, you can never come back here again and if you hold on to your citizenship, you can go to Japan and if you don't like it you can come back here?

A. I don't think that's right though.

In addition, in an overwhelming majority of the cases the renunciants assured the Hearing Officers that they keenly felt allegiance to Japan and rejected any allegiance to the United States. In the light of these circumstances it appears to me that it is reasonable to presume that a person born in the United States of Japanese parents who during a war between the United States and Japan voluntarily renounces his United States citizenship and declares his allegiance to Japan, is, in fact, a national of Japan.

It may be, of course, that there are some cases in which the renunciant can obtain evidence sufficient to carry the burden of persuading the court that, notwithstanding his rejection of United States citizenship and his assertions of loyalty to Japan, he is nevertheless not a Japanese national but is merely stateless. If you find such particular cases, it would be appropriate either to bring the facts to the attention of this Department or to institute habeas corpus proceedings since it will be conceded that persons born in the United States who become stateless are not subject to internment under the existing statute. In view of the persausiveness [*sic*] of the reasoning that the children of enemy aliens who renounce their citizenship in time of war are in fact nationals by the renunciant and his parents that Japanese nationality was rejected or that the birth was not registered at the Japanese Consulate will be sufficient.

You next ask how it is possible for persons born in the United States to be interned. As I have already indicated, the internment is under the authority of the alien enemy act which authorizes the internment of any citizen of any enemy state. The significance of birth within the United States is tht [*sic*] such birth confers citizenship. Once the citizenship is renounced the protection acquired by birth here disappears and the enemy national may be interned like any other alien enemy. In passing, I may say there is nothing peculiar to persons about Japanese origin about this. There are probably several million citizens of German or Italian origin who could be interned if they renounced their citizenship since both Germany and Italy recognize *jus Sanguinis*.

You indicate that your branch of the American Civil Liberties Union contemplates litigation to compel the restoration of citizenship in some cases and to test the validity of detention in others. I certainly do not wish to prevent you from seeking to safeguard what you deem to be essential rights of American citizens or stateless aliens residing in this country. On the other hand, I feel that I should point out to you that it would be necessary for the Government in defending such suits to make the arguments which I have just advanced here. I feel that you should consider carefully whether the prospects of success in the litigation are such as to make it in the public interest at this time to litigate issues such as these and to force the production of evidence such as this in open court. In the event, however, that you do feel prepared to assume this heavy responsibility, I trust that you will find this statement of the Department's position to be of value. Because of his interest in the problem discussed, I am sending a copy of this letter to Mr. Roger Baldwin.

Sincerely,

(signed) Edward J. Ennis

Edward J. Ennis
Director

APPENDIX TWO

The Case for the Renunciants: Tule Lake Administrators Testify Regarding Factors Causing Renunciation

The following documents (edited to remove extraneous material) reveal that the Department of Justice's opposition to the renunciants was not shared by those officials who were directly in charge of the camp in which all but a handful of the renunciations took place. In particular, these documents tend to disagree most strongly with the narrow, legal definition of "coercion" held by the Attorney General's Office in its opposition to restoration of citizenship in the renunciation suits.

AFFIDAVIT OF HARRY L. BLACK

The affiant, Harry L. Black . . . deposes and makes the following statement:

I was employed . . . from September 13, 1943, to May 4, 1946, as Assistant Project Director of the Tule Lake Center. . . . This period of employment extended from the date of the first train movement of the segregation program to the close of the Center. . . .

I was not employed by the War Relocation Authority at the time preparations were being made for the segregation program, and particularly during the time when determinations were being made in Tule Lake as to what residents would be transferred to other centers for ultimate relocation as being "loyal" to the United States; or as to what residents of other centers would be transferred to Tule Lake Center as being "loyal" to Japan. I do know that these determinations were made almost exclusively on the basis of "registration" in which process all residents of all centers with the exception of minor children, were required to submit registration forms, the same as for Selective Service, and in which they were required to give answers to two questions which related to their loyalty to the United States. . . .

Under the pressure of public opinion, under the "yammering" of certain elements of the public press, and under the bedevilment of prominent officials, committees, and agencies of the government itself, the War Relocation Authority had to do a sorting job which affected some 110,000 residents of ten relocation centers within an inconscionably short space of time, and under a procedure so hurried, so inconsiderate of human exigencies, and so complicated by relationships with other government agencies, that no responsible official of the War Relocation Authority itself would maintain that a good job had been done. . . .

The only justifiable conclusion is that factors other than the sole question of "loyalty" either to the United States or Japan were the motivating considerations when the residents were confronted with the necessity of giving some answer to the loyalty questions on the registration questionnaire. The most significant was that in general evacuees did not wish to move, and particularly residents of Tule Lake did not wish to be moved to any other relocation center, especially outside the state of California. Some other considerations, generally applicable to all centers are set forth with clarity in Mr. Burling's affidavit. There was an understandable anxiety on the part of some Issei to return to the homeland; the anxiety of adult children, either Nisei or Kibei, to maintain their family unity and not be separated from their parents; the fear of the Selective Service draft both on the part of eligibles and their family members; the dominance of the parents over their children; the feeling of failure and frustration over the loss of property and assets representing a lifetime of labor and savings through evacuation from prewar homes; discrimination against the Japanese as compared to the treatment of other enemy nationalities; the hopelessness of facing the necessity of starting again from scratch to make a living in a perhaps hostile community outside the West Coast zone where most had previously made their homes; the frustration and depression induced by living abnormal, regimented lives in an abnormal, regimented government center; the crowded, dismal barracks; the unpalatable food of the messhalls; the lack of privacy in the community lavatories and laundry rooms; the "concentration camp" atmosphere of the daily routine; and the feeling that the "rights of man" as applied to other citizens and other aliens did not apply to them. . . .

It should be helpful to understand the effect upon residents of the Japanese centers of the endless requirement of answering questions and filling out questionnaires. From the first registration required by General DeWitt under the terms of the evacuation order, the residents of the reception centers, the assembly centers, and finally the relocation centers were constantly beset with the necessity of providing—not once, but time and again—information about themselves and their family members. The Army, the Department of Justice, the Wartime Civil Control Administration and the War Relocation Authority were only the most important of the agencies which had to compile a mass of records and statistics. In the course of supplying all of this information, it would seem that most of the individuals and family heads were almost "question-naired" to death. And in the course of this endless process of amassing records by questionnaires and interviews, it would be only natural for many a well-intentioned resident to arrive at the conclusion that much of the questioning was irrelevant and whatever answers were given were more or less immaterial. Ultimately, I am sure, many arrived at a point where their answers to questions were neither honest nor sincere. I hold this to be the case with the registration questionnaire. There is no doubt at all in the minds of many responsible former W. R. A. officials that in innumerable cases the failure to give the "Yes-Yes" answer to the loyalty questions was induced by other considerations other than a desire to answer truthfully, honestly and sincerely. The interviewee in instances without number obviously asked himself before answering: "What will happen to me if I say 'Yes'?" "What will happen if I say 'No'?" "What will happen to my family?" "Will I be sent to Arkansas?" "Will I be forced to go to some place I do not like?" "May I be allowed to remain here?" "Can I take my children with me?" And so on ad infinitum until the interviewee learns to get along by giving the "right," or the expedient answer rather than the honest, the true and the sincere answer. There is no doubt also that this philosophy and practice in respect to answering questions carried over in a measure to interrogations regarding the renunciation of citizenship and the later mitigation hearings.

To add further confusion, the policies, the procedures, the programs and the plans of the governmental agencies, including W. R. A., the Army, and the Department of Justice changed so frequently that the evacuees rarely knew what they could depend upon. . . .

With this degree of wavering and indecision on the part of government agencies which had the responsibility to deal with the handling of evacuation, relocation, segregation, renunciation, mitigation, internment, expatriation, repatriation, it is certainly not difficult to understand how many evacuees got befuddled in their own thinking. There were cases in which the Department of Justice had announced that all aliens of such and such list would be deported. These aliens induced their Nisei family members, sometimes adult and sometimes minors, sometimes by persuasion and sometimes by threats, intimidations, and even violence, to renounce their citizenship so that they could all go to Japan as a family, or at least all could be together whatever happened, only to find that ultimately the Department of Justice would determine that the alien parents would not be deported and that they should be relocated, while the now renunciant offspring would face deportation without their parents. . . .

During all of this time the entire colony seethed with unrest. It was mainly a struggle between the fanatical and strongly pro-Japanese element which had given their support to the "Negotiating Committee" and a combination of elements made up of more conservative groups who felt that more could be gained by working with the administration than by demonstrating an attitude of conflict and antagonism. The friction between the groups was enduring and bitter, and resulted in numerous beatings and still more numerous threats of violence. The conservatives were generally on the defensive. They were not organized for fighting, had little resort to measures of violence except for self-protection in case of attack. They looked to the administrative officials for protection, and didn't always get it. . . .

In such an atmosphere of terror, it is easy to see what would be the state of mind of many residents who wanted nothing more than to live in peace and security while they must perforce remain in the Center. Literally, hundreds of older people, men and women, fathers and mothers, joined the subversive societies because they were afraid not to. Likewise, they added their parental admonitions to the threats of fanatics to get their children to join the young men's and young women's groups because they were afraid to incur the displeasure of the group's leaders. Literally hundreds of young people participated in the morning drills against their will, yet not daring to reveal their reluctance. . . .

We in the administration were aware that these things were happening. We knew that many people, both young and old, were forced to join the subversive organizations against their will. We discussed these developments in staff meetings, and we realized the coercion which had been exercised to get many young men, otherwise and ordinarily known to be thoroughly Americanized, to join the "shaved-heads," and that by exactly the same means, many Americanized girls were coerced into membership in the "pigtails."

Weekly reports were made by the Project Director concerning these activities to Mr. Myer and his staff in Washington. . . . It was so utterly patent to us of the staff of the Center at Tule Lake and to the key people of the Washington staff that the practices and tactics of the trouble-making leaders was based on the idea of compelling other people to conform to their own ideas and programs that there was little or no occasion to refer to these compulsions as arising out of coercion. The fanatical leaders gained and kept their followers either by persuasion or coercion. Those who followed by persuasion were of the kind and type of the leaders themselves. They were susceptible to the same feelings and attitudes and were of the material which provided the successive layers of leadership that came to the top as the transfers to internment camps progressed. Those who followed by coercion or compulsion, those who accepted the subversive leadership mainly in order to avoid trouble for themselves and their families, constituted an entirely different segment of the organizations' membership. They joined the groups because they were afraid to resist, and they fell into the pattern of un-American behavior because they felt that their safety, for the time being at least, lay in being on the good side of those who could make it tough on them. There were plenty of examples of how tough things could be made. There were cases of families being so harassed that they were compelled to move out of the block in which they had made their residence, only to find themselves so completely ostracized in their new block that there was no peace of mind for them. There were instances of dismissals and enforced resignations from evacuee jobs. Many times a whole family was made to feel the pressure by being required to sit apart in the messhall and receive inferior servings of food while they winced under the crooked looks and muttered curses of those who had thus ostracized them. There were those who found their names prominently posted on the doors of the latrine with the threatening warning "You're next!" following an untoward event such as the Hitomi murder.

Since all concerned knew what was taking place, there was no need to make reference to such activities and practices as forms of "coercion"; and if Mr. Burling found little or no reference to terms implying coercion in the reports and records of W. R. A., this is very obviously the reason. . . .

I cannot help mentioning a considerable reservation I feel concerning the qualifications of Mr. Burling to speak as an authority on the Japanese, particularly at Tule Lake. He was there only for two brief periods, and he saw mainly a show that was put on for his special benefit. It would be difficult for the Department of Justice people, under Mr. Burling's leadership, to have provided a program better made to order for the purpose of the subversive elements of the Center. And be it said, they took fullest advantage of it. They knew the moves he would make after the first two or three interviews he had held. They knew the program of renunciation hearings as he carried it out. They established a "College of Renunciation Knowledge" and carefully coached those called for hearings on the questions which were to be asked and the answers to be given. Specific instructions were given on what to say and how to act. A definite impression was to be made and they knew how to make it. . . .

It is impossible to bring out the full picture within the framework of this statement, even if the writer had the ability to do so. The main point is, and I am very emphatic about this: Whatever the definition of "coercion" in legal parlance, there was as much compulsion, as much outside impetus, as much influence of terrorism at work on the subjects when they were closeted with the hearing officer and the stenographer in the hearing room as if a shadowy "shave-head" had been standing behind them with a club. These subjects had no assurance or belief that what they did or what they said would not come to the knowledge of those who dominated them. They were afraid not to do what they had been told to do, and they were afraid to report falsely what had actually taken place. They had to act out the part, however, they may have felt about it. And they understood far better than any of the hearing officers ap-

preciated what it was that they were doing, because the hearing officers were
merely concerned with the question of whether the subjects understood what
was happening to them as they went through the renunciation procedure. How
much more the subjects really understood!

By granting somewhat over 3,000 renunciants a mitigation to waive deportation and permit their resettlement in this country as aliens under the law, the
Department of Justice has demonstrated a conviction that their presence in this
country constitutes no danger to the national security of the United States. If
the victims of this tragedy, in these better and calmer times, are not able to
repair the damage which they have done to themselves under the stress which
I have described, then I have the conviction that there is something inequitable
in the law or in the application of the law.

Harry L. Black

AFFIDAVIT OF LOUIS M. NOYES

This affidavit was filed in support of renunciants in the same suit as the
above statement of Harry L. Black.

Louis M. Noyes being duly sworn, deposes and says, as follows:

I was employed by the U. S. Department of the Interior as Attorney on the
staff of the Solicitor of the War Relocation Authority from September 15, 1944
until May 20, 1946. . . . I was assigned to the Tule Lake Segregation Center
in Modoc County, California, where I arrived and assumed the duties of Project Attorney on October 6, 1944.

My general duties included rendering legal advice: to the Project Director,
the chief Government administrative official in charge of the Tule Lake Segregation Center; to the Administrative staff on official problems; and to the
evacuee residents of the Center on all legal problems excepting those in which
the Federal Government was an adverse party. I also submitted periodic reports, usually weekly, to the W. R. A. Solicitor in Washington, D. C. concerning the problems handled and the general situation of the evacuees. . . .

In connection with the . . . statements of Mr. Burling, I wish to explain
that I had been assigned by the Project Director to serve as his liaison officer,
to assist Mr. Burling with respect to securing the necessary facilities and personnel to arrange for the scheduling of interviews and hearings from the first
day that Mr. Burling arrived at the Tule Lake in early December, 1944, and
during all the time that he remained at Tule Lake Center. On occasion of both
his visits, Mr. Burling and I were in very close and intimate contact. Inasmuch
as Mr. Burling was primarily concerned with the holding of hearings he had

comparatively little time within which to familiarize himself with all of the details of the manifold problems which prevailed in the every-day life of an isolated community of over 18,000 people residing within a man-proof barbed wire enclosure, and he therefore of necessity could secure only brief highlights as to the facts concerning the life and problems of evacuees in the Center. . . .

We explained to Mr. Burling that many assaults had been committed upon the evacuee residents of the Camp, who were loyal to the United States but that because of the nature of the evacuee community within the barbed wire enclosure, the victims of such assaults could not be induced to identify either their assaulters or the persons whom they suspected of instigating the assaults. . . . To me, as well as to most all of the other members of the War Relocation Authority Staff at the Center, it was quite evident that a great sense of fear was exhibited among most of the evacuees in the center. At times we could perceive a state of terror on the part of the evacuees, usually occurring after some evacuees had been assaulted by other unidentified evacuees. . . .

Under the conditions of such an abnormal community existence, the residents became more and more confused in their thinking, and their sense of values became so distraught and degenerated that they lost all concept of the realities of life. The resentment of many against evacuation and detention became transformed into a zeal for repatriation or expatriation to Japan. It is my opinion that this zeal for return to Japan was a cumulation of an escape phobia. They regarded themselves as victims of racial discrimination whose only ultimate place of refuge was Japan where they would not be constantly reminded of the fact that "a Jap, is a Jap." This expression grew out of the statement "Once a Jap, always a Jap" which the residents attributed to General DeWitt and resented very bitterly.

As nearly as I was able to determine from personal interviews and investigations there were approximately 600 male adult evacuee center residents who had been either honorably discharged from the United States Army or transferred to the Reserves and released from military duty in February 1942. The certificates of honorable discharge gave as the reason for discharge "for the convenience of the Government." Many of these ex-servicemen stated to me that they resented their discharge very bitterly. They explained to me how they had pleaded in vain with their commanding officers for the opportunity to fight for the country of their birth and of which they were citizens and the only country to which they owed loyalty, the United States. They related with intense bitterness the humility of distrust implied by their certificate of honorable discharge with the inscription, I quote again, "For the convenience of the Government," and they told me how from a month to three months after returning to their homes they and their families were evacuated and herded into detention centers and how they were angered when they were then again ordered to register for Selective Service. One extremely bitter such ex-service-man stated to me that he told his commanding officer, ''I know why I'm dis-charged. It's because I'm a Jap. Well, why don't you discharge the Germans and Italians, too?. . .''

These resentful, discharged soldiers in voicing their resentments undoubt-edly helped crystallize the belief among a great many of the other camp resi-dents that they would never again be acceptable to our Government or our people.

This was the background for the growth and development of a militant, fa-natical Japanese nationalistic movement within the camp that caused the un-foreseen and unexpected stampede among the citizen residents to renounce their citizenship.

It was a matter of common knowledge to those who had the opportunity of observing at first hand the reactions and emotions of the evacuees in the Tule Lake Relocation Center that the resentful bitterness caused by the evacuation and the several years of detention, gradually changed into an emotion of pes-simistic resignation to the fact that they were persona non grata to the Amer-ican public and to the United States Government. Furthermore, most of the camp residents had lost their homes and their friends, and had been forced to liquidate, give away, or abandon, their farm equipment, merchandise and such other valuables and personal property they had. Through no fault of their own even before evacuation they had been discriminated against because of their race and had been generally ostracized from the Caucasian society. . . . Evacuation, therefore, in addition to subjecting them to the bitter and cruel outburst of racial discrimination also had the effect of severing the only strong roots which they were permitted to develop, namely; their economic roots. Having lost practically all economic security and having no social, political and economic hope for the future in this country, their thinking naturally turned to finding racial and social refuge and security in Japan the only other land known to them; the land of their ancestors and relatives.

The program of the government following evacuation had the effect of forc-ing the evacuees to choose between repatriation or expatriation to Japan or accepting the indignations and committing themselves to a future in this coun-try which did not seem to offer them any hope whatsoever.

The purpose of the segregation program was allegedly to segregate the so-called ''disloyal'' from the loyal. Theoretically, all of the ''disloyal'' were to have been segregated to the Tule Lake Center, that being the only segregation center established by the War Relocation Authority. As a practical matter, it was necessary to resort to arbitrary tests and standards having no legal or sci-entific basis in making a determination as to which of the evacuees were loyal and which were disloyal. . . .

One of the consequences of the segregation program was the transferring to

Tule Lake of most or nearly all of the disciplinary and administrative "problem children" from all of the other relocation centers thus greatly adding to the confusion and abnormality of the Tule Lake community. Among these were the alleged pro-Japanese agitators and leaders, some of whom imposed their authority and leadership upon a substantial portion of the bewildered and confused population.

The struggle for power and control among the would-be leaders was in general disregarded by the authorities as long as it did not interfere with the ordinary problems of administration. There developed a strong compulsion among the evacuees to cling to the imaginary security within the barbed wire enclosure, and a consuming fear of possibly being compelled to another and more abhorrent readjustment into a community on the outside which they deemed hostile and dangerous. This fact is significant because it compelled the people to do a great many things to reassure themselves that they would not be eligible for release which meant to them eviction from the security of the camp. That, in turn, made it appear to many who were not aware of these confusing and conflicting emotions, that these people were affirming and reaffirming their loyalty to Japan and, therefore, affirmatively demonstrating their disloyalty to the United States. . . .

As a result of the confusion and unrest which came about from a mass reshuffling of evacuees under the segregation program, a group quickly formed at the Tule Lake Segregation Center, calling themselves the true Japanese. This group took the position that Tule Lake was no place for loyal Americans or persons whom they termed "fence sitters." They circulated a petition which they called the petition for resegregation, and at the same time conducted an intense and bitter campaign for the expulsion from the segregation center of all persons whom they deemed either loyal Americans or "fence sitters." Many people signed the resegregation petition solely in self-defense. . . .

On December 6, 1944, Mr. John L. Burling, Special Assistant to the Attorney General arrived at the Tule Lake Center and commenced hearings for Center residents, whose identity Mr. Burling would determine on the basis of the hearings and information he secured from the W. R. A. Administration, would be removed to Department of Justice Internment Camps. . . .

It was undoubtedly the intent of both the Authority and the Justice Department that removing the known leaders and more obstreperous members of the Japanese nationalistic groups would release the Center population from coercion and intimidation, thereby enabling the remaining people to make their own free decisions concerning repatriation or relocation. This was probably in anticipation of General Pratt's lifting of the Mass Exclusion Order. Unfortunately, the timing of the Justice Department's renunciation hearings and removals proved extremely ill timed from the standpoint of helping to free the residents from domination and terrorism at the hands of pro-Japanese leaders.

Rumors of the impending lifting of the Mass Exclusion Order had apparently reached the Center residents and they were overcome by a sense of nervous tension, distrust, insecurity and a general state of fear. In December, 1944, immediately preceding the lifting of the Mass Exclusion Order, and during Mr. Burling's first series of hearings, the power of the Sokuji Kikoku Hoshi Dan and the Hokoku Seinen Dan was at its lowest state and it then seemed that these organizations would fade into utter insignificance. However, the Center residents were upset and confused by reason of the following three successive events:

1. The renunciation hearings from December 6 to 14, 1944.
2. The announcement of the lifting of the Mass Exclusion Order on December 18, 1944; and
3. The spectacular apprehension and removal to internment camps by the Department of Justice on December 27, 1944 of some seventy leaders of the Hoshi Dan and Seinen Dan.

As a consequence, the terrorists and propagandists gained a stronger foothold than ever for their pro-Japanese organizations. The hush-hush which preceded these three events lead to general community fear of imaginary horrors, and the remaining leaders of the Hoshi-Seinan Dan immediately took advantage of that condition by embarking upon an intensive membership drive. They knew the people's fears of relocation, and fanned those fears into an hysterical pitch by spreading false rumors faster and more effectively than the Administration could refute and counteract.

It was the consensus of opinion among the members of the Administrative Staff, as well as among the more sober, intelligent and responsible evacuee residents, that the holding of renunciation hearings at the Tule Lake Center during January, February and March of 1945 was a serious mistake. Without their first having been psychologically prepared for it, the Center residents were tragically confused and terrified by the sudden lifting of the Mass Exclusion Order, and as a consequence they were easily stampeded into believing the propagandists and terrorists that renunciation of membership [sic—should be "renunciation of citizenship"] was the only security they had against separation of citizen members from alien members and the immediate drafting into the American Armed Forces of citizen males over the age of eighteen years. This rumor seemed to the residents to have been substantiated by the fact that although the renunciation Act did not specify an age minimum, Mr. Burling, while at the Center, announced that only citizens who had passed their eighteenth birthday would be permitted to apply for renunciation of their citizenship. The Department of Justice also played into the hands of the propagandists and terrorists by concentrating on the members of the Sokuji Kikoku Hoshi

Dan, Hokoku Seinen Dan, and Hokoku Joshi Seinen Dan, thus lending credence to assertions of the leaders of those organizations that renunciation could only be secured by membership in such organizations. Once this mistaken notion took hold, all efforts on the part of the Administration to discredit it were in vain, and incalculable harm resulted. Other factors which added to the state of confusion and fear were:

1. The sensationalized newspaper stories concerning terrorism against evacuees who returned to the West Coast.
2. The lack of information concerning the individual exclusion orders which were being served by the Western Defense Command Process Servers, and particularly the meaning and significance of the question ''Have you applied for renunciation of citizenship?'' which was asked by the Process Servers of each excludee simultaneously with the service upon him of the Individual Exclusion Order. This question let [*sic*] the residents to imagine that the government had a scheme in mind to trick them in the same way as they thought they had been tricked in the loyalty questionnaire. . . .

As stated elsewhere in this affidavit, the demonstrations and the stampede to renounce citizenship were, in the opinion of this affiant and in the opinion of many other Government officials and their observers of a hysterical nature and not based upon a conscious and free choice of loyalties. Unfortunately this opinion was neither shared nor given consideration by those who determined the time, place and procedure for holding the renunciation hearings.

The opinion expressed in the preceding paragraph was, in a measure later confirmed by many renunciants and by citizens who survived the mass political suicide psychosis. One of the most intelligent young men in the camp who was among the twenty per centum of the citizens who survived said to me after the renunciation program ceased as he pointed to an equally intelligent, and I have no doubt, equally loyal young man, ''There go I but for the grace of God, and for my very close contact with you and other members of the staff because of being employed in the Administrative area.''

Toward the end of the renunciation hearing program, some of the renunciants began to come out of their psychotic state and called at my office for advice as to what steps they should take to cancel their renunciation. After the hearings closed and the hearing officers departed for Washington, D. C., my office was deluged with inquiries from renunciants who wanted to ''renounce their renunciation of citizenship.'' All inquiries were referred to the Alien Enemy Control Unit of the Department of Justice in Washington, D. C. It is my understanding that a very substantial number of the renunciants wrote to Washington, D. C., requesting cancellation of their renunciation, and a sizeable number even sent telegrams to the Director of the Alien Enemy Control

Unit stating their desire to cancel their renunciation after hearing unofficial reports that all renunciants would be deported to Japan.

Louis M. Noyes

LETTER BY RAY BEST

The following letter by Ray Best, Project Director of the Tule Lake Segregation Center, vividly describes how fears over forced resettlement in hostile and potentially dangerous communities outside of the relocation centers forced citizens to trade their citizenship for safety within the confines of Tule Lake.

United States Department of the Interior
Tule Lake Center, Newell, California

January 12, 1945

Confidential
Airmail

Mr. Dillon S. Myer
Director
War Relocation Authority
Barr Building
Washington 20, D. C.

Dear Mr. Myer:

There has been an acceleration of applications for renunciation of citizenship and from reports received from various sources, independent of each other, it is definitely clear to me that the evacuee citizens of this center are resorting to renunciation as a means of assuring detention, at least for the duration, very much in the same manner as they did in connection with segregation.

Considerable confusion has resulted from their uncertainty as to their status—that is, the possibility of their having to leave—and to this has been added further confusion by minor conflicts and inconsistencies in information which has been disseminated by WRA. These conflicts, though minor, under abnormal conditions are almost deliberately misconstrued by the evacuees in their frantic and desperate efforts to find refuge from the spectre of relocation. The net result, as I have stated before, [is that the rush toward renunciation] has been continued and accelerated by the irrepressible rumors that renunciation will assure them of detention and protect them against expulsion from this center.

Unfortunately the evacuees are not the only ones who are in need of additional clarifications. For example, we are still trying to determine as a matter of certainty what should be done, insofar as WRA is concerned, respecting the right of evacuee citizens who have applied for renunciation but who are "not designated by name for exclusion", etc., if they wish to leave after January 2, 1945.

Clarification is also needed respecting the right of excludees at this center to leave after January 20, 1945. Public Proclamation No. 21 . . . rescinds Public Proclamation No. 8, effective midnight, January 20, 1945, and also as of that time and date rescinds Civilian Restrictive Orders No. 18, 19, 20, 23, 24, and 30, "except as to those persons who have been designated individually for exclusion or other control," etc. Civilian Restrictive Order No. 26 which applies to Tule Lake War Relocation Project Area is not rescinded and therefore remains in full force and effect. What significance does this have since it is issued pursuant to Public Proclamation No. 8 and that Proclamation is rescinded?

It appears that excepting for the failure to rescind Civilian Restrictive Order No. 26, the Tule Lake Project is in the same category as are all other projects, and that the restrictions of Proclamation No. 8 apply only to those persons who have been or may be designated for exclusion or control. It would therefore seem to follow that all other citizens at this center, no matter what their loyalty record or our opinion may be, are free to leave after midnight, January 20, 1945.

From the scraps of information which we have so far obtained from the army and from an examination of the white, or cleared list, it seems likely that some of the most pro-Japanese in the center will not be individually designated by the army at all. . . . If, however, some persons not individually designated are not free to go after January 20, who is to detain them and under what authority? This discussion does not exhaust the perplexities but highlights the legal and practical difficulty which we foresee. In honesty, I will state that neither I nor my staff clearly understand the situation and as a result our efforts to explain it to the evacuees, together with statements issued from Washington, by the army, and appearing in the public press, have resulted in the greatest confusion in the colony. The central theme of evacuee thought at the present time is focused not on how to leave the center, but on how to remain in it. Most of the adult evacuees have given negative loyalty answers or have otherwise placed themselves in a position making war-time relocation extremely difficult. They have become emotionally conditioned to accepting the promise previously extended to them here that this camp would remain open to them as a haven during the War. They now see themselves faced with the choice of having the camp closed and being forced to relocate or in someways persuading some agency of the Government that they are dangerous and they must be detained. At the present time the evacuees hope to persuade the Department of Justice to intern them either here or in Santa Fe by renouncing their citizenship. If the Department of Justice should refuse to shelter them, notwithstanding renunciation, more drastic and possibly violent measures may be resorted to, to insure detention. Thus, in my opinion, the policy of forced relocation from this center at the present time will not succeed in relocating any significant number of persons but at best will force the evacuees to renounce their citizenship and, worse, might lead to an incident.

The seriousness of the situation in which many citizens are being led to renounce their citizenship solely for the protection against having to relocate warrants, in my opinion, a clear and unqualified announcement that no resident will be forced either directly or indirectly out of this center for the duration of the war, and either this center or a similar center will be available to the present residents of Tule Lake on a voluntary basis whether or not they renounced their citizenship. I have discussed this problem with members of my staff and they concur in my opinion that it would very likely prevent a situation such as that which followed segregation and registration.

Mr. Burling of the Department of Justice who, as you know, is here conducting renunciation of citizenship hearings, has approached me and has expressed grave concern over the enormous increase in the number of applications for renunciation over the figure anticipated. He independently expressed the view that this increase is, to an important extent, caused by the apparent application of the policy of forced relocation to this center. He has pointed out that under the act, it is almost impossible for him to stop the wave of renunciation of citizenship. I understand that he feels, therefore, that the Department of Justice has an interest in urging the abandonment of the policy of relocation at this particular center and that he has made a report to that effect to his superiors in Washington.

Because of the fact that once applications for renunciation are made, the process always goes through to its conclusion, and because of the speed with which center morale is deteriorating and with which undesirable attitudes are crystalizing, I recommend that the underlying policy again be considered at the earliest possible moment.

Sincerely,
R. R. BEST,
Project Director

APPENDIX THREE

The Renunciants Speak for Themselves

As early as March, 1945, even before the last renunciation hearings were held, a movement away from renunciation of citizenship had begun. It started slowly and developed into a flood that nearly equalled the earlier rush to renounce. Renunciants pleaded with the Department of Justice requesting cancellation of renunciation and sought the aid of the American Civil Liberties Union, individual attorneys, and anyone else who would listen.

LETTERS TO EDWARD J. ENNIS

Many of the letters received by the Department of Justice were heart-rending, pleading with the Department to understand the renunciants' plight, to forgive what had been done in confusion, misunderstanding, frustration, and/or fear. The writers received replies which expressed sympathy but refused their requests. The following two letters, written from Tule Lake in July, 1945 to Edward J. Ennis, Director of the Alien Enemy Control Unit of the Department of Justice, are representative.

Dear Mr. Ennis:

I wrote to you about my wife June 30 and your reply taking away all hope came yesterday.

You are a man who I am sure can put yourself in my place. May I tell you something of my awful situation and please, Mr. Ennis, please do something for my little family.

I am one of the block managers and have a place of responsibility in this center. I have been block manager since September, 1944. One of my duties is to stop all the rumors but have you ever tried to put out a forest fire or stop the tide from coming in? We were up against a real tide when the Department of Justice hearings were on. My wife picked up all the rumors and believed them. She thought if she renounced she would stay in here. Otherwise she would be pushed out. We are from Hood River and that was a dangerous place. My wife was afraid to go there if we were made to leave. She felt that some way she must fix things so the family could stay here together and her "fixing" was to renounce. Night after night I pleaded with her not to do such a thing. She tried to get me to renounce also but I would not. Nothing could change her mind. She was completely hysterical and unbalanced with fear and worry. Well, she renounced in spite of all I could do.

We found the rumors false and she began to change her mind but according to your letter, it was too late. Do you know what it means in a few minutes of hysteria to throw away your happiness, your family, your future, seemingly for ever? When I read your letter to her all hope left her and she collapsed. All night long she cried. When there had been hope of cancellation we had talked of going out and raising our children to be good citizens. Then your letter came. She told me to go on out and take the children who are anxious to leave . . . and she would stay behind alone and commit suicide. So now I must not go, knowing I had killed my wife and my children must remain in this abnormal atmosphere and so must I. Don't you see what a tragedy a few minutes has made for us?

And now, Mr. Ennis, isn't there some way that we can go out? Even if my wife's citizenship is gone, can't she go out as an alien? She did not renounce out of disloyalty. She would never do anything against this country. She only wanted us to be together. Isn't there some way by which our little family can relocate? Don't you see how awful our situation is? Do help us if you can.

Dear Mr. Ennis:

As you told me in the refusal of the application in my letter I know now I am an alien. For I renounced my citizenship.

As to why I, then renounced, foolishly, I wish you listen to my reason. It was very blind of me that time and I was, to the great extent, influenced and lead by the Hoshidan, the jingoistic and fanatic Patriotic Group, who propagated that those who want and hold U. S. Citizenship would not be able to be accepted by Japan when entering Japan. I have much to tell, but, to cut short, I was taken by what the said group urged and cajoled the colonists in the community.

Of course, as the authority of Tule Lake Center could show, I am perfectly out of the said patriotic group mentally and officially, and getting realized how much I was crazy to have lost my sense and common sense.

Shortly after the renounciation of citizenship was applied I was called to the office for the hearing at which I all answered that everything was by my own will. But I could honestly tell you that I did not know what I was doing then. I tried to express as I meant then, but, without interpreter, I did not know how and what I made by expression in my poor English. How I wanted then to have an interpreter for me. Of course I was childishly crazed and intoxicated by the so called prevailing mass opinion, which I soon found out that there were very few who was of that opinion comparing to those who did not believe so.

I want to relocate now. . . . Whether or not I could relocate I want to take back my U. S. Citizenship. I deeply regret what I mistakenly have done.

Would you be so kind to give me one more chance to be interviewed at rehearing in order that I fully express my thoughts and opinion of then and thereafter?

LETTER TO TOM CLARK

Many of the renunciants refused to plead with the Department of Justice and instead demanded the restoration of their citizenship rights and freedom within the United States. A large number of these demands were mass-produced by mimeograph and sent to the pertinent government officials. Some persons were unable to obtain such forms and sent their own handwritten and typed versions. Many copies of the following form letter were viewed by the author in the files of Wayne Collins, who drafted the letter for the renunciants.

_____

_____ ,

194_

HONORABLE TOM CLARK,
Attorney General of the United States,
Department of Justice Building
Washington, D. C.

Dear Sir:

On or about _____ , 194_, I signed an application for renunciation of U. S. Nationality at the Tule Lake Center, Newell, Modoc County, California.

I hereby repudiate, withdraw, retract and revoke the said renunciation upon the following grounds and for the following reasons:

(1) The circumstances under which said renunciation form was signed by

me did not constitute a fair and impartial hearing and was a denial of my constitutional guaranty of due process of law and of the equal protection of the laws;

(2) I was not a free agent at the time when and the place where said renunciation form was signed but then and there was held in duress and was the victim of fraud, menace, undue influence and mistake of fact and law;

(3) I then and there was and for a period of time prior thereto had been detained in said Tule Lake Center by official authority and was deprived of substantially all my constitutional rights, liberties, privileges and immunities as an American citizen and was treated as though I were an alien enemy and thus was discriminated against solely by reason of the Japanese nationality of my ancestors;

(4) I was intimidated, coerced and compelled to sign said renunciation form by reason of the duress in which I was held by the government and the duress against which the government failed to protect me.

Because of the foregoing reasons the said renunciation was fictitious and is invalid and void.

I am not a citizen or subject of Japan and I do not and never have owed or given that country or nation any allegiance. I am not an alien enemy. I am a native American by birth and choice. I have no dual citizenship through any act or acceptance upon my individual part.

I demand that you withdraw and set aside the said renunciation form, and the approval thereof if any approval thereof was given.

I am ready and willing to have this matter re-opened and a hearing be granted me in order to prove the said renunciation application was executed under the circumstances above-mentioned when I was not a free agent in any sense of the word but was acting under duress, menace, fraud, undue influence and mistake of fact and law.

I respectfully request your immediate consideration of this urgent matter.

Very truly yours,

_____

(Name)

Address: _____

EXTRACTS FROM LETTERS FROM RENUNCIANTS

There were many opinions expressed concerning the "why's" of renunciation. Officials of the Department of Justice, the War Relocation Authority, the Department of the Interior, and Caucasian observers in

Tule Lake listed the reasons as they viewed them. The renunciants reg-istered their own versions of what had happened in thousands of letters to attorneys and government agencies pleading for aid in helping undo the damages caused by their renunciation of citizenship. The following excerpts from those letters reveal fears of forced relocation in outside communities; efforts to avoid family separation; avoidance of the draft; fear of violence from the radical organizations; family pressure; and the effects of rumors on the isolated Tule Lake community as among the factors influencing decisions to renounce.

Renouncing my citizenship was a great mistake. In this camp, they all said they be forced out if they don't renounce it, so with our large family with nothing on hand, and no money to support ourselves, we have to go without foods, no house to live in, so I thought it was alright to renounce it for the duration.

I signed against my will. Whatever my husband do I have to be loyal to him.

We have been kicked around all time in this country. Since I was sore, I an-swered ''no'' to question 28. Then I was thrown in the stockade. I renounced my citizenship because I felt I might as well, because I had come this far as a disloyal citizen.

I was a member of the Hokoku Seinen Dan, and was told that unless I re-nounce my U. S. citizenship by the end of February, the U. S. Army would draft us . . . after WRA forces us to go outside.

Those Hokoku men somehow kept track of those who had renounced and who had not. They knew I had not. Every day some of those men in my block would ask whether I had renounced or when I would renounce. In a short time, block people refused to talk to me; and it seemed that everyone was shunning me. When I finally decided to renounce, the pressure was off me. I didn't get cold stares any more.

I never wished to renounce but to stop my parents pleading and sobbing I went and told them ''I am renouncing because my parents wished to take me to the old country.''

My Issei parents believed that all aliens here would be deported to Japan, while all the citizens would be forced to remain here. We were therefore confronted with the problem of preventing family separation.

Notes

Chapter 1. Introduction

1. U. S., Department of the Interior, War Relocation Authority, *WRA: A Story of Human Conservation* (Washington, D. C.: Government Printing Office, 1946), p. 44.

2. Roger Daniels, *The Politics of Prejudice: The Anti-Japanese Movement in California, and the Struggle for Japanese Exclusion* (Berkeley and Los Angeles: University of California Press, 1962), p. 107.

3. U. S., Congress, House, *Expatriation of Certain Nationals of the United States*, Hearings, on H. R. 2701, H. R. 3012, H. R. 3489, H. R. 3446, and H. R. 4103, 78th Cong., 1st sess., 1944, p. 63.

4. Harry H. L. Kitano, *Japanese Americans: The Evolution of a Subculture* (Englewood Cliffs, N. J.: Prentice-Hall, Inc., 1969), pp. 78, 101–3.

5. *Ibid.*, pp. 107–9.

6. Eric Woodrum, "An Assessment of Japanese American Assimilation, Pluralism, and Subordination," *American Journal of Sociology*, LXXXVII (July, 1981), 161.

7. Kitano, *Japanese Americans*, pp. 107–9; Tamotsu Shibutani, *The Derelicts of Company K* (Berkeley: University of California Press, 1978), p. 25; Yoshiko Uchida, *Desert Exile* (Seattle: University of Washington Press, 1982), p. 57; John W. Connor, *Tradition and Change in Three Generations of Japanese Americans* (Chicago: Nelson-Hall, 1977), pp. 10–11, 21–44; Darrel Montero, *Japanese Americans: Changing Patterns of Ethnic Affiliation over*

Three Generations (Boulder, Colo.: Westview Press, 1980), pp. 16–17, 21–22.

8. Kitano, *Japanese Americans*, pp. 67–68; S. Frank Miyamoto, "An Immigrant Community in America," in: Hilary Conroy and T. Scott Miyakawa, eds., *East across the Pacific* (Santa Barbara, Calif.: American Bibliographic Center, Clio Press, 1972), pp. 227 30.

9. War Relocation Authority, *WRA*, p. 8.

10. *Ibid.*; Roger Daniels and Harry H. L. Kitano, *American Racism: Exploration of the Nature of Prejudice* (Englewood Cliffs, N. J.: Prentice-Hall, Inc., 1970), pp. 46–47.

11. Dorothy Swaine Thomas, *The Salvage: Japanese American Evacuation and Resettlement* (Berkeley and Los Angeles: University of California Press, 1952), p. 44; Milton R. Konvitz, *The Alien and the Asiatic in American Law* (Ithaca: Cornell University Press, 1946), pp. 22–23 and Chapter III; William Petersen, *Japanese Americans: Oppression and Success* (New York: Random House, Inc., 1971), pp. 47–48; Roger Daniels, *Concentration Camps North America: Japanese in the United States and Canada During World War II* (Malabar, Fla.: Robert E. Krieger Publishing Company, Inc., 1981), pp. 19–20.

12. Forrest E. LaViolette, *Americans of Japanese Ancestry* (Toronto: Canadian Institute of International Affairs, 1946), pp. 36, 40.

13. Harry H. L. Kitano, "Japanese," *Harvard Encyclopedia of American Ethnic Groups* (Cambridge, Mass.: Belknap Press of Harvard University Press, 1980), p. 566.

14. The Kibei varied in their attitudes toward the United States and Japan. While some displayed strongly pro-Japanese and anti-American feelings, others settled down easily among their peers and supported the United States when war came. Hundreds of Kibei provided invaluable service as instructors in military language-training programs, as interpreters and translators in the Pacific theater, and as psychological warfare specialists. Staff Sergeant Kenny K. Yasui, a Kibei, served with Merrill's Marauders in Burma, where he was awarded the Silver Star. Another Kibei, Pfc. Sadao S. Munemori, earned the Congressional Medal of Honor for service in Italy. Bill Hosokawa and Robert Wilson, *East to America: A History of the Japanese in the United States* (New York: William Morrow and Company, Inc., 1969), pp. 412–13, 415–16.

15. U. S., Department of the Interior, War Relocation Authority, *Wartime Exile: The Exclusion of the Japanese Americans from the West Coast* (Washington, D. C.: Government Printing Office, 1946), pp. 92–96.

16. *Ibid.*, p. 30.

17. *Ibid.*, p. 23.

18. *Ibid.*, p. 30.

Chapter 2. Evacuation

1. U. S., Department of the Interior, War Relocation Authority, *Impounded People: Japanese Americans in the Relocation Centers* (Washington, D. C.: Government Printing Office, 1946), pp. 6–9.

2. Morton Grodzins, *Americans Betrayed: Politics and the Japanese Evacuation* (Chicago: University of Chicago Press, 1949), p. 63.

3. *Ibid.*, p. 377.

4. War Relocation Authority, *Wartime Exile*, p. 104.

5. War Relocation Authority, *Impounded People*, pp. 32–34; Roger Daniels, *The Decision to Relocate the Japanese Americans* (Philadelphia: J. B. Lippincott Company, 1975), pp. 10–11; Shibutani, *Derelicts of Company K*, pp. 43–44.

6. U. S., Congress, House, *National Defense Migration*, H. Report 1911 Pursuant to H. Res. 113, 77th Cong., 2d sess., 1942, p. 14.

7. U. S., Department of the Interior, War Relocation Authority, in collaboration with the War Department, *Nisei in Uniform* (Washington, D. C.: Government Printing Office, 1944), unpaged.

8. War Relocation Authority, *Wartime Exile*, pp. 106–8; Grodzins, *Americans Betrayed*, pp. 185–86; Milton S. Eisenhower, *The President Is Calling* (Garden City, N. Y.: Doubleday & Company, Inc., 1974), pp. 106, 110.

9. War Relocation Authority, *Impounded People*, p. 2.

10. War Relocation Authority, *WRA*, p. 10; Michi Weglyn, *Years of Infamy: The Untold Story of America's Concentration Camps* (New York: William Morrow and Company, Inc., 1976), p. 49.

11. Grodzins, *Americans Betrayed*, p. 377; Daniels, *Decision*, pp. 21–22.

12. U. S., House, *National Defense Migration*, H. Rept. 1911, pp. 3–5.

13. General DeWitt, as Commanding Officer of the Western Defense Command, was charged with "the defense of the Pacific Coast . . . against attacks by land, sea, and air; and the local protection of establishments and communications vital to the National Defense for which adequate defense cannot be provided by local civilian authorities." Jacobus tenBroek; Edward N. Barnhart; and Floyd W. Matson, *Prejudice, War and the Constitution* (Berkeley and Los Angeles: University of California Press, 1954), p. 100.

14. U. S., Army, Western Defense Command, *Final Report: Japanese Evacuation from the West Coast, 1942* (Washington, D. C.: Government Printing Office, 1943), p. 34; Daniels, *Decision*, pp. 24–25; Eisenhower, *President Is Calling*, pp. 110–11.

15. War Relocation Authority, *WRA*, pp. 13, 25–26; Grodzins, *Americans Betrayed*, pp. 206–7; Weglyn, *Years of Infamy*, p. 69; Eisenhower, *President Is Calling*, p. 127.

16. War Relocation Authority, *WRA,* p. 26; Western Defense Command, *Final Report,* p. 43; Uchida, *Desert Exile,* p. 58; Bill Hosokawa, *JACL in Quest of Justice* (New York: William Morrow and Company, 1982), pp. 169–72.

17. War Relocation Authority, *WRA,* p. 24.

18. Eisenhower, *President Is Calling,* pp. 114–18.

19. War Relocation Authority, *WRA,* pp. 32–33; Dillon S. Myer, *Uprooted Americans: The Japanese Americans and the War Relocation Authority During World War II* (Tucson: University of Arizona Press, 1971), pp. 257–59.

20. War Relocation Authority, *WRA,* pp. 20–23; Eisenhower, *President Is Calling,* pp. 119–22.

21. Carey McWilliams, "Moving the West Coast Japanese," *Harper's Magazine,* CLXXXV (September, 1942), 360–61; Weglyn, *Years of Infamy,* pp. 79–83.

22. War Relocation Authority, *Impounded People,* pp. 36, 38.

23. *Ibid.,* pp. 38–39.

24. War Relocation Authority, *Impounded People,* pp. 39–42; Uchida, *Desert Exile,* pp. 106–11; Myer, *Uprooted Americans,* pp. 31–32.

25. War Relocation Authority, *Impounded People,* pp. 42–44, 48–51, 60, 64; Weglyn, *Years of Infamy,* pp. 89–91, 116–21; Myer, *Uprooted Americans,* pp. 59–61; Daniels, *Concentration Camps: North America,* p. 105.

26. War Relocation Authority, *Impounded People,* pp. 88–93; Myer, *Uprooted Americans.* pp. 61–62.

27. War Relocation Authority, *WRA,* pp. 49–50; Hosokawa, *JACL,* pp. 205–7; Weglyn, *Years of Infamy,* pp. 122–25.

28. War Relocation Authority, *WRA,* p. 50.

Chapter 3. The Registration Crisis

1. The terms "loyal" and "disloyal" were frequently misused during and after World War II in reference to persons of Japanese descent. Quotation marks are used in all cases in which the author believes the terms to refer to evacuees acting from frustration, confusion, or resentment, rather than allegiance to any nation.

2. Louise Merrick Van Patten, "Public Opinion on Japanese Americans," *Far Eastern Survey,* XIV (August 1, 1945), 207.

3. War Relocation Authority, *WRA,* p. 111; Leo Katcher, *Earl Warren: A Political Biography* (New York: McGraw-Hill, 1947), p. 148; War Relocation Authority, *Impounded People,* p. 97; Uchida, *Desert Exile,* pp. 53–54.

4. War Relocation Authority, *Impounded People,* p. 98; Petersen, *Japanese Americans,* p. 84.

5. This policy led to criticism of the League by those Nisei who did not hold this view. Some members of this group enlarged the organization's acronym (JACL) to read "JACKAL." Hosokawa, *JACL*, pp. 197–201, 209–11.

6. Hosokawa, *Nisei*, p. 363; Hosokawa, *JACL*, pp. 190, 193–94, 197–200.

7. War Relocation Authority, *Impounded People*, pp. 97–98; U. S., Department of the Interior, War Relocation Authority, *Community Government in War Relocation Centers* (Washington, D. C.: Government Printing Office, 1946), pp. 37–38; War Relocation Authority, *WRA*, p. 54.

8. War Relocation Authority, *WRA*, pp. 37–38, 43, 45–46.

9. The term "relocation" was used originally to refer to the movement of the evacuees from their homes to relocation centers. After this was accomplished, however, it came to mean "resettlement" in normal communities outside the centers, but beyond the exclusion zone.

10. War Relocation Authority, *WRA*, pp. 54–55; Shibutani, *Derelicts of Company K*, pp. 51–52.

11. War Relocation Authority, *Impounded People*, p. 99.

12. Hosokawa, *JACL*, pp. 214–16; "Outline of Events Leading to Renunciation," (Unpublished pamphlet prepared for plaintiffs in the renunciation cases by their attorney, Wayne Collins, n.d.), p. 2, Personal Files of Wayne Collins, San Francisco.

13. War Relocation Authority, *Impounded People*, p. 100.

14. "Outline of Events," p. 2.

15. Dorothy S. Thomas and Richard S. Nishimoto, *The Spoilage* (Berkeley: University of California Press, 1946), pp. 95–96; Hosokawa, *JACL*, pp. 214–16; Weglyn, *Years of Infamy*, pp. 136–39.

16. Record, p. 248, Clark v. Inouye 175 F. 2d 740 (9th Cir. 1949); War Relocation Authority, *Impounded People*, p. 104.

17. War Relocation Authority, *Impounded People*, p. 104; "Outline of Events," p. 2; Weglyn, *Years of Infamy*, pp. 135–36.

18. War Relocation Authority, *Impounded People*, pp. 105–6.

19. *Ibid.*, p. 109; Weglyn, *Years of Infamy*, pp. 139–40.

20. War Relocation Authority, *Impounded People,* p. 111.

21. *Ibid* pp. 111–12; Shibutani, *Derelicts of Company K*, pp. 52–54; U. S., Department of the Interior, War Relocation Authority, *The Evacuated People: A Quantitative Description* (Washington, D. C.: Government Printing Office, 1946), pp. 164–65.

22. The most complete account of the registration program in the Tule Lake Relocation Center is given in Thomas and Nishimoto, *The Spoilage*, pp. 72–83. This work is part of a three-volume study of the evacuation program by

the University of California, prepared from reports made by Caucasians and evacuees living in the centers. *The Spoilage* was presented as evidence by both sides in the renunciation cases.

23. Thomas and Nishimoto, *Spoilage*, p. 73; War Relocation Authority, *Impounded People*, p. 103.

24. War Relocation Authority, *Impounded People*, p. 103.

25. Thomas and Nishimoto, *Spoilage*, p. 74.

26. *Ibid.*, p. 75; War Relocation Authority, *Community Government*, pp. 39–40; Daisuke Kitagawa, *Issei and Nisei: The Internment Years* (New York: Seabury Press, 1967), pp. 118–19.

27. Thomas and Nishimoto, *Spoilage*, p. 75.

28. *Ibid.*, p. 76.

29. *Ibid.*, p. 77; Weglyn, *Years of Infamy,* pp. 147–48.

30. Thomas and Nishimoto, *Spoilage*, p. 78; War Relocation Authority, *Community Government*, pp. 40–41.

31. Thomas and Nishimoto, *Spoilage*, p. 81; Weglyn, *Years of Infamy*, pp. 149–51.

32. Thomas and Nishimoto, *Spoilage*, pp. 81–82; Weglyn, *Years of Infamy*, pp. 149–50.

33. War Relocation Authority, *Evacuated People*, p. 164.

34. *Ibid.*; War Relocation Authority, *WRA*, p. 57.

35. War Relocation Authority, *WRA*, p. 57.

36. War Relocation Authority, *Evacuated People*, p. 30.

37. War Relocation Authority, *WRA*, p. 57.

38. tenBroek, *Prejudice*, p. 161; Hosokawa, *JACL* pp. 227–28.

39. tenBroek, *Prejudice*, pp. 161–62.

40. *Ibid.*, p. 163; War Relocation Authority, *Evacuated People*, p. 169.

41. War Relocation Authority, *Impounded Peoole*, p. 132; Hosokawa, *JACL* p. 269; Myer, *Uprooted Americans*, pp. 76–77.

42. War Relocation Authority, *Impounded People*, pp. 130–32; Weglyn, *Years of Infamy*, pp. 157–58.

43. tenBroek, *Prejudice*, p. 163.

44. War Relocation Authority, *Impounded People*, p. 129.

Chapter 4. The Failure of Moderate Leadership in Tule Lake

1. Brief for Appellees, pp. 53–54, McGrath v. Abo, 186 F. 2d 766 (9th Cir. 1951); War Relocation Authority, *Impounded People*p. 134; Thomas and Nishimoto, *Spoilage*, p. 106.

2. War Relocation Authority, *Impounded People*, pp. 133–34.

3. Record, p. 247, Clark v. Inouye.

4. Brief for Appellants, Appendix C, p. vii, Acheson v. Murakami, 176 F. 2d 953 (9th Cir. 1949).

5. War Relocation Authority, *Evacuated People*, p. 169.

6. Morton Grodzins, "Making Un-Americans," *American Journal of Sociology*, LX (May, 1955), 572–80.

7. Record, pp. 335–36, McGrath v. Abo, 186 F. 2d 766 (9th Cir. 1951).

8. It is important to remember that the groups were not static. Individuals and groups vacillated constantly as they were swayed by events, news, and rumors. A resented administrative policy or a newspaper report of an assault upon Japanese Americans residing outside of the centers would, for a period of time, increase the number of evacuees who believed that the United States held no future for them. This tendency was vastly greater in Tule Lake than in any other center. The prolonged feelings of insecurity and indecision prevalent in the segregation center were sufficient to unbalance even individuals who possessed great mental stability. A substantial majority of the center residents had been in a state of uncertainty for years. As a result, throughout the entire two-and-a-half–year history of the segregation center, the population tended to believe even the most fantastic rumors; people frequently did not think or act logically; they were prone to take whatever appeared to be the immediate path to safety; and they were predisposed to fall into mass anxiety, which on several occasions rose to panic. *Ibid.*, p. 337.

9. Thomas and Nishimoto, *Spoilage*, p. 111; War Relocation Authority, *Impounded People*, p. 135.

10. Brief for Appellants, Appendix C, p. xxii, Acheson v. Murakami; War Relocation Authority, *Impounded People*, pp. 135—37.

11. Brief for Appellants, Appendix C, pp. xx-xxi, Acheson v. Murakami; tenBroek, *Prejudice*, p. 164.

12. Brief for Appellants, Appendix C, pp. xxiv-xxv, Acheson v. Murakami.

13. Rosalie Hankey Wax, "The Destruction of a Democratic Impulse," *Human Organization*, XII (Spring, 1953), 12.

14. Pseudonyms are used in this work only when the author has been unable to determine the actual names of persons involved. The pseudonyms found herein were taken from Thomas and Nishimoto's *Spoilage*.

15. Thomas and Nishimoto, *Spoilage*, pp. 113–14.

16. *Ibid.*, p. 115.

17. *Ibid.*, p. 119; Wax, "Destruction," p. 14.

18. Thomas and Nishimoto, *Spoilage*, p. 119.

19. The block, composed of fourteen barracks, was the basic unit of the evacuee community. The next unit of community organization was the ward, made up of nine blocks. The wards were separated by firebreaks.

20. Wax, "Destruction," pp. 14–15.

21. *Ibid.*, p. 15.

22. Thomas and Nishimoto, *Spoilage*, p. 121.

23. *Ibid.*

24. Wax, "Destruction," p. 15.

25. Thomas and Nishimoto, *Spoilage*, p. 21.

26. Wax, "Destruction," p. 15.

27. *Ibid.*, p. 16.

28. *Ibid.*, p. 17.

29. *Ibid.*, p. 18; Thomas and Nishimoto, *Spoilage*, p. 130.

30. Wax, "Destruction," pp. 18–19; Thomas and Nishimoto, *Spoilage*, pp. 130–31; Weglyn, *Years of Infamy*, p. 162.

31. War Relocation Authority, *WRA*, pp. 66–67; Thomas and Nishimoto, *Spoilage*, 137; Myer, *Uprooted Americans*, pp. 78–79.

32. Thomas and Nishimoto, *Spoilage*, pp. 138–40; Weglyn, *Years of Infamy*, p. 162.

33. Wax, "Destruction," p. 18.

34. *Ibid.*, p. 19.

35. *Ibid.*; Rosalie Hankey Wax, "The Development of Authoritarianism: A Comparison of the Japanese American Relocation Centers and Germany" (unpublished Ph.D. dissertation, University of Chicago, 1951), p. 134; Thomas and Nishimoto, *Spoilage*, p. 148.

36. Wax, "Destruction," p. 19; Wax, "Development," p. 135; Thomas and Nishimoto, *Spoilage*, p. 148.

37. Rosalie Hankey Wax, *Doing Fieldwork* (Chicago: University of Chicago Press, 1971), pp. 97–98.

38. Audrie Girdner and Anne Loftis, *The Great Betrayal: The Evacuation of the Japanese Americans during World War II* (New York: Macmillan, 1969), p. 323. The power of the Japanese government to ease conditions in the relocation centers lay in its ability to retaliate against American citizens held in Japanese concentration camps. On at least one occasion, the Japanese adopted restrictive measures toward prisoners in the Santo Tomas camp in the Philippines in response to trouble at Tule Lake. This fact was recognized by such persons as United States Attorney General Francis Biddle, who opposed continued Army control of Tule Lake and who took the stand before the Dies Committee to warn that Japan was watching the treatment of the people at the segregation center.

39. Thomas and Nishimoto, *Spoilage*, pp. 142, 151.

40. Wax, "Development," p. 135.

41. Thomas and Nishimoto, *Spoilage*, p. 153.

42. Wax, "Development," p. 137.

43. Thomas and Nishimoto, *Spoilage*, p. 157.

Chapter 5. Martial Law and the Rise of the Radical Underground

1. War Relocation Authority, *Impounded People*, pp. 140, 175.

2. Wax, "Development," p. 142.

3. *ACLU News* (San Francisco), August, 1944, p. 2; Weglyn, *Years of Infamy*, p. 166.

4. Coincident with the development of these divergent organizations came a sharpening of the distinction between the "disloyal" and "loyal" evacuees, an intensification of race-consciousness, and a wave of hate, fear, and suspicion toward dissenters, "fence-sitters," collaborationists, and informers. The climate of fear and hate which developed during the period of martial law continued throughout 1944 and most of 1945. Such conditions may be blamed primarily on the Resegregationists and to a lesser extent on the Coordinating Committee, both of which used unprincipled tactics to encourage such feelings among the people. The culmination of their efforts was a general hatred of "*inu*" (i.e., "dog" in Japanese), which infected virtually the entire population. The term *inu* during this period referred not only to dissenters, fence-sitters, collaborationists, and informers, but it was frequently used by various individuals to blacken the name of any person they might dislike. The greatest amount of hatred and suspicion was directed toward the administration. This meant that anyone who was seen merely talking to a Caucasian might be labeled an *inu*. The punishment for being an *inu* was social ostracism: friends and neighbors ceased speaking to them; they were segregated at separate tables in the messhalls; and children would bark like dogs as they passed. Few persons were willing to submit to such severe punishment. Record, pp. 327–28, McGrath v. Abo.

5. Thomas and Nishimoto, *Spoilage*, pp. 161–62; Weglyn, *Years of Infamy*, p. 167.

6. Thomas and Nishimoto, *Spoilage*, p. 162; Brief for Appellees, p. 66, McGrath v. Abo; Wax, "Development," pp. 144–45; Weglyn, *Years of Infamy*, p. 166.

7. Thomas and Nishimoto, *Spoilage*, p. 163; Brief for Appellees, p. 66, McGrath v. Abo.

8. Thomas and Nishimoto, *Spoilage*, p. 167, Wax, "Development," p. 146.

9. War Relocation Authority, *Impounded People*, p. 177.

10. Wax, "Development," p. 150.

11. *Ibid.*, p. 151.

12. *Ibid.*, p. 147.

13. *Ibid.*, pp. 150–51.

14. *Ibid.*, p. 153; Weglyn, *Years of Infamy*, p. 205.

15. Wax, "Development," p. 155.

16. *Ibid.*; Thomas and Nishimoto, *Spoilage*, p. 183.

17. Wax, *Fieldwork*, p. 109.

18. *Ibid.*, pp. 115–17.

19. Wax, "Development," pp. 165–66. See footnote number four for a definition of "*inu.*"

20. *Ibid.*, p. 165; War Relocation Authority, *Impounded People*, pp. 178–79; Weglyn, *Years of Infamy*, pp. 170–71, 207.

21. War Relocation Authority, *Impounded People*, p. 179.

22. Thomas and Nishimoto, *Spoilage*, p. 193.

23. *Ibid.*, pp. 200–201, 203, 211, 213–15.

24. Wax, "Development," pp. 170–71; Weglyn, *Years of Infamy*, p. 207.

25. Thomas and Nishimoto, *Spoilage*, p. 216.

26. Wax, "Development," p. 171.

27. *Ibid.*, p. 172.

28. Thomas and Nishimoto, *Spoilage*, p. 306.

29. Wax, "Development," p. 173.

30. *Ibid.*, p. 174.

31. Thomas and Nishimoto, *Spoilage*, p. 306.

32. *Ibid.*, p. 375; Record, p. 344, McGrath v. Abo.

33. Record, pp. 344–45, McGrath v. Abo.

34. Thomas and Nishimoto, *Spoilage*, p. 306.

35. Wax, "Development," p. 177.

36. Thomas and Nishimoto, *Spoilage*, pp. 304–5.

37. The term "colony" was used to refer to the residential section of the center set aside for persons of Japanese descent.

38. Thomas and Nishimoto, *Spoilage*, p. 229.

39. Wax, *Fieldwork*, p. 120.

40. Wax, "Development," p. 177.

41. Record, p. 346, McGrath v. Abo.

42. Wax, *Fieldwork*, p. 120.

43. Record, p. 347, McGrath v. Abo.

44. Thomas and Nishimoto, *Spoilage*, p. 235.

45. *Ibid.*

46. *Ibid.*, pp. 236–37; Wax, *Fieldwork*, pp. 125–26; Wax, "Development," p. 183.

47. Thomas and Nishimoto, *Spoilage*, p. 236.

48. *Newell Star*, (Tule Lake Segregation Center, California), May 25, 1944, p. 1.

49. Wax, *Fieldwork*, p. 129.

50. Thomas and Nishimoto, *Spoilage*, p. 246.

51. Wax, *Fieldwork*, p. 130.

52. Thomas and Nishimoto, *Spoilage*, p. 245.

53. Wax, "Development," p. 187.

Chapter 6. Prelude to Renunciation

1. *Newell Star*, May 25, 1944, p. 2.

2. War Relocation Authority, *WRA*, p. 71.

3. Record, p. 267, Clark v. Inouye.

4. Record, p. 348, McGrath v. Abo.

5. Wax, "Development," p. 192.

6. Thomas and Nishimoto, *Spoilage*, pp. 261, 265.

7. *Ibid.*, p. 264.

8. *Ibid.*, p. 263.

9. *Ibid.*, p. 307.

10. Wax, *Fieldwork*, p. 137; *Newell Star*, July 6, 1944, p. 1.

11. Record, pp. 257–61, Clark v. Inouye.

12. Thomas and Nishimoto, *Spoilage*, p. 274.

13. *Newell Star*, July 20, 1944, extra edition, p. 1.

14. Wax, *Fieldwork*, p. 144; Record, p. 350, McGrath v. Abo; Thomas and Nishimoto, *Spoilage*, p. 280.

15. Wax, *Fieldwork*, p. 144; Wax, "Development," pp. 200–1.

16. Wax, "Development," pp. 203–4.

17. *ACLU News,* September 1944, pp. 1–4; Unpublished "Statement of Wayne M. Collins," prepared by Collins, San Francisco, July 10, 1958, Personal Files of Wayne Collins; Weglyn, *Years of Infamy*, pp. 215–16.

18. Thomas and Nishimoto, *Spoilage*, pp. 309–10.

19. *Ibid.*, p. 310.

20. War Relocation Authority, *Wartime Exile* p. 30; Anne Reeploeg Fisher, *Exile of a Race* (Seattle: F. and T. Publishers, 1965), p. 99.

21. *Congressional Record*, LXXXIX, 8467–68.

22. War Relocation Authority, *Impounded People,* p. 140.

23. Committee on Immigration and Naturalization, *Expatriation of Certain Nationals*, p. 26.

24. Record, pp. 156–57, McGrath v. Abo; Weglyn, *Years of Infamy*, pp. 229–30.

25. *Ibid.*, p. 157.

26. Committee on Immigration and Naturalization, *Expatriation of Certain Nationals*, p. 36. The Department was somewhat equivocal on the number of "disloyals" in Tule Lake which it hoped might take advantage of Biddle's bill and renounce. On January 25, 1944, Biddle told the Committee on Immigration and Naturalization that it was between 1,500 and 2,500. In a letter to the

Speaker of the House of Representatives, written within the same month, he revised this to between three thousand and one thousand persons. Ennis, in a letter to Ernest Besig on August 22, 1945, said the figure was "well over a thousand."

27. Edward J. Ennis, letter to Ernest Besig, Washington, D. C., August 22, 1945, Personal Files of Wayne Collins, San Francisco.

28. Record, p. 160, McGrath v. Abo.

29. Committee on Immigration and Naturalization, *Expatriation of Certain Nationals*, pp. 34–46; Ennis, letter to Besig.

30. Record, p. 159, McGrath v. Abo.

31. War Relocation Authority, *WRA* p. 72.

32. War Relocation Authority, *Impounded People*, pp. 183–85.

33. Wax, "Development," pp. 204–5; Thomas and Nishimoto, *Spoilage*, p. 308.

34. War Relocation Authority, *Impounded People*, p. 187.

35. Wax, *Fieldwork*, p. 145; Weglyn, *Years of Infamy*, pp. 230–32.

36. Wax, *Fieldwork,* p. 144; Wax, "Development," pp. 351–52.

37. Wax, *Fieldwork*, p. 145.

38. Wax, "Development," p. 206.

39. *Ibid*.

40. Thomas and Nishimoto, *Spoilage*, p. 312; Weglyn, *Years of Infamy*, p. 232.

41. Record, pp. 256–57, McGrath v. Abo; Brief for Appellees, pp. 66–71, McGrath v. Abo, 186 F. 2d 776 (9th Cir. 1951).

42. Record, p. 352, McGrath v. Abo; Wax, "Development," p. 207.

43. Record, pp. 260–61, 352, McGrath v. Abo; Wax, "Development," p. 207.

44. Wax, "Development," p. 208.

45. *Ibid.*, pp. 210–11; Wax, *Fieldwork*, pp. 152–54.

46. Record, pp. 259–60, Clark v. Inouye.

47. Wax, "Development," p. 208.

48. Thomas and Nishimoto, *Spoilage*, p. 315.

49. Record, pp. 354–55, McGrath v. Abo.

50. Wax, "Development," p. 212.

51. Wax, *Fieldwork* pp. 153–54.

52. Record, p. 356, McGrath v. Abo.

53. *Ibid.*, pp. 357–59; Wax, "Development," pp. 213–14; Wax, *Fieldwork*, pp. 154–55.

54. Wax, "Development," p. 215.

55. *Ibid.*, p. 216.

56. Record, pp. 358–59, McGrath v. Abo.

57. *Ibid.*, p. 361.

58. Wax, *Fieldwork*, pp. 156, 159.

59. Record, p. 259, McGrath v. Abo.

60. Thomas and Nishimoto, *Spoilage*, p. 322.

61. *Ibid.*, pp. 322–23.

62. *Ibid.*, pp. 324–25.

63. Thomas and Nishimoto, *Spoilage*, p. 326. According to Thomas and Nishimoto, persons who wanted to remain in the United States found comfort in the rumor that renunciants would be permitted to remain in this country as aliens after the war. Kira himself offered comfort to those holding this view with his statement that "the Denationalization Bill is a wartime law, and I think it's unconstitutional, because you can't discriminate against a certain portion of the population because of their color and race. They evacuated us, and then they try to pin us down to a citizens duties. Once a person is thrown into a camp and pushed around, he looks at things emotionally. We cannot be held responsible for what we do in camp. After the war the entire picture will be changed. The United States will not deport those who renounce their citizenship."

64. Record, p. 364, McGrath v. Abo.

65. *Ibid.*, p. 366.

Chapter 7. Renunciation of Citizenship

1. Record, pp. 164–65, McGrath v. Abo.

2. *Ibid.*

3. *Ibid.*, p. 165; *Newell Star*, October 26, 1944, pp. 1–2, November 16, 1944, p. 1.

4. Record, pp. 369–70, McGrath v. Abo.

5. *Ibid.*, pp. 165–66. Up to this time, the WRA had kept conditions in the center, including the growth of the Resegregationists and their activities, secret from other agencies of the federal government and from the general public. Thus, it was only upon Burling's arrival in the camp on December 5, 1944, that the Department of Justice learned the actual state of affairs there.

6. *Ibid.*, pp. 165–67.

7. Record, p. 218, Clark v. Inouye.

8. *Ibid.*, p. 231.

9. Record, p. 30, McGrath v. Abo; Wax, *Fieldwork*, pp. 163–66.

10. Record, pp. 371–72, McGrath v. Abo.

11. Thomas and Nishimoto, *Spoilage*, p. 324.

12. Record, p. 374, McGrath v. Abo.

13. *Newell Star*, December 19, 1944, extra edition, pp. 1–3.

14. Record, pp. 374–75, McGrath v. Abo.

15. Thomas and Nishimoto, *Spoilage*, pp. 334–35.

16. *Ibid.* p. 345.

17. *Ibid.*, p. 347.

18. *Ibid.*; Record, p. 381, McGrath v. Abo; Weglyn, *Years of Infamy*, pp. 234–35.

19. *Ibid.*

20. Thomas and Nishimoto, *Spoilage*, p. 335.

21. *Ibid.*, pp. 336–37; Weglyn, *Years of Infamy*, p. 235.

22. Record, pp. 374–75, McGrath v. Abo.

23. *Ibid.*, pp. 375–76.

24. *Ibid.*, p. 376; Weglyn, *Years of Infamy*, p. 235.

25. Thomas and Nishimoto, *Spoilage*, p. 339.

26. *Ibid.*

27. Record, p. 188, McGrath v. Abo; Weglyn, *Years of Infamy*, p. 240.

28. Record, pp. 307–8, Clark v. Inouye; Weglyn, *Years of Infamy*, pp. 235–36.

29. Thomas and Nishimoto, *Spoilage,* p. 339; Weglyn, *Years of Infamy*, pp. 236–37.

30. Thomas and Nishimoto, *Spoilage*, p. 340; *Newell Star*, January 11, 1945, p. 2; Wax, *Fieldwork*, pp. 166–67; Weglyn, *Years of Infamy*, pp. 237–38.

31. Thomas and Nishimoto, *Spoilage*, pp. 340–41.

32. Wax, *Fieldwork*, p. 167.

33. Record, p. 378, McGrath v. Abo.

34. Thomas and Nishimoto, *Spoilage*, p. 342.

35. *Ibid.*, pp. 324, 347–48.

36. Record, p. 234, Clark v. Inouye.

37. Record, p. 201, McGrath v. Abo.

38. *Ibid.*, pp. 406–7.

39. Wax, *Fieldwork*, pp. 167–68.

40. Record, pp. 232–34, Clark v. Inouye.

41. *Ibid.*, p. 234.

42. *Ibid.*, p. 281; Myer, *Uprooted Americans*, pp. 88–90.

43. Record, pp. 193–94, McGrath v. Abo.

44. *Ibid.*, pp. 244, 261–62.

45. *Ibid.*, p. 172.

46. *Ibid.*, pp. 174, 186–87.

47. *Ibid.*, pp. 188, 190.

48. *Ibid.*, pp. 188–89.

49. *Ibid.*, pp. 172–75.

50. *Ibid.*, p. 178.

51. Brief for Appellees, pp. 83–84, McGrath v. Abo.

52. Thomas and Nishimoto, *Spoilage*, p. 303; Weglyn, *Years of Infamy*, pp. 241–42.

53. Record, p. 379, McGrath v. Abo.

54. *Ibid.*; Daniels, *Concentration Camps: North America*, pp. 116–17.

55. Record, p. 378, McGrath v. Abo.

56. *Ibid.*, pp. 237–38, 243–44, 262.

57. John L. Burling, letter to Tsutomu Higashi and Masao Sakamoto, Tule Lake Segregation Center, California, January 18, 1945, Personal Files of Wayne Collins, San Francisco.

58. Record, pp. 382, 384, McGrath v. Abo; Weglyn, *Years of Infamy*, p. 242.

59. Record, p. 385, McGrath v. Abo.

60. *Ibid.*, p. 383.

61. *Ibid* , p. 182.

62. Thomas and Nishimoto, *Spoilage*, pp. 356–57.

63. Record, p. 183, McGrath v. Abo.

64. *Ibid.*

65. *Ibid.*, pp. 184–85.

66. *Ibid.*, p. 378.

67. Record, pp. 266–67, Clark v. Inouye.

68. Record, p. 185, McGrath v. Abo.

69. *Ibid.*, p. 184.

70. Charles M. Rothstein returned to Tule Lake in July, 1945 and conducted approximately two hundred additional renunciation hearings.

71. War Relocation Authority, *Evacuated People*, p. 178; Brief for Appellees, p. 86, McGrath v. Abo.

72. Brief for Appellees, p. 85, McGrath v. Abo; Record, p. 239, McGrath v. Abo.

73. Record, p. 198, McGrath v. Abo.

74. *Ibid.*, pp. 198–205.

75. *Ibid.*, pp. 391–94.

76. *Ibid.*, pp. 394–95.

77. *Ibid.*, p. 396.

78. Numerous letters from renunciants expressing their reasons for renouncing were examined by the author in the files of attorney Wayne Collins in San Francisco and in the Japanese American Evacuation File, at the Bancroft Library, University of California at Berkeley.

79. Thomas and Nishimoto, *Spoilage*, pp. 358–59.

80. *Ibid.*, pp. 350–60.

81. *Ibid.*, p. 361.

Chapter 8. Reaction against Renunciation

1. Brief for Appellees, p. 96, McGrath v. Abo. Many of the names on the list had been added, without the individuals' knowledge, to convince other residents and the administration that the Resegregationists had more members

than they actually possessed. This resulted in arrests and internment of some unwitting persons.

2. War Relocation Authority, *Story* p. 73. Jacobus tenBroek, in *Prejudice, War, and the Constitution*, p. 177, states that a total of 1,416 men, including 1,098 renunciants and 318 aliens, were sent to Department of Justice internment camps. Since the four shipments made by the Department between December 27, 1944 and March 4, 1945 totaled 1,016, the remaining 400 would be the total removed at the WRA's request during June and July, 1945.

3. War Relocation Authority, *Impounded People*, pp. 214–15; *ACLU News*, August 15, 1945, p. 1; Weglyn, *Years of Infamy*, p. 244.

4. War Relocation Authority, *Impounded People*, p. 215; Record, pp. 252–53, McGrath v. Abo.

5. War Relocation Authority, *Impounded People*, p. 215.

6. *Ibid.*, pp. 215–16.

7. Girdner and Loftis, *Great Betrayal*, p. 421.

8. tenBroek, *Prejudice*, p. 180.

9. Record, pp. 262–63, McGrath v. Abo.

10. *Ibid.*, pp. 242–43, 262–63.

11. *Ibid.*, pp. 395–96.

12. *Ibid.*, pp. 299–300.

13. Record, p. 235, Clark v. Inouye.

14. Record, pp. 191–92, McGrath v. Abo.

15. War Relocation Authority, *Evacuated People*, p. 178.

16. Herbert Wechsler, letter to each person whose application for renunciation of citizenship was accepted by the Attorney General, Washington, D. C., circa 1945–46, Personal Files of Wayne M. Collins, San Francisco. Only eighty-four approvals of renunciation applications were made after April 18, 1946. However, Wayne Collins, in an interview with the author on April 8, 1972, charged that Attorney General Tom Clark continued to approve applications made in Tule Lake for several years after the center closed, despite the fact that thousands of renunciants were in court attempting to have such applications cancelled.

17. Edward Ennis, letter to Ernest Besig, Washington, D. C., August 22, 1945, Personal Files of Wayne Collins, San Francisco.

18. The devastation of Hiroshima, Japan by an atomic bomb on August 6, 1945, was a terrible blow since approximately a third of the residents in Tule Lake were either from that city or had relatives there.

19. Edward Ennis, form letter sent to renunciants, Washington, D. C., circa 1945–46, Personal Files of Wayne Collins, San Francisco; Weglyn, *Years of Infamy*, pp. 246–47.

20. Brief for Appellees, pp. 6–7, Barber v. Abo, 186 F. 2d 775 (9th Cir. 1951).

21. *Ibid.*, p. 3.

22. Fisher, *Exile of a Race*, p. 229.

23. Unpublished "Statement of the Tule Lake Defense Committee," (n.d.) p. 2, Personal Files of Wayne Collins, San Francisco.

24. Record, pp. 253, 266, McGrath v. Abo.

25. Girdner and Loftis, *Great Betrayal*, p. 447; Wayne Collins, private interview with the author, San Francisco, March 31, 1972.

26. Weglyn, *Years of Infamy*, pp. 253–54; Girdner and Loftis, *Great Betrayal*, p. 447; Wayne Collins, private interview with author, San Francisco, March 31, 1972.

27. Unpublished "Statement of Wayne M. Collins," pp. 9, 14; Wayne Collins, private interview with the author, San Francisco, March 31, 1972.

28. *ACLU News*, August, 1945, p. 1.

29. *Ibid.*, September, 1945, p. 3.

30. Unpublished "Statement of Wayne M. Collins," July 10, 1958, pp. 6–8, Personal Files of Wayne Collins, San Francisco.

31. *Ibid.*, p. 9.

32. Girdner and Loftis, *Great Betrayal*, p. 447; Weglyn, *Years of Infamy*, p. 253.

33. "Statement of Wayne M. Collins," pp. 11–12; Weglyn, *Years of Infamy*, p. 253.

34. "Statement of Wayne M. Collins," pp. 13–14.

35. *Ibid.*, p. 14.

36. Girdner and Loftis, *Great Betrayal*, p. 447.

37. Wayne M. Collins, private interview with the author, March 31, 1972; Weglyn, *Years of Infamy*, p. 254.

38. Wayne M. Collins, private interview with author, March 31, 1972.

39. Thus, except for the year of radical control, the residents of the center preferred to put important decisions in the hands of democratically elected bodies.

40. "Statement of the Tule Lake Defense Committee," pp. 4–5.

41. Wayne M. Collins, private interview with author, March 31, 1972; Weglyn, *Years of Infamy*, p. 254.

42. Wayne M. Collins, private interview with author, March 31, 1972.

43. *Ibid.*

44. *Ibid.*

45. War Relocation Authority, *WRA*, p. 74.

46. tenBroek, *Prejudice*, p. 179.

47. Blair Stewart, Chairman of the Committee to Aid Relocation, letter to Attorney General Tom Clark, Portland, Oregon, October 25, 1945, Japanese American Evacuation Files, Bancroft Library, University of California at Berkeley.

48. War Relocation Authority, *WRA*, p. 74; Weglyn, *Years of Infamy*, pp. 251–52.

49. War Relocation Authority, *WRA*, p. 74; Weglyn, *Years of Infamy*, pp. 256–57.

50. War Relocation Authority, *Impounded People*, p. 216. For approximately a month after the suits were filed, the Department of Justice remained committed to the removal of all renunciants without exception. In the meantime, however, only persons leaving voluntarily were removed. On November 25, a group of over 426 "die-hards" from Tule Lake and about a thousand from the other internment camps—all unattached males—embarked for Seattle. In this and later shipments, the hard-core Resegregationist leaders and members left, thereby decreasing the remaining fears of the residents and freeing many of them to join Collins' lawsuits.

51. War Relocation Authority, *Impounded People*, p. 216; Weglyn, *Years of Infamy*, p. 256.

52. *Newell Star*, December 10, 1945, "extra" edition, p. 1; tenBroek, *Prejudice*, p. 179.

53. tenBroek, *Prejudice*, p. 180; Myer, *Uprooted Americans*, p. 220.

54. *ACLU News*, January, 1946, p. 1.

55. *Ibid.*, February, 1946, p. 3.

56. Record, p. 303, McGrath v. Abo; Weglyn, *Years of Infamy*, p. 257.

57. *ACLU News*, February, 1946, p. 3.

58. Record, p. 306, McGrath v. Abo; Brief for Appellees, p. 101, McGrath v. Abo.

59. *ACLU News*, February, 1946, p. 3.

60. Brief for Appellees, p. 101, McGrath v. Abo. Jacobus tenBroek, in *Prejudice, War, and the Constitution*, p. 180, lists only 406.

61. *ACLU News*, March, 1946, p. 3.

62. Brief for Appellees, pp. 101–2, McGrath v. Abo.

63. *ACLU News*, March, 1946, p. 3.

64. tenBroek, *Prejudice*, p. 180.

65. *ACLU News*, April, 1946, p. 1; War Relocation Authority, *Annual Report, 1946*, p. 390.

66. War Relocation Authority, *Annual Report, 1946*, p. 390. An account in the *ACLU News*, April, 1946, p. 1, stated that 2,792 were released from Tule Lake.

67. U. S., Department of the Interior, War Agency Liquidation Unit, *People in Motion: The Postwar Adjustment of the Evacuated Japanese Americans* (Washington, D. C.: Government Printing Office, 1947), pp. 33–34.

68. Wayne Collins, letter to a renunciant, San Francisco, September 16, 1946, Personal Files of Wayne Collins, San Francisco.

69. Wayne Collins, letter to all renunciant-plaintiffs, San Francisco, October 5, 1946, Personal Files of Wayne Collins, San Francisco.

70. War Relocation Authority, *Evacuated People*, p. 196.

71. *Newell Star*, December 14, 1945, p. 2.

72. Girdner and Loftis, *Great Betrayal*, p. 452.

73. *Pacific Citizen* (Los Angeles), December 25, 1948, p. 14.

74. Girdner and Loftis, *Great Betrayal*, p. 452; Gladys Ishida, "The Japanese American Renunciants of Okayama Prefecture: Their Accommodation and Assimilation to Japanese Culture" (unpublished Ph.D. dissertation, University of Chicago, 1956).

75. *Ibid.*, pp. 452–53.

Chapter 9. The Renunciation Cases

1. *ACLU News*, December, 1945, p. 1.

2. Brief for Appellees, pp. 106–15, McGrath v. Abo; Wayne Collins, letter to renunciant-plaintiff, San Francisco, March 19, 1951, Personal Files of Wayne Collins, San Francisco; Weglyn, *Years of Infamy*, pp. 255–56.

3. Record, pp. 157–60, McGrath v. Abo.

4. Tom Clark, interview with the author, Marietta, Georgia, April 30, 1971; Daniels, *Decision to Relocate*, p. 48.

5. *Ex parte Abo*, 76 F. Supp. 664, at 665 (N.D. Cal. 1947).

6. Record, pp. 64, 73, Barber v. Abo, 186 F. 2d 775 (9th Cir. 1951).

7. *ACLU News*, January, 1946, p. 1, February, 1946, p. 3.

8. Record, pp. 94–95, Barber v. Abo; Brief for Appellees, pp. 13–14, Barber v. Abo.

9. Record, pp. 131–32, Barber v. Abo; *ACLU News*, October, 1946, p. 3.

10. Record, pp. 134–44, Barber v. Abo.

11. *ACLU News*, August, 1947, p. 3; Collins, letter to renunciant-plaintiffs, March 19, 1951.

12. *Ex parte Abo*, 76 F. Supp. 664, at 666–67.

13. Petition for Writs of Certiorari to the United States Court of Appeals for the Ninth Circuit and Brief in support thereof, pp. 8–9, Aoki v. Barber. This was presented to the United States Supreme Court at its October term, 1950, by Wayne Collins. The case was not, apparently, accepted by the Court. Personal Files of Wayne Collins, San Francisco.

14. tenBroek, *Prejudice*, p. 181.

15. Barber v. Abo, 186 F. 2d 775, at 777.

16. *Ibid.*, p. 778.

17. Wayne Collins, letter to each renunciant-plaintiff in the habeas corpus

cases, San Francisco, May, 1952, Personal Files of Wayne Collins, San Francisco.

18. Record, p. 222, McGrath v. Abo; Brief for Appellees, p. 11, McGrath v. Abo.

19. Abo v. Clark, 77 F. Supp. 806, at 808.

20. Abo v. Clark, 77 F. Supp. 806, at 812; Weglyn, *Years of Infamy*, p. 261.

21. Record, pp. 491–500, McGrath v. Abo.

22. Abo v. Clark, 77 F. Supp. 806; McGrath v. Abo, 186 F. 2d 766, at 768. Wayne Collins, in his Petitions for Writs of Certiorari, p. 13, McGrath v. Abo, to the United States Supreme Court, October term, 1950, states that the final number in the equity cases in the District Court was 4,410.

23. Record, pp. 544–45, McGrath v. Abo. Specially printed for the United States Supreme Court, October term, 1951. Personal Files of Wayne Collins, San Francisco.

24. *Ibid.*, pp. 550–59.

25. *Ibid.*, pp. 567–68.

26. *Ibid.*, p. 569.

27. Record, pp. 408a–408b, McGrath v. Abo; Weglyn, *Years of Infamy*, p. 261.

28. Record, pp. 455–59, McGrath v. Abo.

29. Ernest Besig, interview with the author, San Francisco, April 5, 1972; Dwight MacDonald, "Profiles: In Defense of Everybody," *New Yorker*, XXIX (July 18, 1953), 50–53; Peggy Lamson, *Roger Baldwin, Founder of the American Civil Liberties Union* (Boston: Houghton Mifflin Company, 1976), pp. 238–40; Weglyn, *Years of Infamy*, pp. 111–12; American Civil Liberties Union, Board of Directors, *Minutes*, November 23, 1944, p. 1, July 30, 1945, p. 1, August 13, 1945, and several other references show frequent instances of problems between the national board and the Northern California Branch of the ACLU.

30. Ernest Besig, interview with the author, San Francisco, April 5, 1972; Wayne Collins, interview with the author, San Francisco, March 31, 1972.

31. Besig, interview with the author.

32. Wayne Collins, letter to renunciant-plaintiffs, March 19, 1951; American Civil Liberties Union, Press Service, *News Release* (New York), April 23, 1946, pp. 1–2.

33. *Pacific Citizen*, January 24, 1948, p. 2.

34. ACLU, Press Service, *Bulletin* (New York), Number 1186 (July 9, 1945), pp. 1–2, Number 1219 (February 25, 1946), p. 1, Number 1230 (May 13, 1946), p. 2, Number 1323 (March 1, 1948), p. 2, Number 1338 (June 14, 1948), p. 1.

35. Besig, interview with the author; Ernest Besig, letter to A. L. Wirin,

San Francisco, February 9, 1946, Personal Files of Wayne Collins, San Francisco. After this book was all but complete, a new work appeared which has significance to the roles of A. L. Wirin, Wayne Collins, Ernest Besig, and the national office of the ACLU and its Northern California Branch in the legal history of Japanese Americans during and after World War II. Although Peter Irons' book, *Justice at War: The Story of the Japanese American Internment Cases* (New York and Oxford: Oxford University Press, 1983) is limited solely to cases involving the government's evacuation and internment program, it contains important new information on the above individuals and organizations who also worked as allies and/or adversaries in the renunciation cases. Irons details the close ties of the national office of the ACLU to the Roosevelt administration which caused the civil rights group to throw roadblocks in the way of a number of its branches and attorneys that attempted to represent Japanese American clients. While not mentioned by Irons, this hindrance extended to the efforts of Wayne Collins, Ernest Besig, and the Northern California Branch of the ACLU to aid the renunciants.

It should be noted, in the light of the role played by Wayne Collins in the renunciation cases, that Irons presents a (perhaps unnecessarily) negative image of the San Francisco attorney. In one example, Ernest Besig is described (p. 169) as fearful that "Collins lacked both the temperament and competence to prepare an adequate brief and to make a persuasive argument before the Court." Irons contradicts this statement with several examples of public and private support for Collins by Besig—e.g., Collins' preparation of the amicus brief for Besig's Northern California Branch for presentation to the U. S. Supreme Court in the *Hirabayashi* case (p. 192) and Besig's sense of outrage at the national office of the ACLU for forcing Collins into a subordinate role in the *Korematsu* case (p. 360). Irons' criticism of A. L. Wirin, on the other hand, is comparatively mild, pointing briefly to his ambitious nature and his confusion of his private practice and role as an ACLU counsel (p. 111).

36. American Civil Liberties Committee of Northern California, Agenda of the Executive Committee for November 1, 1945 (Mimeographed).

37. Collins, letter to renunciant-plaintiffs, March 19, 1951.

38. Besig, interview with the author; Wayne Collins, letter to the Tule Lake Defense Committee, San Francisco, May-July, 1948, Personal Files of Wayne Collins, San Francisco. A. L. Wirin, through a letter from his law partner Fred Okrand, dated June 14, 1972, declined the author's request for information concerning his (Wirin's) role in the renunciation cases.

39. Besig, letter to Wirin, February 9, 1946.

40. Besig, interview with the author.

41. Defense Committee, form letter to renunciants, Tule Lake, California, October 8, 1945, Personal Files of Wayne Collins, San Francisco.

42. Form which was to be signed by individual renunciants authorizing A.

L. Wirin and J. B. Tietz to represent them and for the selection of a Trust Committee to administer funds for this purpose, Tule Lake, California, February, 1946, Personal Files of Wayne Collins.

43. Clark v. Inouye, 175 F. 2d 740 (9th Cir. 1949).

44. *ACLU News*, April, 1949, p. 1.

45. Acheson v. Murakami, 176 F. 2d 953, at 954 (9th Cir. 1949).

46. *Ibid.*, pp. 954–58.

47. *Ibid.*, pp. 962–63; Collins, letter to renunciant-plaintiffs, March 19, 1951.

48. Collins, letter to renunciant-plaintiffs, March 19, 1951.

49. *Ibid.*

50. *ACLU News*, March, 1949, p. 1.

51. *New York Times*, October 27, 1949, p. 17.

52. *Ibid.*, January 21, 1951, p. 80.

53. Record, p. 383, McGrath v. Abo.

54. *Ibid.*, pp. 380–84.

55. Collins, letter to renunciant-plaintiffs, March 19, 1951.

56. Record, pp. 379–80, McGrath v. Abo.

57. *ACLU News*, February, 1951, p. 1; Weglyn, *Years of Infamy*, p. 262.

58. Collins, letter to renunciant-plaintiffs, December 24, 1952.

59. Wayne Collins, letter to Tule Lake Defense Committee, San Francisco, October 16, 1953, Personal Files of Wayne Collins, San Francisco.

60. *Ibid.*; Wayne Collins, letter, San Francisco, April 22, 1957, Personal Files of Wayne Collins, San Francisco.

61. U. S., Department of Justice, form letter to the United States Attorney in San Francisco, Washington, D. C., n.d., Personal Files of Wayne Collins, San Francisco.

62. *Ibid.*

63. Collins, letter, April 22, 1957.

64. Collins, interview with the author, March 31, 1972.

65. This judgment was made based on a personal examination of the files of the renunciants' attorney, Wayne Collins, by the author.

66. Collins, letter, April 22, 1957.

67. Tule Lake Defense Committee, form letter to renunciants, Los Angeles, December 21, 1955, Personal Files of Wayne Collins, San Francisco.

68. *New York Times*, August 14, 1956, p. 27.

69. Collins, letter, April 22, 1957.

70. *New York Times*, May 21, 1959, p. 5.; Girdner and Loftis, *Great Betrayal*, p. 454.

71. Girdner and Loftis, *Great Betrayal*, p. 454; Wayne Collins, "Statement of Counsel for Plaintiffs," unpublished concluding statement by Collins at the last hearing in the mass suits, March 6, 1968, Personal Files of Wayne Collins; U. S., Commission on Wartime Relocation and Internment of Civil-

ians, *Personal Justice Denied* (Washington, D. C.: Government Printing Office, 1982), p. 251.

72. Girdner and Loftis, *Great Betrayal*, p. 454.

73. tenBroek, *Prejudice*, pp. 320–21.

Bibliography

Books

Barron, Milton L. *American Minorities: A Textbook of Readings in Intergroup Relations*. New York: Alfred A. Knopf, 1958.

Biddle, Francis. *In Brief Authority*. Garden City, New York: Doubleday and Co., Inc., 1962.

Bonacich, Edna, and Modell, John. *The Economic Basis of Ethnic Solidarity: Small Business in the Japanese American Community*. Berkeley: University of California Press, 1980.

Broom, Leonard, and Kitsuse, John I. *The Managed Casualty: The Japanese American Family in World War II*. Berkeley and Los Angeles: University of California Press, 1956.

————, and Riemer, Ruth. *Removal and Return: The Socio-economic Effects of the War on Japanese Americans*. Berkeley and Los Angeles: University of California Press, 1949.

Cole, Stewart G., and Cole, Mildred Wiese. *Minorities and the American Promise: The Conflict of Principle and Practice*. New York: Harper and Brothers, 1954.

Conn, Stetson; Engelman, Rose C.; and Fairchild, Byron. *Guarding the United States and Its Outposts*. Washington, D. C.: Department of the Army, Office of the Chief of Military History, 1964.

Connor, John W. *Acculturation and the Retention of an Ethnic Identity in Three Generations of Japanese Americans*. San Francisco: Robert D. Reed and Adam S. Eterovich, 1977.

————. *Tradition and Change in Three Generations of Japanese Americans.* Chicago: Nelson-Hall, 1977.

Conroy, Hilary, and Miyakawa, T. Scott, eds. *East across the Pacific.* Santa Barbara, California and Oxford, England: American Bibliographic Center, Clio Press, 1972.

Daniels, Roger. *Concentration Camps: North America; Japanese in the United States and Canada during World War II.* Malabar, Florida: Robert E. Krieger Publishing Co., 1981.

————. *The Decision to Relocate the Japanese Americans.* Philadelphia: J. B. Lippincott Co., 1975.

————. *The Politics of Prejudice: The Anti-Japanese Movement in California, and the Struggle for Japanese Exclusion.* Berkeley and Los Angeles: University of California Press, 1962.

————, and Kitano, Harry H. L. *American Racism: Exploration of the Nature of Prejudice.* Englewood Cliffs, New Jersey: Prentice-Hall, Inc., 1970.

Eisenhower, Milton S. *The President Is Calling.* Garden City, New York: Doubleday & Co., Inc., 1974.

Fisher, Anne Reeploeg. *Exile of a Race.* Seattle: F. and T. Publishers, 1965.

Girdner, Audrie, and Loftis, Anne. *The Great Betrayal: The Evacuation of the Japanese Americans during World War II.* Tucson: University of Arizona Press, 1969.

Grodzins, Morton. *Americans Betrayed.* Chicago: University of Chicago Press, 1949.

Hansen, Arthur A., and Mitson, Betty E. *Voices Long Silent: An Oral Inquiry into the Japanese American Evacuation.* Fullerton: Japanese American Project, California State University, Fullerton Oral History Program, 1974.

Hosokawa, Bill. *JACL: In Quest of Justice.* New York: William Morrow and Co., Inc., 1982.

————. *Nisei: The Quiet Americans.* New York: William Morrow and Co., Inc., 1969.

————, and Wilson, Robert A. *East to America: A History of the Japanese in the United States.* New York: William Morrow and Co., Inc., 1980.

Irons, Peter. *Justice at War: The Story of the Japanese American Internment Cases.* New York and Oxford: Oxford University Press, 1983.

Katcher, Leo. *Earl Warren: A Political Biography.* New York: McGraw-Hill, 1967.

Kiefer, Christie W. *Changing Cultures, Changing Lives: An Ethnographic Study of Three Generations of Japanese Americans.* San Francisco: Jossey-Bass Publishers, 1974.

Kitagawa, Daisuke. *Issei and Nisei: The Internment Years.* New York: Seabury Press, 1967.

Kitano, Harry H. L. *Japanese Americans: The Evolution of a Subculture*. Englewood Cliffs, New Jersey: Prentice-Hall, 1969.

Konvitz, Milton R. *The Alien and the Asiatic in American Law*. Ithaca, New York: Cornell University Press, 1946.

Lamson, Peggy. *Roger Baldwin, Founder of the American Civil Liberties Union*. Boston: Houghton Mifflin Co., 1976.

LaViolette, Forrest E. *Americans of Japanese Ancestry*. Toronto: Canadian Institute of International Affairs, 1946.

Leighton, Alexander H. *The Governing of Men*. Princeton, New Jersey: Princeton University Press, 1945.

McWilliams, Carey. *Brothers under the Skin*. Boston: Little, Brown, 1951.

————. *Prejudice, Japanese Americans: Symbols of Racial Intolerance*. Boston: Little, Brown, 1944.

————. *Witch Hunt: The Revival of Heresy*. Boston: Little, Brown, 1950.

Montero, Darrel. *Japanese Americans: Changing Patterns of Ethnic Affiliation over Three Generations*. Boulder, Colorado: Westview Press, 1980.

Myer, Dillon S. *Uprooted Americans: The Japanese Americans and the War Relocation Authority during World War II*. Tucson: University of Arizona Press, 1971.

Nelson, Douglas W. *Heart Mountain: The History of an American Concentration Camp*. Madison: State Historical Society of Wisconsin for the Department of History, University of Wisconsin, 1976.

Ogden, August Raymond. *The Dies Committee: A Study of the Special House Committee for the Investigation of Un-American Activities, 1938–1944*. Washington, D. C.: Catholic University of America, 1945.

Okubo, Mine. *Citizen 13660*. New York: Columbia University Press, 1946.

Penrose, Eldon. *California Nativism: Organized Opposition to the Japanese, 1890–1913*. San Francisco: Robert D. Reed, 1973.

Petersen, William. *Japanese Americans: Oppression and Success*. New York: Random House, 1971.

Shibutani, Tamotsu. *The Derelicts of Company K: A Sociological Study of Demoralization*. Berkeley: University of California Press, 1978.

Smith, Bradford. *Americans from Japan*. Philadelphia and New York: Lippincott, 1948.

Spicer, Edward H.; Hansen, Asael T.; Luomala, Katherine; and Opler, Marvin K. *Impounded People: Japanese Americans in the Relocation Centers*. Tucson: University of Arizona Press, 1969.

Stegner, Wallace. *One Nation*. Boston: Houghton Mifflin Co., 1945.

tenBroek, Jacobus; Barnhart, Edward N.; and Matson, Floyd W. *Prejudice, War and the Constitution*. Berkeley and Los Angeles: University of California Press, 1954.

Thomas, Dorothy Swaine. *The Salvage: Japanese American Evacuation and*

Resettlement. Berkeley and Los Angeles: University of California Press, 1952.

———, and Nishimoto, Richard S. *The Spoilage*. Berkeley and Los Angeles: University of California Press, 1946.

Uchida, Yoshiko. *Desert Exile: The Uprooting of a Japanese American Family*. Seattle and London: University of Washington Press, 1982.

Wax, Rosalie H. *Doing Fieldwork: Warnings and Advice*. Chicago: University of Chicago Press, 1971.

Weglyn, Michi. *Years of Infamy: The Untold Story of America's Concentration Camps*. New York: William Morrow and Co., 1976.

Articles

Bendiner, Robert. "Cool Heads or Martial Law," *The Nation*, CLIV (February 14, 1942), 183–84.

Bennett, L. Howard. "Race Conditions in the United States," *American Year Book: A Record of Events and Progress, Year 1946*. New York: Thomas Nelson and Sons, 1947.

Blakemore, Thomas L., Jr. "Recovery of Japanese Nationality as a Cause for Expatriation in American Law," *American Journal of International Law*, XL (July, 1949), 441–59.

Bogardus, Emory S. "The Japanese Return to the West Coast," *Sociology and Social Research*, XXXI (January-February, 1947), 226–33.

Costigan, Howard. "The Plight of the Nisei," *The Nation*, CLIV (February 14, 1942), 184–85.

Cox, Oliver C. "Nature of the Anti-Asiatic Movement on the Pacific Coast," *Journal of Negro Education*, XV (October, 1946), 603–14.

Derrick, Edith W. "Effects of Evacuation on Japanese-American Youth," *School Review*, LV (June, 1946), 356–62.

Deschin, Celia S. "Tule Lake—Social Science in Inaction," *Journal of Educational Sociology*, XXI (February, 1948), 368–81.

"Duress Voids Renunciation of Citizenship," *Stanford Law Review*, II (December, 1949), 217–21.

"Editorial: Epilogue to a Sorry Drama," *Life*, LXII (April 28, 1967), 4.

Fisher, Anne M. "Debt of Dishonor," *The Reporter*, VI (February 5, 1952), 21–23.

Fisher, Galen M. "Japanese Evacuation from the Pacific Coast," *Far Eastern Survey*, XI (June 29, 1942), 145–52.

———. "Resettling the Evacuees," *Far Eastern Survey*, XIV (September 26, 1945), 265–68.

"Gallup and Fortune Polls," *Public Opinion Quarterly*, VII (Spring, 1943), 177.

Gerhard, Paul F. "The Plight of the Japanese Americans during World War II," *University of Wichita Bulletin*, XXXIX (November, 1953), 1–21.

Goater, Richard G. "Civil Rights and Anti-Japanese Discrimination, (1913–1948)," *University of Cincinnati Law Review*, XVIII (January, 1949), 81–89.

Grodzins, Morton. "Making Un-Americans," *American Journal of Sociology*, LX (May, 1955), 570–82.

Howard, Harry Paxton. "Americans in Concentration Camps," *Crisis*, XLIX (September, 1942), 281–82, 301.

Iglehart, Charles. "Citizens behind Barbed Wire," *The Nation*, CLIV (June 6, 1942), 649–51.

Intelligence Officer, An. "The Japanese in America: The Problem and the Solution," *Harper's Magazine*, CLXXXV (October, 1942), 489–97.

"Issei, Nisei, Kibei," *Fortune*, XXIX (April, 1944), 8, 22, 32, 74, 78, 84, 94, 106, 118.

Jackson, Norman R. "Collective Protests in Relocation Centers," *American Journal of Sociology*, LXIII (November, 1957), 264–72.

Kimble, G. Eleanor. "The Disloyal at Tule Lake," *Common Ground*, VI (Winter, 1946), 74–81.

Kiser, Clyde V., and Kiser, Louise K. "Race Conditions in the United States," *American Year Book: A Record of Events and Progress, Year 1942*. New York: Thomas Nelson and Sons, 1943. (Further articles in this series appeared in the 1944–46 editions.)

Kitano, Harry H. L. "Japanese," *Harvard Encyclopedia of American Ethnic Groups*. Cambridge, Massachusetts: Belknap Press of Harvard University Press, 1980.

LaViolette, Forrest. "The American-Born Japanese and the World Crisis," *Canadian Journal of Economics and Political Science*, VII (November, 1941), 417–27.

Letter forwarded by Marion Randal Parsons to the editors of *The Nation*, CLIV (June 6, 1942), 666.

Luomala, Katherine. "Fellow Californians . . . Fellow Americans," *Journal of the American Association of University Women*, XXXIX (Summer, 1946), 208–11.

MacDonald, Dwight. "Profiles: In Defense of Everybody," *New Yorker*, XXIX (July 18, 1953), 29–59.

Marshall, Jim. "West Coast Japanese," *Collier's*, CVIII (October 11, 1941), 14–15.

McDonald, Carey. "Moving the West-Coast Japanese," *Harper's Magazine*, CLXXXIV (September, 1942), 365–69.

Meany, Thomas, Jr. "Citizens—Renunciation of Citizenship—Necessity of Animus Renunciandi," *Notre Dame Lawyer*, XXVI (Summer, 1951), 723–27.

Mitchell, Donald W. "Scapegoats and Facts," *The Nation*, CLIV (February 7, 1942), 155–57.

"Nisei, California Casts an Anxious Eye upon the Japanese-Americans in Its Midst," *Life*, IX (October 14, 1940), 75–82.

"Nisei Face East," *Business Week*, No. 837 (September 15, 1945), 36.

Osburn, Worth J. "Civil Liberties in Wartime," *School and Society*, LVI (September 5, 1942), 188–89.

Pickett, Clarence E., and Morris, Homer L. "From Barbed Wire to Communities," *Survey Midmonthly*, LXXXIX (August, 1943), 210–13.

"Postwar Jobs for Japanese," *Far Eastern Survey*, XIV (March 14, 1945), 62.

"Races: Square Deal for the Japanese," *Time*, XLII (November 29, 1943), 21.

"Renunciation of Citizenship by Japanese Americans," *Illinois Law Review*, XLIV (March-April, 1949), 106–12.

Roche, John P. "The Loss of American Nationality—The Development of Statutory Expatriation," *University of Pennsylvania Law Review*, XVIX (October, 1950), 56–61.

Rostow, Eugene V. "The Japanese American Cases—A Disaster," *Yale Law Journal*, LIV (June, 1945), 489–533.

———. "Our Worst Wartime Mistake," *Harper's Magazine*, CXCI (September, 1945), 193–201.

Roucek, Joseph S. "American Japanese, Pearl Harbor, and World War II," *Journal of Negro Education*, XII (Fall, 1943), 733–49.

"Should All Japanese Continue to Be Excluded from the West Coast for the Duration?" *Town Meeting*, IX (July 15, 1943), 1–24.

Smith, Bradford. "Experiment in Racial Concentration," *Far Eastern Survey*, XV (July 17, 1946), 214–18.

———. "Legalized Blackmail," *Common Ground*, VIII (Winter, 1948), 34–36.

Thomas, Dorothy Swaine. "Some Social Aspects of Japanese-American Demography," *Proceedings of the American Philosophical Society*, XCIV (October, 1950), 459–80.

"Tule Lake," *Life*, XIV (March 20, 1944), 25–35.

"Twenty Years After," *Time*, LXXVIII (August 11, 1961), 15–16.

Van Patten, Louise Merrick. "Public Opinion on Japanese Americans," *Far Eastern Survey*, XIV (August 1, 1945), 207–8.

Warren, George L. "The Refugee and the War," *Annals of the American Academy of Political and Social Sciences*, CCXXIII (September, 1942), 92–99.

Wax, Rosalie H. "The Destruction of a Democratic Impulse," *Human Organization*, XII (Spring, 1953), 11–21.

Weltfish, Gene. "American Racism: Japan's Secret Weapon," *Far Eastern Survey*, XIV (August 29, 1945), 233–37.

White, Magnar. "Between Two Flags," *Saturday Evening Post*, CCXII (September 30, 1939), 14–15, 73–75.

Woodrum, Eric. "An Assessment of Japanese American Assimilation, Pluralism, and Subordination," *American Journal of Sociology*, LXXXVII (July, 1981), 157–69.

Newspapers

ACLU News, (San Francisco), 1942–60.

American Civil Liberties Union, Press Service, *Weekly Bulletin*, (New York City), 1944–49.

Conscientious Objector, The, (New York City), 1939–46.

JACL Reporter, (Salt Lake City), 1945–52.

Newell Star. (Tule Lake Segregation Center), 1944–46.

New York Times, 1941–59.

Pacific Citizen, (Los Angeles), 1942–55.

Tulean Dispatch, (Tule Lake Relocation Center), 1942–43.

Government Publications

U. S. Army. Western Defense Command. *Final Report, Japanese Evacuation from the West Coast, 1942*. Washington, D. C.: Government Printing Office, 1943.

U. S. Bureau of Selective Service. *The 3rd Report of the Director of Selective Service, 1943–44*. Washington, D. C.: Government Printing Office, 1945.

U. S. Bureau of Selective Service. *The 4th Report of the Director of Selective Service, 1944–45*. Washington, D. C.: Government Printing Office, 1946.

U. S. Commission on Wartime Relocation and Internment of Civilians. *Personal Justice Denied*. Washington, D. C.: Government Printing Office, 1982.

U. S. Congress. *Congressional Record*. 1942–44.

U. S. Congress. House. Committee on Immigration and Naturalization. *Expatriation of Certain Nationals of the United States*. Hearings. Hearings before the Committee on Immigration and Naturalization, House of Representatives, on H. R. 2701, H. R. 3012, H. R. 3489, H. R. 3446, and H. R. 4103, 78th Cong., 1st sess., 1944.

U. S. Congress. House. *National Defense Migration*. H. Reps. 1879, 1911,

2124, 2396, and 2589 Pursuant to H. Res. 113, 77th Cong., 2d sess., 1942.

U. S. Congress. House. *Providing for Loss of United States Nationality under Certain Circumstances.* H. Rep. 1075 to Accompany H. R. 4103, 78th Cong., 2d sess., 1944.

U. S. Congress. House. *Report and Minority Views of the Special Committee on Un-American Activities in Japanese War Relocation Centers.* H. Rept. 717, 78th Cong., 1st sess., 1943.

U. S. Congress. Senate. Committee on Immigration and Naturalization. *Study of Problems Relating to Immigration and Deportation and Other Matters.* Hearings before a subcommittee of the Committee on Immigration and Naturalization, Senate, on H. Res. 52, 79th Cong., 1st sess., 1945–46.

U. S. Congress. Senate. Committee on Military Affairs. *War Relocation Centers.* Hearings before a subcommittee of the Committee on Military Affairs, Senate, on S. 444, 78th Cong., 1st sess., 1943–44.

U. S. Congress. Senate. *Custody of Japanese Residing in the United States.* S. Rept. 1496 to Accompany S. 2293, 77th Cong., 2d sess., 1942.

U. S. Congress. Senate. *Providing for the Loss of United States Nationality under Certain Circumstances.* S. Rept. 1029 to Accompany H. R. 4103, 78th Cong., 2d sess., 1944.

U. S. Congress. Senate. *Segregation of Loyal and Disloyal Japanese in Relocation Centers.* S. Doc. 96, Report on S. Res. 166, 78th Cong., 1st sess., 1943.

U. S. Department of Justice. *Annual Report of the Attorney General of the United States for the Fiscal Year Ended June 30, 1946.* Washington, D. C.: Government Printing Office, 1946.

U. S. Department of Justice. *Annual Report of the Attorney General of the United States for the Fiscal Year Ended June 30, 1947.* Washington, D. C.: Government Printing Office, 1947.

U. S. Department of Justice. Immigration and Naturalization Service. *Annual Report of the Commissioner of Immigration and Naturalization to the Attorney General, for the Fiscal Year Ended June 30, 1947.* Washington, D. C.: Government Printing Office, 1947.

U. S. Department of the Army. Office of the Chief of Military History. *Command Decisions.* Washington, D. C.: Government Printing Office, 1960.

U. S. Department of the Interior. War Agency Liquidation Unit. *People in Motion: The Postwar Adjustment of the Evacuated Japanese Americans.* Washington, D. C.: Government Printing Office, 1947.

U. S. Department of the Interior. War Relocation Authority. *Annual Report.* Washington, D. C.: Government Printing Office, 1942–46.

U. S. Department of the Interior. War Relocation Authority. *Community Gov-*

ernment in War Relocation Centers. Washington, D. C.: Government Printing Office, 1946.

U. S. Department of the Interior. War Relocation Authority. *The Evacuated People: A Quantitative Description.* Washington, D. C.: Government Printing Office, 1946.

U. S. Department of the Interior. War Relocation Authority. *Impounded People: Japanese Americans in Relocation Centers.* Washington, D. C.: Government Printing Office, 1946.

U. S. Department of the Interior. War Relocation Authority. *Legal and Constitutional Phases of the WRA Program.* Washington, D. C.: Government Printing Office, 1946.

U. S. Department of the Interior. War Relocation Authority. *The Relocation Program.* Washington, D. C.: Government Printing Office, 1946.

U. S. Department of the Interior. War Relocation Authority. *Semi-Annual Report.* Washington, D. C.: Government Printing Office, 1943–46.

U. S. Department of the Interior. War Relocation Authority. *WRA: A Story of Human Conservation.* Washington, D. C.: Government Printing Office, 1946.

U. S. Department of the Interior. War Relocation Authority. *The Wartime Handling of Evacuee Property.* Washington, D. C.: Government Printing Office, 1946.

U. S. Department of the Interior. War Relocation Authority. *Wartime Exile: The Exclusion of the Japanese Americans from the West Coast.* Washington, D. C.: Government Printing Office, 1946.

U. S. Department of the Interior. War Relocation Authority and the War Department. *Nisei in Uniform.* Washington, D. C.: Government Printing Office, 1944.

Theses and Dissertations

Ishida, Gladys. "The Japanese American Renunciants of Okayama Prefecture: Their Accommodation and Assimilation to Japanese Culture." Unpublished Ph.D. dissertation, University of Michigan, 1956.

————. "The Background and Effects of the Renunciation by Japanese Americans in World War II." Unpublished Master's thesis, University of Chicago, 1946.

Kirk, David Henry. "The Loyalties of Men in Crisis: An Exploratory Study of Some Dimensions of Allegiance." Unpublished Master's thesis, Cornell University, 1950.

Klish, Rupert. "Loss of United States Citizenship." Unpublished Master's thesis, University of Georgia, 1956.

Turner, Albert Blythe. "The Origins and Development of the War Relocation
    Authority." Unpublished Ph.D. dissertation, Duke University, 1967.
Wax, Rosalie Hankey. "The Development of Authoritarianism: A Compari-
    son of the Japanese American Relocation Centers and Germany." Un-
    published Ph.D. dissertation, University of Chicago, 1951.
Yatsushiro, Toshio. "Political and Socio-cultural Issues at Poston and Man-
    zanar Relocation Centers—A Themal Analysis." Unpublished Ph.D.
    dissertation, Cornell University, 1953.

Interviews (Tape recordings in possession of the author)

Clark, Tom, with the author, April 30, 1971, Marietta, Georgia.
Collins, Wayne M., with the author, March 31, 1972 and April 8, 1972, San
    Francisco.
Besig, Ernest, with the author, April 5, 1972, San Francisco.

Manuscript Collections

American Civil Liberties Union. Records and Publications, 1917–1975. (Mi-
    crofilm copy)
Personal Files of Wayne M. Collins, San Francisco. Most, if not all, of these
    materials are now in the Bancroft Library, University of California at
    Berkeley.
University of California at Berkeley. Bancroft Library, Japanese American
    Evacuation Files.

Legal Documents

Federal Reporter Series

Acheson v. Murakami, 176 F. 2d 953 (9th Cir. 1949).
Barber v. Abo, 186 F. 2d 775 (9th Cir. 1951).
Ex parte Abo, 76 F. Supp. 664 (N. D. Cal. 1947).
Ex parte Endo, 323 U. S. 283 (1944).
Hirabayashi v. United States, 320 U. S. 81 (1943).
Inouye v. Clark, 73 F. Supp. 1000 (S. D. Cal. 1947).
Inouye v. Clark, 175 F. 2d. 740 (9th Cir. 1949).
Korematsu v. United States, 323 U. S. 214 (1944).
McGrath v. Abo, 186 F. 2d 766 (9th Cir. 1951).
Tadayasu Abo v. Clark, 77 F. Supp. 806 (N. D. Cal. 1948).
U. S. v. Kuwabara, 56 F. Supp. 716 (N. D. Cal. 1944).

Transcripts of Record

Record, Abo v. McGrath, Nos. 112 and 121, United States Supreme Court, October term, 1951. (This case was denied certiorari and is not listed in the *United States Reports*.)

Record, Acheson v. Murakami, 176 F. 2d 953 (9th Cir. 1949).

Record, Aoki v. Barber, Nos. 113 and 122, United States Supreme Court, October term, 1951. (This case was denied certiorari and is not listed in the *United States Reports*.)

Record, Barber v. Abo, 186 F. 2d 775 (9th Cir. 1951).

Record, Inouye v. Clark, 175 F. 2d 740 (9th Cir. 1949).

Record, McGrath v. Abo, 186 F. 2d 766 (9th Cir. 1951).

Legal Briefs

Appellants' Reply Brief, Barber v. Abo, 186 F. 2d 775 (9th Cir. 1951).

Appellants' Reply Brief, McGrath v. Abo, 186 F. 2d 776 (9th Cir. 1951).

Appellees' Petition for a Rehearing, Barber v. Abo, 186 F. 2d 775 (9th Cir. 1951).

Appellees' Petition for a Rehearing, McGrath v. Abo, 186 F. 2d 776 (9th Cir. 1951).

Brief for Appellant, Barber v. Abo, 186 F. 2d 775 (9th Cir. 1951).

Brief for Appellants, Clark v. Inouye, 175 F. 2d 740 (9th Cir. 1949), and Acheson v. Murakami, 176 F. 2d 953 (9th Cir. 1949).

Brief for Appellants, McGrath v. Abo, 186 F. 2d 766 (9th Cir. 1951).

Brief for Appellees, Barber v. Abo, 186 F. 2d 775 (9th Cir. 1951).

Brief for Appellees, McGrath v. Abo, 186 F. 2d 776 (9th Cir. 1951).

Brief for Respondents in Opposition, McGrath v. Abo, and Barber v. Aoki, Nos. 121–122, United States Supreme Court, October term, 1951. (This case was denied certiorari and is not listed in the *United States Reports*.)

Petition for Writs of Certiorari to the United States Court of Appeals for the Ninth Circuit and Brief in support thereof, Aoki v. Barber, and Wakabayashi v. Barber, No. 113, United States Supreme Court, October term, 1950. (These cases were denied certiorari and are not listed in the *United States Reports*.)

Petition for Writs of Certiorari to the United States Court of Appeals for the Ninth Circuit and Brief in support thereof, McGrath v. Abo, No. 112, United States Supreme Court, October term, 1950. (This case was denied certiorari and is not listed in the *United States Reports*.)

Index

Abo v. Clark, 125
Abo v. Williams, 125
Acheson v. Murakami, 135-38, 140
ACLU. *See* American Civil Liberties Union (ACLU)
ACLU News (of Northern California), 136
Alden, John, Dr., 92
Alien Enemy Act of 1798, 110-11, 127-28
Alien land laws, 8, 120, 133
American Civil Liberties Union (ACLU), 103; national office, 132, 134, 194-95 n.35; of Northern California, 112, 115, 132-33, 194-95 n.35; of Southern California, 133
American Legion, 12, 22
Anti-Japanese/Oriental activities, 6, 8-9, 12-14, 70-71, 107; violence against returnees, 89-90
Aoyama, Mr., 68
Army, U. S., 19, 32, 46-47, 50, 52, 60, 64-65, 107; guard relocation centers, 17; leave-clearance hearings in Tule Lake, 90-91; loyalty registration for male Nisei, 23-25, 31; oppressiveness of martial law under, 50; radicals include former soldiers, 161-62; searches and arrests in Tule Lake, 46, 49, 51
Assembly centers, 17-19
Austin, Verne, Colonel, 45-46, 50

Baldwin, Roger, 132-33
Besig, Ernest, 132, 145, 194-95 n.35
Best, Raymond, 50, 55, 69, 81, 113; attends Nisei funeral, 64-65; criticizes election failure, 62; letter from, 166-68; recruits strikebreakers, 40-41; removed as defendant, 129; requests recission of center closing, 93
Biddle, Francis, 59, 124, 138, 149; and development of renunciation legislation, 71-73, 146; on Japan's awareness of conditions in Tule Lake, 182 n.38
Bismarck Internment Camp (North Dakota), 106, 111, 118-19
Black, Harry L., 59, 101, 136, 155-60
Burger, Warren E., 139

Burling, John L., 64, 71-72, 87, 93-
    96, 100-102, 147; concern over
    number of renunciations, 168;
    critical of Tule Lake officials,
    109, 159-64; open letter to radical
    leaders, 98-99; solicits *Hokoku*
    leaders' renunciations, 86-87, 92

California, 5, 10, 13-14, 16, 79; at-
    tacks on returning evacuees, 89-
    90; choosing segregation to re-
    main in, 33; largest Japanese pop-
    ulation, 6; reactivates alien land
    laws, 121
California Joint Immigration Com-
    mittee, 12
Civic Association (Tule Lake), 51
Clark, Tom, 113, 116, 125, 139,
    171-72, 190 n.16
Collins, Wayne M., 4, 69, 111-15,
    117, 119-20, 123-34, 136-44, 190
    n.16, 194 n.22, 194-95 n.35;
    ACLU attempts to undercut, 132-
    33; becomes attorney for renun-
    ciants, 114-15; breaks with na-
    tional ACLU, 132; decides on
    mass suits, 123-24; prevents de-
    portation of renunciants, 117,
    124-25
Congress, U. S., 5-6, 9, 13, 22, 53,
    71, 73, 147
Cooperative Enterprises (Tule Lake),
    67, 69, 74
Coordinating Committee (Tule
    Lake), 48, 52-57, 59-61, 66, 183
    n.4; lack of administration support
    for, 52; resignation, 54-55, 60-61;
    unpopular with residents, 54
Court of Appeals, U. S., Ninth Cir-
    cuit, 127-28, 135-40
Cozzens, Robert, 69
Crystal City Internment Camp
    (Texas), 111, 126-27

Daihyo Sha Kai, 39-52, 54-56, 58,
    62, 70, 114; arrest of leaders or-
    dered, 46; formation of, 39-40;
    meeting with Myer, 42
De Amat, Francisco, 45
Denman, William, 127-28, 135-39
Deportation Commission, 71
DeWitt, John L., 15-16, 26, 125,
    139, 156, 177 n.13; anti-Japanese
    prejudice of, 15; opposition to re-
    turn of evacuees, 22
Dickstein, Samuel, 111, 134
Dies Committee, 71, 182 n.38
District Court, U. S. (Los Angeles),
    135
District Court, U. S. (San Fran-
    cisco), 117, 125-32, 135, 137,
    140
Divisional Responsible Men (Tule
    Lake), 51, 66
Draft, military, 25-26, 30, 156;
    Army teams register male Nisei,
    23; reopening for Nisei favored,
    22-23
Doi, H. (pseudonym), 39
Doi, Sumio, 89
Doub, George C., 142

Eisenhower, Milton S., 17
Ellison, Enoch E., 139
Engle, Clair, 70
Ennis, Edward, 71, 133, 145-53,
    169-71, 185-86 n.26
Equity cases. *See* Mass equity suits
Espionage and sabotage, 95; DeWitt
    predicts, 15; not grounds for de-
    tention, 88
Evacuation from West Coast, 12,
    15-25; exclusion zones defined,
    16. *See also* Exclusion from West
    Coast
Exclusion from West Coast, 18, 97;
    effects of rescission, 88-89; exclu-

sion hearings, 90-91, 96; exclusion orders, 16, 18; exclusion orders rescinded, 87-88, 107; exclusion zones established, 16; opinion poll, 22
Executive Order 9066, 15
Ex parte Endo, 87, 112, 149
Expatriation. *See* Repatriation/expatriation to Japan

Federal Bureau of Investigation (FBI), 13, 49, 140
Ford, Leland, 14
Fujii v. California, 120
Furuya v. Clark, 125
Furuya v. Williams, 125

Gentlemen's Agreement, 8
Gila River Relocation Center (Arizona), 19
Goodman, Louis, 126-27, 129-31, 135, 138-41
Granada Relocation Center (Colorado), 19
Greater East Asia Language School (Tule Lake), 77, 100, 148
Grubbs, Thomas W., 109

Habeas corpus cases. *See* Mass habeas corpus suits
Hankey (Wax), Rosalie, 64, 88, 102-3, 108
Heart Mountain Relocation Center (Wyoming), 19
Hennessey, F. J., 112
Higashi, Tsutomu, 98
Hirabayashi v. United States, 112, 194-95 n.35
Hiroshima, Japan, 190 n.18
Hitomi, Tasaku, 65
Hitomi, Yaozo, 65; murder of, 67-68, 95

Hokoku Joshi Seinen-dan (Joshi-dan), 100, 104, 165. *See also* Resegregation Group; Resegregationists; Underground movement (Tule Lake)
Hokoku Seinen-dan (named changed from *Sokoku Kenkyu Seinen-dan*), 76-82, 85, 87, 90, 103-4, 148-49, 164-65, 173; aims of, 76; influence declines, 164; internment of members, 92-93, 99-100; leaders receive warning, 98-99; name change, 82
Hoshi-dan. See *Sokuji Kikoku Hoshi-dan (Hoshi-dan)*

Ickes, Harold, 117, 133
Immigration Act of 1924 (Oriental Exclusion Act), 9
Inouye v. Clark, 135
Interior Department, U. S., 150; urges leniency for renunciants, 129
Internment camps (Department of Justice), 32, 86-87, 92-93; internees from Tule Lake, 190 n.2; radicals sent to, 99-100, 105-6; Tule Lake becomes, 108, 116. *See also names of specific camps*
Irons, Peter, 194-95 n.35
Ishida, Gladys, 122
Ishikawa, Torakichi (pseudonym), 59, 75, 79
Issei, 13, 25-27, 37, 70, 77, 113-14; definition, 9; lead radical groups, 37, 82; quandry regarding allegiance question, 27; retain cultural traits, 6-8

Jackson, Robert M., 143
Japan, 8, 14, 64, 70, 76, 118, 127-29; deportations to, 116, 192 n.50; influence on center condi-

Japan (con't.)
    tions, 182 n.38; radicals' desire
    for recognition by, 56; renunciants
    in, 120-22; Spain represents inter-
    ests of, 45, 70; surrender of, 107,
    113-14
Japanese American Citizens League
    (JACL), 20, 58, 132-33; favors
    draft for Nisei, 22-23; favors seg-
    regation, 32; Nisei criticize, 179
    n.5; refusal to cooperate with re-
    nunciants, 108, 134
Japanese language schools, 37-38,
    77, 107
Jerome Relocation Center (Arkan-
    sas), 19
Jochi-iin, 75, 81
Johnson, J. LeRoy, 71
Joshi-dan. See Hokoku Joshi Seinen-
    dan (Joshi-dan)
Justice Department, U. S., 73, 75,
    83-87, 93-94, 96, 98-102, 105,
    108-11, 115-19, 125-27, 134,
    137-42, 145-53, 159, 163, 190
    n.2; alone in opposing renun-
    ciants, 129; assumes control of
    Tule Lake, 108; "coercion" nar-
    rowly interpreted by, 84, 102; dis-
    agreement with WRA, 94; files
    designations, 129-31; lack of un-
    derstanding of Tule Lake situa-
    tion, 86, 159, 160-61; position on
    renunciations, 145-53

Kibei, 28, 37, 138; believed dis-
    loyal, 72, 102; definition, 9; life
    in Japan after war, 122; in U. S.
    Army, 176 n.14
Kido, Saburo, 133-34
Kira, Stanley (pseudonym), 58, 66,
    68, 75-76, 79-81, 187 n.63
Kitano, Harry, 6-7
Knox, Frank, 14

Korematsu v. United States, 112,
    132, 143, 194-95 n.35
Kuratomi, George, 39, 48, 58
Kuwabara v. United States, 127

Lowry, Lloyd, 70
Loyalty/leave clearance registration,
    23-34, 155-56, 179-80 n.22; loy-
    alty questionnaire, 23-26, 102,
    147, 155-57; loyalty questions,
    24-26, 31-32, 147; poorly planned
    questionnaire, 23

McCarthy, Joseph, 138
Manzanar Relocation Center (Cali-
    fornia), 19-21, 31, 58
Martial law (Tule Lake), 46-52, 72-
    73, 75
Mass equity suits, 125, 129-31, 137-
    42; administrative clearance, 139-
    41; Court of Appeals decision,
    137-39; designations, 130-31,
    140; District Court decree, 130-
    31; number of plaintiffs, 194
    n.22. See also Mass suits
Mass habeas corpus suits, 119, 125-
    28, 152. See also Mass suits
Mass suits, 132, 135-39, 141-42; in-
    itiated, 115, 117; reasons for,
    123-25; reasons for loss of, 138-
    39. See also Mass equity suits;
    Mass habeas corpus suits
Mathes, William C., 135
Meek, Colonel, 50
Minidoka Relocation Center (Idaho),
    19, 32
Mitigation hearings, 117-19, 125,
    157
Morison, H. Graham, 137
Munemori, Sadao S., 176
Murakami v. Acheson, 135-38, 140
Myer, Dillon, 16, 56, 66, 69, 79,
    94, 97, 129, 133; meeting with

Negotiating Committee, 42, 58; primary concern for loyal centers, 53; segregation by loyalty, 23

Nakamura, Tetsujiro, 98, 108
Narumi, Jutaro, 108
Nationality Act of 1940, 6-7, 73, 146
Native Sons of the Golden West, 12, 70
Negotiating Committee (Tule Lake), 40-41, 45-46, 48-49, 58, 62, 69; arrest of, ordered, 46; meeting with Myer, 42
Nevada, 16
Newell Star (Tule Lake), 61-62, 64, 69-70, 73, 88, 97, 117, 120
Nisei, 9-10, 14, 17, 19-34, 38, 70-73, 76-77, 80-81, 83, 87-88, 97, 120, 138; attempted deportation of, 70; and coercion, 77, 158-60; constitutionality of detention of, 17, 87, 112, 149; definition, 9; dual citizenship of, 10, 70, 72-73, 126-28, 151-52; efforts to demonstrate loyalty, 10-11; loyalty, registration of, 23-34; parental pressures on, 7-8, 27
Noyes, Louis M., 94, 98, 109, 113, 136, 160-66

Okamoto, Shoichi James, 64-65
Okrand, Fred, 195 n.38
Okubo, Zenshiro, 108
Old Tuleans, 42, 52, 66, 69, 104; definition, 37
Oyama, Fred, 133

Pacific Citizen, 121
Pearl Harbor, attack on, 12, 78, 95
Pedicord, R., Dr., 43
Perlman, Philip B., 128

Portland Citizens Committee to Aid Relocation (Oregon), 116
Poston Relocation Center (Arizona), 19, 20, 41
Presidential Proclamation No. 2525, 126
Presidential Proclamation No. 2655, 126

Registration. *See* Loyalty/leave clearance registration
Relocation, 23, 25, 31, 167-71; a cause of renunciation, 102; definition, 179 n.9; resumption in Tule Lake, 107-8, 120
Relocation centers, 17-20, 23, 31-33; description of, 19-20. *See also names of specific centers*
Renunciation cases. *See* Mass equity suits; Mass habeas corpus suits; Mass suits
Renunciation Law, 5-6, 70-73, 113, 124, 128, 143; constitutionality of not ruled on, 143; historical background, 71-73; radical leader on constitutionality of, 187 n.63; role of Justice Department in, 145-47
Renunciation of citizenship, 69-73, 83, 122, 124-32, 134-37, 139-42, 190 n.2; causes of, 101-4; community duress as cause of, 126, 133, 136; cultural factors, 6-10; deportation efforts, 124-25, 192 n.50; duress as cause of, 147, 150, 158-60; estimate of potential renunciations, 185-86 n.26; as goal of Resegregationists, 79-80; government duress as cause of, 115, 124, 129, 133, 136, 139; historical factors, 6-11; initiation of mass suits, 115, 125; Justice Department blamed for, 94; Justice Department's position on,

Renunciation of citizenship (*con't.*)
145-53; late approvals of, 190
n.16; late hearings for, 189 n.70;
legal and economic restrictions resulting from, 120; letters and
statements by renunciants, 169-73;
movement toward citizenship restoration, 105-22; pressures on
Nisei cause, 97-98; procedures
for, 84-85; reasons behind anxiety
for, 87; reasons for, 84; rise of issue in Tule Lake, 69-70; Tule
Lake administrators on, 155-68;
Tule Lake officials aid renunciants, 108-9
Repatriation/expatriation to Japan,
29, 32-33, 59, 82, 94, 161; Biddle on, 72; desired by "disloyal"
groups, 74; expatriation law proposed, 147; radical pamphlet in-
sists on, 79
Representative Committee (Tule
Lake), 62
Resegregation Group, 58-61, 65-66,
68, 75, 78-81, 83; established, 58;
unleash "hot heads," 65. *See also*
Resegregationists; Resegregation
of loyal/disloyal (Tule Lake); Underground movement; *names of
specific organizations*
Resegregationists, 48, 59, 62-63,
65-69, 85-86, 92, 97-102, 104-8,
112, 117, 126, 136, 155-68, 183
n.4, 187 n.5, 189-90 n.1, 192
n.50; beatings and threats by, 65-
67, 80-81; coaching of renunciants, 100-101; description of
radical group, 74-78; leaders ordered to cease pressures on Nisei,
98; leaders sent to internment
camps, 92, 99; organizational
changes, 81-82; pressure others to
renounce, 97-98; zeal to renounce,

85-86. *See also* Resegregation
Group; Resegregation of
loyal/disloyal (Tule Lake); Under-
ground movement; *names of spe-
cific organizations*
Resegregation of loyal/disloyal (Tule
Lake), 53, 56-61, 64-65, 79, 83,
86-87; a goal of underground
groups, 56-57; petitions for, 58-
61, 64-65, 79. *See also* Segrega-
tion of loyal/disloyal
Rocky Shimpo, 134
Rogers, William P., 142
Rohwer Relocation Center (Arkan-
sas), 19
Roosevelt, Franklin D., President,
15, 23, 89, 133, 194-95 n.35
Roosevelt, Theodore, President, 8
Rostow, Eugene V., 142
Rothstein, Charles M., 118, 189
n.70
Russell, Sam M., 71
Rust, Clarence E., 112

Sabotage and espionage, 95; DeWitt
predicts, 15; as grounds for deten-
tion, 88
Saikakuri Seigan, 58, 81
St. Sure, Adolphus F., 112, 126
Sakamoto, Masao, 98
Salt Lake City Conference, 17
San Francisco Chronicle, 8
Santa Anita Assembly Center (Cali-
fornia), 18
Santa Fe Internment Camp (New
Mexico), 99-100, 106, 111, 118-
19, 126
Santo Tomas Japanese Concentration
Camp (Philippines), 182 n.38
Sasaki, Masami, 98, 108
Seabrook Farms (Bridgton, New Jer-
sey), 119, 126-27

Segregation of loyal/disloyal, 23, 31-33, 35-37, 95, 162-63; to aid relocation program, 23; classes of segregants, 32; loyalty questionnaire as basis for, 31; reasons for failure in Tule Lake, 36-37

Selective Service, 25-26, 30, 156; Army teams register male Nisei, 23; reopening for Nisei favored, 22-23

Shimokon, Minekichi, 68

Sokoku Kenkyu Seinen-dan. See *Hokoku Seinen-dan*

Sokuji Kikoku Hoshi-dan (Hoshi-dan), 81-82, 93, 97-98, 100, 103, 164-65

Spanish Consul, 49, 60, 66, 70

Spanish Embassy, 60, 64

Spanish government, 45, 70

Special Project Regulations (Tule Lake), 106, 112

Spoilage, The, 179-80 n.22

State Committee on Japanese Resettlement (California State Senate), 89

State Department, U. S., 129

Stimson, Henry L., 15-16, 23

Stockade (Tule Lake), 48-51, 53-54, 62, 67, 69, 112; authorization for, 38; closing of, 69; effects on morale, 62; WRA opposes releases from, 54

Supreme Court, U. S., 8-9, 87-88, 128, 132-33, 139, 143

Takahashi, Kaoru, 108

Tietz, J. B., 134, 195-96 n.42

Topaz Relocation Center (Utah), 19, 41

Truman, Harry S., President, 110, 143

Tule Lake Defense Committee, 114-15, 119, 122-23, 134, 139, 141

Tule Lake Relocation Center (California), 19-20, 32; loyalty/leave clearance registration, 27-31

Tule Lake Segregation Center (California), 32-44, 46-62, 64-70, 73-75, 79-81, 86-92, 94, 96-99, 106-8, 110-12, 116-20, 126, 130, 134, 136, 146, 155, 157-59, 161-64, 166-68, 181 n.8; Army take-over, 43-44; beginning of violence, 64; closing of center, 120, 126; description of "disloyal" groups, 74-75; disruptive nature of population, 35-36; hostility to administration, 40-42, 44, 52; hostility toward *inu*, 53, 55, 58, 61, 66-69, 183 n.4; isolation of administration from residents, 53-54, 61-62; martial law, 46, 50, 52; mass hysteria, 91-92, 97; murder of resident, 67-69; November 1 incident, 42-43; petitions for resegregation, 58-61, 79-81; prevalence of Japanese way of life, 37-38; renunciation hearing teams arrive, 96; return to "normalcy" after strike, 51-53, 55-56, 61-62, 66; rise of radical underground, 56-58; rise of renunciation issue, 69-70; shipments to internment camps, 190 n.16; shooting of resident by sentry, 64-65; "status quo," 49-51, 55; strike, 39-41, 51-52, 55-56

Underground movement (Tule Lake), 53, 55-59, 64, 78; movement into the open, 75-76, 79; seek separation of "true Japanese," 56, 58-59

War Department, U. S., 22-25, 28, 30

War Relocation Authority, 16-18,
     22, 25-26, 31-32, 35, 41, 44-50,
     52-54, 56, 65, 73, 78-79, 87-89,
     93-94, 97-98, 105-9, 116-17, 129,
     150, 155-68, 187 n.5; announces
     loyalty segregation policy, 32;
     aware of coercion by radicals, 79;
     disapproves of renunciation pro-
     gram, 94; disliked by Tule Lake
     residents, 52; effort to break radi-
     cal power, 105-7; fears harm to
     national relocation, 78; leave
     clearance registration planned, 23;
     misunderstands Tule Lake resi-
     dents, 53; opposes deportation of
     renunciants, 116-17; opposes re-
     leases from stockade, 54; urges
     leniency toward renunciants, 129
Warren, Earl, 22

Wartime Civilian Control Authority,
     16, 18
Watanabe, Taro (pseudonym), 39
Wax, Rosalie Hankey, 64, 88, 102-
     3, 108
Wechsler, Herbert, 109
Western Defense Command, 15, 17,
     89-90, 149, 177 n.13; rescinds
     exclusion orders, 87-89, 107
Wirin, Abraham Lincoln, 123; aid to
     Japanese Americans, 133; criti-
     cism of, 133-36, 194-95 n.35; and
     Murakami case, 134-36, 138;
     seeks cases in Tule Lake, 134,
     195-96 n.42

Yamashita, Koshiro (pseudonym),
     58, 66, 75-76, 79, 81
Yasui, Kenny K., 176 n.14

About the Author

DONALD E. COLLINS is an Associate Professor at East Carolina University in Greenville, North Carolina. He earned his Ph.d. in History at the University of Georgia in 1975. His articles have been published in *Journal of Library History, The Alabama Review,* and *Catholic Library World.*